A FORGOTTEN VOICE:

A Biography of
Leta Stetter Hollingworth

Ann G. Klein, Ed.D.

Great Potential Press, Inc.
www.giftedbooks.com

A Forgotten Voice: A Biography of Leta Stetter Hollingworth

Cover Design: ATG Productions
Interior Design/Layout: The Printed Page

Published by Great Potential Press, Inc.
(formerly Gifted Psychology Press, Inc.)
P.O. Box 5057
Scottsdale, AZ 85261
www.giftedbooks.com

Printed and bound in the United States of America

05 04 03 02 01   6 5 4 3 2 1

Library of Congress Cataloging-in-Publication Data

Klein, Ann G., 1939-
  A forgotten voice : the biography of Leta Stetter Hollingworth /
by Ann G. Klein.
     p. cm.
   Includes bibliographical references and index.
   ISBN 0-910707-53-7 (trade pbk. : alk. paper)
   1. Hollingworth, Leta Stetter, 1886-1939. 2. Women psychologists—United States—Biography. 3. Psychologists—United States—Biography.   I. Title.
   BF109.H6K57 2002
   150'.92—dc21
   [B]

2002012772

Most biographies deal with unevenly developed folks,
neurotic geniuses, single-minded zealots, and the like... .
But best of all are the people who are alive in all
directions, and who have many kinds of faculties in use
their whole lives through. They are less famous than the
people of one idea, but in the long run believe they add
more to the value and joy of life.
—Mary Ware Dennett

Acknowledgments

My thanks to the University of Wisconsin-Eau Claire for its generous financial support. My gratitude is extended to Rhoda Miller, John Soderberg, Kathy Kearney, Linda Silverman, Jane Piirto, Michael Piechowski, Annemarie Roeper, Dana Sommerfeld, Margaret Soderberg, Susan McIntyre, Loris Akervik, Kenneth Schmidt. I am appreciative of the many archivists and librarians who facilitated my research, and to Jen Ault Rosso for her perceptive reading of the manuscript. A particular thank-you is extended to Jim Soester, Coordinator for Library Services/Information Services Librarian, King Library, Chadron State College, Chadron, Nebraska. I am indebted to my sister, Marcia Klein, for believing in me and for reading so many drafts of the manuscript. My publishers/editors Jim Webb and Janet Gore were as committed to the notion of publishing a new biography of Leta Hollingworth as I, and I thank them for running this marathon with me.

Finally, this book would never have been written had it not been for my (now adult) children, Brian and Elizabeth—their gifts inspired me to learn more about the perplexities such highly talented children share.

Preface

I came to write this book in a rather serendipitous way. In 1992, I ordered several back issues of the *Roeper Review: A Journal on Gifted Education*. I randomly selected several from a list of journals *Roeper* was discounting. I was struck by one issue in particular, dated March 1990. The cover was graced by a 4" x 5" black-and-white photograph—a profile of a middle-aged woman with her hair pulled back in a bun, wearing a simple dark dress with a white collar. The photo was labeled, "Leta Stetter Hollingworth, 1886-1939." The hundred or so pages that followed were devoted to this woman's life and work. I read and re-read the journal many times, intrigued with Leta Stetter Hollingworth. Despite my serious involvement in gifted education and educational psychology, including a teaching career spanning nearly four decades and two graduate degrees, her name was new to me. Yet here was an entire issue of the prestigious journal, *Roeper Review*, devoted to a woman who was apparently one of the most eminent psychologists of the twentieth century and founder of the field of gifted education. Why was her name unfamiliar to me? From the *Roeper* article, it was clear that this woman was every bit as significant as John Dewey, Lewis Terman, and many other "giants" in the history of education and psychology. Why was her name not as well known? I had to find out.

To paraphrase Tennessee Williams, it was the kindness of strangers that made this book possible. After ruminating about Leta for another year or so, I decided to telephone Dr. Linda Silverman, guest editor for that particular *Roeper Review* tribute. With trepidation, I introduced myself and asked the question, "Are you planning to write a biography of Leta Hollingworth?" She responded, "No, I'm doing her work. You write it."

My quest to learn more about Leta Hollingworth thus began in earnest. My guiding questions were the most basic ones: Who was she? Where did she come from? What did she do? Why did she do it? Why was her work either marginalized or ignored altogether for so many years?

Very little primary source material was available. The only biography of Leta was written by her grief-stricken husband Harry "Holly" Hollingworth. Within months of her death from cancer in 1939, Holly wrote a two-volume autobiography, *Born in Nebraska* and *The Years at Columbia*. He later extrapolated material from these manuscripts for the book *Leta Stetter Hollingworth, A Biography*, published in 1942. His own autobiographical works were never published, although they were revised several times in hopes of publication. These works provide most of the available data about Leta Hollingworth's personal life.

Harry Hollingworth also revealed that he destroyed Leta's personal correspondence and gave many of her uncompleted studies and lab notes to her colleagues. These papers, unfortunately, have never surfaced.

Over a period of several years, I traveled across the United States—from New York City to Valentine, Nebraska—searching for Leta's voice. I deliberately chose to drive from Eau Claire, Wisconsin to Valentine, Nebraska so that I could experience the vastness of the prairie and the beauty of the Sandhills of Leta's youth. In Valentine, I talked with Leta's first cousin Helen Stetter (who was 101 years old in 1996 when I met her) and Helen's great-nephew Richard Boyer. I walked through the large white house on Cherry Street belonging to Leta's beloved Uncle Henry (Stetter), Aunt Mary, and cousins Helen, Anna, John, and Luther. Leta and her sisters spent many hours basking in the warmth of their love. Cherry County Historical Society member Iola Stewart personally escorted me through Leta's high school.

Kathleen Rutledge (Leta's second cousin once removed) met me on several occasions in Lincoln, Nebraska, and we made a memorable visit to Leta's grave in Wyuka Cemetery. She secured wonderful photographs of the Stetters from her father, Richard Fischer, a great-nephew of Leta's. I interviewed Virginia Weischer Florence, the daughter of the Hollingworths' housekeeper, Josefine Weischer, at her home in Weston, Connecticut. Virginia grew up in the Hollingworths' Morningside Heights apartment and in their Montrose, New York home. When Josefine married Harry Hollingworth in 1946, Virginia became his stepdaughter. Virginia Florence also loaned me original drafts of Harry Hollingworth's autobiography and many photographs of Leta and Holly.

I traveled to Waterville, Ohio, to meet with a great-niece of Leta's, Patricia Johnson. Her great-grandmother was Leta's sister, Margaret Carley Stetter. Pat shared important insights into Leta's psyche from her great-grandmother's perspective and gave me beautiful photographs of Leta and her sisters, as well as a detailed genealogical chart of the Stetter family. The latter was particularly valuable as I tried to sort out all the Margarets.

My most unusual contact was with television talk show hostess Sally Jesse Raphael, who was at the time (in 1996) living in "Hollywyck," once home to Leta and Holly. I had hopes that, perhaps during renovation, Sally had found something—anything—of Leta's—maybe letters buried in the backyard or lab notes discovered in the attic. Perhaps a poem of Leta's had slipped behind a radiator. Ms. Raphael graciously replied to my letter and informed me that, while she was happy to know that such a wonderful person had once lived in her home, no artifacts were found. Ms. Raphael subsequently sold Hollywyck and has moved.

The story of Leta Stetter Hollingworth is one that needs to be told, for despite her many contributions to the fields of psychology, feminism, and gifted education, she continues to be a forgotten voice. I hope you will enjoy her story as much as I have enjoyed discovering it.

—AGK

Contents

Introduction

Leta Stetter Hollingworth, who founded the field of gifted education with her studies and observations of gifted children, was born on the Nebraska frontier in 1886. She is best known for her work in the psychology and education of gifted children. She endured many hardships on the prairie, which may have given her great strength and determination to retain her pioneering spirit throughout her all-too-short life.

Leta Hollingworth's greatest intellectual passion was the study of children so bright that many educators mistakenly think they can learn on their own. In an autobiographical summary, she wrote: "I consider this one of the most important of all problems for the development of social science—the problem of how to recognize, educate, foster, and utilize the gifted young."[1] Through meticulous research and intense commitment, she invented ways to teach and counsel gifted children that are still being used today. It was Leta Hollingworth who first recognized that gifted children have unique social and emotional needs and that not all gifted children are necessarily alike, differentiating among the "high" and "still higher." She was instrumental in creating the first public school for gifted children in New York City, and she conducted the first longitudinal study of children above 180 IQ.

Gifted education was not the only area in which she lectured, studied, and published. She was intrigued by both individual differences and marginalized populations. She contributed seminal works on the status of women, adolescents, learning disabled children,

children with special talents, and cognitively challenged children. Additionally, she was instrumental in the professionalization of both clinical and school psychology. She was a well-known public figure because of her writings in popular magazines and her talks on nation-wide radio broadcasts, and she was widely recognized as a vocal advocate for children and adolescents.

During her years as a graduate student at Columbia University, Leta Hollingworth published a chapter in a textbook, five articles, a master's thesis, and a Ph.D. dissertation. Ultimately, she authored nine books and more than eighty scholarly articles. Who better to be a founder of gifted education than one who was herself profoundly gifted? Who better to understand the social and emotional needs of gifted children than one who was herself so greatly impacted by her own intense emotions? The gifted children she studied, taught, and counseled were her soulmates.

Fifty years after Leta Hollingworth died, a conference convened in her memory at the University of Nebraska, her alma mater. Julian Stanley, an eminent gifted educator known for his SMPY program (Study for Mathematically Precocious Youth) at Johns Hopkins University, offered a toast in which he honored the two most significant researchers of gifted education in the twentieth century—Lewis Terman and Leta Hollingworth. He said:

> Whereas Lewis Terman…deservedly gets credit for providing the United States its first major tool for objectively identifying intellectually talented individuals in order to study them further, Leta Hollingworth took the next important step, to nurture them academically…. It took both of them working hard and largely independently on opposite coasts to get the movement started. Both were towering pioneers…"paradigm shifters."[2]

Lewis Terman is deservedly well known today among psychologists and educators specializing in gifted education. He is known for his long-term studies of gifted youth and for the development of the Stanford-Binet Intelligence Test. Leta Hollingworth is considerably less well known. Although she achieved eminence in her lifetime, many contemporary psychologists and educators are still unfamiliar with her numerous and significant contributions to gifted education and psychology. Her work was marginalized, trivialized, and in many instances, overlooked entirely. For example, in *Terman's Kids* (1992), Joel Shurkin mistakenly refers to Leta Hollingworth as "one of his [Terman's] female assistants."[3] In fact, some of Terman's research assistants received their master's degrees and doctorates from Teachers College, Columbia University under the tutelage of Leta.

Her impact on future leaders in psychology and education was widespread. During the 1925-1926 academic year, for example, Leta inspired one particular student to undertake a career in psychology rather than the ministry. His name was Carl Rogers, the now famous founder of client-centered psychotherapy, which emphasizes unconditional acceptance of the client as its cornerstone.[4] He found Dr. Hollingworth's class "fascinating, especially because she seemed to him to be so interested in children and people in general."[5] Rogers enrolled for a second course in clinical psychology with Leta. "It was under her supervision that I first came in actual clinical contact with children—testing them, talking with them, dealing with them as fascinating objects of study, helping to make plans for their welfare."[6]

Leta Hollingworth's influence reached far and wide. Why was she forgotten? It was partly the time she lived in. Carol Heilbrun suggests that the writing of a woman's biography presents a special challenge.

> While biographers of men have been challenged on the "objectivity" of their interpretations, biographers of women have had not only to choose one interpretation over another, but far more difficult, actually to reinvent the lives their subjects led, discovering from what evidence they could find the processes and decisions, the choices and the unique pain, that lay beyond the life stories of these women.[7]

Leta's story may be viewed in two ways—first, as a case study of one highly gifted individual's struggle to comprehend her world and to contribute to it, and second, as the life story of a woman psychologist and educator who attained eminence during the 1920s and 1930s despite obstacles placed in her path due to her gender. Leta Hollingworth struggled mightily to achieve her goals and was able to succeed despite being female. Eminent women of her day varied in ethnicity as well as social and economic status, but they shared one overriding life theme—they had fallen in love with an idea, and this passion sustained them more than any other. Leta Hollingworth clearly fell in love with the psychology and education of gifted children.[8]

She was a psychometrician—one of the few very early psychologists who developed and used tests to measure mental functioning, and she was enthusiastic about the new Binet-Simon test of intelligence and its successor, the Stanford-Binet. Like so many of her contemporaries in psychology, she believed that heredity was the primary factor that determined people's lives, and she was an advocate for eugenics, a term which is applied to selective breeding for humans. Despite living in New York City—one of the most diverse cities in the United States—for almost three decades, her friends were almost exclusively white, Anglo-Saxon, and Protestant. There are even some small hints of anti-Semitism in family reminiscences of others about her. Yet she was ethnicity-blind when children were concerned. The subjects for her first experiment in gifted education (Public School 165) were overwhelmingly Jewish children, and she formed deep, emotional ties with this group of children that lasted until her death. In her P.S. 500 (Speyer School) experiment, she worked hard to ensure that the gifted classes were as diverse as possible.

After World War II, the "science" of eugenics was thoroughly discredited, particularly since Nazi atrocities had been based upon eugenic theory. Attempts to selectively breed a master race and the systematic, senseless murder of millions of "defectives" (e.g., Jews, homosexuals, communists, gypsies, cognitively and physically disabled persons) would have horrified Leta.

Leta Hollingworth was not a saint; she was a human being. As repugnant as some of her beliefs were, they do not negate her academic accomplishments or her seminal contributions to the psychology and education of the gifted. Lewis Terman is similarly criticized today, in his case for favoring boys over girls in his studies and for not including students of diverse backgrounds. Yet he is still seen as making great contributions to the general understanding of gifted young people. In a contemporary review of Lewis Terman's work, Vialle makes the following observation that is as true of Leta Hollingworth as it is of Lewis Terman:

> The benefit of hindsight is invoked frequently in all manner of discourse as, with smugness, we denigrate the commonly held beliefs of previous generations. Our smugness is in essence an unwillingness to acknowledge that each of us is firmly anchored in time and space and that none one of us can predict what succeeding generations will make of our attitudes and assumptions. Science is as much a part of this basic human frailty as any other endeavor.[9]

Leta Hollingworth's personal life, as well as her professional writings and actions, are rooted in the time and space of the late nineteenth century and the first four decades of the twentieth century. These were years of great social and technological changes.

At the time of Leta's birth in 1886, Sigmund Freud was thirty, Mark Twain was forty-one, and Susan B. Anthony was sixty-six years old. Composer Franz Liszt died that year. Only six years earlier, Wilhelm Wundt founded the first psychological laboratory in Leipzig, Germany, and Thomas Alva Edison invented the incandescent light bulb in the U.S. The telephone and the manual typewriter were new, and few people owned such amenities. There were no automobiles, airplanes, radios, or televisions. Grover Cleveland was President of the United States, and Queen Victoria ruled in England. Women could not vote, and an act of Congress made it a federal crime to distribute materials or devices relating to birth control or abortion. The great educator John Dewey, the psychoanalyst Carl Jung, the eminent psychologists Edward Lee Thorndike and James McKeen Cattell, the feminist author Charlotte Perkins Gilman, and the birth control advocate Margaret Sanger—all were contemporaries and acquaintances of Leta.

By the year of her death in November 1939, the world had changed dramatically. World War I was over, and the nation was mired in the Great Depression. Franklin Roosevelt was in his second term as president, and World War II was underway in Europe and Asia.

In this re-telling of Leta Stetter Hollingworth's story, every attempt has been made to do so within the context of her own time and space. Describing, or as Heilbrun says, "Reinventing" the life of Leta Stetter Hollingworth begins with her encounter with an eight-year-old boy known only as "Child E."

CHAPTER 1

A Child Called "E"

*I perceived the clear and flawless working of his
mind against a contrasting background of dull and
foolish minds. It was an unforgettable observation.[1]*
—Leta Stetter Hollingworth, 1942

When Leta Stetter Hollingworth was thirty years old, an eight-
year-old boy totally changed her life. Later, she explained:

It was in November, 1916, shortly after taking appointment as instructor in educational psychology at Teachers
College, Columbia University, that I saw for the first
time, a child testing above 190 IQ (S-B). I was teaching a
course in the psychology of mentally deficient children,
and it seemed to me that my class should if possible
observe under test conditions one bright child for the
sake of contrast. I asked whether any teacher present could
nominate a very intelligent pupil for demonstration.

Miss Charlotte G. Garrison and Miss Agnes Burke,
teachers in the Horace Mann School, Teachers College,
New York City, thereupon nominated the child who is
called E.... . E was presented at the next meeting of the
class. It required two full classroom periods to test this
child to the limits of the Stanford-Binet Scale, which had
just the been published. E exhausted the scale without

being fully measured by it, achieving an IQ of at least 187. He was on that date 8 years 4 months old.

The IQ of at least 187 placed E in Galton's Class X of able persons, i.e., more than six "grades" removed from mediocrity.... This appeared as sufficiently striking to warrant permanent recording, since it would rate E as one in a million for statistical frequency, assuming "zeal and power of working" to be also abundantly present.

I did not at that time have any expert knowledge of highly intelligent children. I had been working for some years in the hospitals of New York City with persons presented for commitment to reformatories, prisons, and institutions for mental defectives. I had tested thousands of incompetent persons, a majority of them children, with Goddard's Revision of the Binet-Simon Scale, scarcely ever finding anyone with an IQ rating as high as 100. This thoroughgoing experience of the negative aspects of intelligence rendered the performance of E even more impressive to me than it would otherwise have been. I perceived the clear and flawless working of his mind against a contrasting background of dull and foolish minds. It was an unforgettable observation.[2]

This experience was clearly a defining moment for Leta. Child E struck a deep, internal chord with her because she recognized that she had met a compatriot. Leta was as profoundly gifted as he. Well aware of the absence of research on profoundly gifted children, she then began to "look for children like E, to observe them with reference to the principles of education."[3] Her quest was to continue until her death in 1939. In the ensuing twenty-three years, she found only twelve children with IQs above 180 on the Stanford-Binet Intelligence Scale, and she continued to be in contact with several of them for many years. It was in part because of Child E that Leta modified her research focus, shifting it from the study of the psychology and sociology of women to the "comprehension of the extent, nature and origin of individual differences in mental caliber,"[4] which later evolved into the study of giftedness.

What is giftedness? As recently as 1991, a group of prominent gifted educators met in Columbus, Ohio to discuss the concept of giftedness and "took issue with the widespread emphasis on performance and achievement in defining giftedness, arguing that the qualitatively different inner experiences of the gifted child lie at the heart of the phenomenon."[5] Incorporating the works of Kazimierz Dabrowski, Jean Charles Terrassier, Alfred Binet, and Lev S. Vygotsky, this group (now known as The Columbus Group) agreed upon a description of giftedness that provides a conceptual framework for this book on Leta Stetter Hollingworth's life.

The Columbus Group emphasized that giftedness is characterized by uneven—or asynchronous—cognitive development, coupled with heightened emotional sensitivities and intensities. They further agreed that the disparity between precocious intellectual development on the one hand and normal physical and skill development on the other creates inner experiences and awarenesses for the gifted child (and adult) that are qualitatively different from the norm. As Leta Hollingworth explained, "To have the intelligence of an adult, and emotions of a child combined in a childish body, is to encounter certain difficulties."[6]

This asynchrony and dissonance may create emotional turmoil and social isolation for people with profound intellectual and creative gifts. Profoundly gifted herself, Leta struggled her whole life to make sense of her unusual cognitive, social, and emotional abilities and behaviors. From infancy, she experienced uneven emotional and cognitive development, coupled with the intense sensitivities that are so typical of highly gifted individuals. Her intellect and logic were more than that of others, but so were her emotions. She loved more deeply, hurt more deeply, and felt more deeply. The song of a bird or the sight of a glorious sunset often pushed her emotions to tears. The first time her husband-to-be kissed her, she wrote a poem about it. (Writing poetry became a life-long avocation.) A slight was rarely forgiven. A kindness was rarely forgotten. Hers was a personality replete with more energy, enthusiasm, sadness, outrage, empathy, commitment, and resilience than most people ever experience. But with her prodigious talents, Leta was also extremely emotionally vulnerable throughout her entire life.

🌿 CHAPTER 2 🌿

The Lone Pine

I shall never cease to rejoice that I was born on the
limitless prairies, to grow up on their expanse
means to see in long stretches, to scorn boundaries,
to go free all one's life.[1]
—Leta Stetter Hollingworth, 1943

It is remarkable, given her childhood, that Leta Hollingworth was as resilient as she was. Perhaps her years living on the prairie helped her go free, as her quote above suggests.

Emotional and physical stresses were nearly constant during her childhood and early adolescence. In rugged prairie life, all families had hard times, but Leta's was harder than most. First, her mother died when she was three years old; then, her father deserted the family for quite some time. Raised for ten years by her supportive and caring maternal grandparents, Leta and her two younger sisters were then suddenly wrenched away from these caregivers when their father remarried. This stepmother terrorized and terrified the Stetter sisters in ways that were almost sadistic. Leta never forgave her father for abandoning his children to such a stepmother and for failing to intervene when she treated his children so cruelly.

Ironically, it may have been these stressors that shaped Leta's character in ways that promoted her path to eminence. Gifted children often develop coping skills—resilience, determination, and stamina—when living under difficult psychological conditions.[2] "It may be that the development of very high levels of talent and eminence require motivation and characteristics born from childhood tragedy and unmet, compelling psychological needs," suggests Paula Olszewski-Kubilius.[3] If so, the traumas and unhappy times that Leta endured as a child may have had some redeeming value in the positive outcome in her adult life.

PIONEERS

The Nebraska frontier of the late 1800s was beautiful but also challenging, dangerous, and unpredictable. In many ways, it may have been an ideal physical setting for this young, profoundly gifted child. The rugged landscape and lifestyle no doubt fed Leta's imagination, curiosity, and creativity, for she found pioneer life invigorating, not intimidating. There were outlets for her intense physicality. She could race her horse for miles on the limitless wild grass prairie, unhindered by a single fence. This was one of her greatest pleasures. Highly gifted people are known to enjoy and sometimes crave solitude and isolation. The western Nebraska frontier of Leta Stetter Hollingworth's childhood, it seems, took hold of her psyche and never let go.

> I shall never cease to rejoice that I was born on the limitless prairies, to grow up on their expanse means to see in long stretches, to scorn boundaries, to go free all one's life. Down around Fremont one sees carefully tilled eighty-acre farms, and sleepy domesticated animals. But two hundred miles west begin the rolling plains; and how one's heart leaps up to behold them![4]

These words proved to be metaphorical because Leta did "see in long stretches," far beyond her contemporaries; she did "scorn boundaries," and in doing so, she did "go free."

Leta's pioneer parents arrived in Nebraska at approximately the same time, but by very different routes. Like hundreds of thousands of other hopeful settlers, they came west to improve the quality of their lives. It is hard to imagine the enormity of the westward movement. Between 1854 and 1880, Nebraska's population swelled from 2,700 to 450,402. By 1890, that population had more than doubled again.[5]

Two factors were central to this exponential growth. The first was the expansion of railroad lines. "Because of the railroad, Nebraska became a territory; because of it she thrived. Under its aegis, farmers settled, town began."[6] Receiving land grants to offset the costs of construction, the railroads enticed settlers to purchase property by using aggressive advertising campaigns throughout the United States and even in Europe. One railroad brochure exclaimed:

> You have only to tickle it [the land] with a plow and it will laugh a harvest that will gladden your hearts and make joyous your homes.... The bright sky, pure water, and clear, life-inspiring atmosphere of this region give to men and animals the vitality and inspiration of youth... the paradise of invalids... anti-bilious, anti-consumptive and anti-dyspeptic. Old men and women grow young.[7]

Leta's pioneer parents initially migrated to Nebraska with their families because of the economic opportunities that the railroads provided. The aftermath of the Civil War left many eager to seek their fortune elsewhere. The railroad companies needed workers. Samuel and Will Danley (Leta's maternal grandfather and uncle) enlisted as rail graders between the two towns of O'Neill and Valentine, Nebraska. As merchants, the Stetter brothers knew that a burgeoning population would bring an increasing supply of customers.

A second factor contributing to western growth was the Homestead Act, enacted by Congress in 1862. It stipulated that "any person who was the head of a household, including widows and single males, is entitled to 160 acres of federal land."[8] The homesteader had several months to prove that the land was intended for permanent habitation by building some type of shelter. After five years of permanent residence, the land then officially belonged to the settler at a cost of $1.25 an acre. "What a blessing this wise and human legislation will bring to many a poor, but honest and industrious family,"

Nebraska's Governor Alvin Saunders exclaimed. "Its benefits can never be estimated in dollars and cents. The very thought, to such people, that they can now have a tract of land that they can call their own, has a soul-inspiring effect upon them."[9]

"Soul-inspiring" though it might have been, actually staying on a homestead for five continuous years was often difficult. Homesteader Jane Aldrich wrote a poem in 1877 describing the unfortunate ordeal that so many newcomers experienced.

Alone

The shades come stalking forth
From out the canyon, rough and black,
While from the northwest rolling clouds
Proclaim the Storm Fiend on the track.
I stand within my lowly sod-built walls
watching shadows, and the lightning's flame
And moan, Oh God, the wretchedness
Of holding down a claim.

Alone. To hear no voice in speech
Only the howling coyote in the glen
To 'fright me in the lowly watching
In my home so near his den.
And four year more I must stay here and wait
And in the morn think on the shades of night,
Then when it comes again, I shivering lie
And pray all night through for morning light. [10]

It is estimated that half the original filers gave up their claims before they could be given title to the land. Although the acreage was cheap, the financial and emotional costs that went with it were often simply too great. One Nebraska pioneer wrote:

My mother-in law did a lot of cooking in the early days for the travelers in her two-roomed soddy. People always seemed so happy coming to a new country. On some wagon covers were printed these words, "We're going to victory." But in a few short years on their return to the east, printed on the same wagon covers were these words, "In God we trusted, in Nebraska we busted."[11]

Leta's great-grandfather, Levi Danley, was one of the more fortunate early pioneers. He had accumulated a considerable amount of property in Illinois under the terms of the Homestead Act and prospered. But Leta's grandfather, Samuel Danley, lost the Nebraska family homestead in 1886. The paternal grandfather of Harry Hollingworth (who later became Leta's husband) also purchased a homestead in Nebraska, but like Samuel Danley, could not successfully cultivate and maintain the land.

These early Nebraska settlers described hardships of Biblical proportions. Fire, floods, blizzards, drought, locusts, and grasshoppers plagued the area. Any one of these could destroy in minutes what had taken years to build. Because wood was scarce, many settlers constructed dugouts and sod homes from the earth—the only available and cheap building material. Settlers referred to these sod bricks as "Nebraska Marble." Leta spent her early years living in an earthen dugout, a home that was literally dug out of a riverbank or hill. A sod house, which Leta lived in later in her childhood, was a bit more elaborate. At least it was built of sod bricks and was above ground.

Despite the best efforts of frontier sod architects, snakes and insects routinely fell from the dirt walls and roofs of these homes into food and bedding. The pioneers quickly learned to shake out their linens vigorously and to sift carefully through their food before eating. If the settler's home was mostly underground, it was possible that a horse or cow or buffalo might stumble through the sod roof into their home. One sod house dweller, Jane Shellhase, reminisced, "One day father was out on horseback, and he stopped on a small knoll the better to view the countryside At his very feet a man came out of the ground and said, "Mister, would you please get off the roof of my house?"[12]

Estelle Chapman, another prairie sod house dweller, keenly describes in her *Sod House Memories* journal both the dangers and the beauty of the stark prairie at that time:

> I have seen the land burned dry, and I have watched the young crops being beaten into the earth by severely, violently punishing hailstorms, while my poor young parents stood by, my father with his hands twisting in pain and agony, tears in his eyes. I have seen the swiftly rushing waters from the spring that go down the draw in the back of our soddy. I have seen the glory of this land in the spring. And again the richness of harvest. [13]

While prairie life was physically challenging, it could also be psychologically devastating. Many miles separated homesteads, and the isolation exacted a toll on the newcomers, particularly the women. Often there was no one nearby to assist them in childbirth or to help if a child or husband was seriously injured. With whom could they share their stories? "We made quilts as fast as we could so our families would not freeze, and as beautiful as we could, so our heart would not break," wrote one pioneer woman.[14] Such was the Nebraska frontier of Leta's childhood.

CHADRON AND VALENTINE

As a child, Leta lived for several years in two small frontier towns of western Nebraska—Chadron and Valentine. Chadron was so far west that it was almost in Wyoming, just ten miles south of the South Dakota state line. Valentine was 150 miles east of Chadron in the gently rolling Nebraska sand hills and was similarly just below the South Dakota border. These towns were interesting places in 1885, just one year before Leta's birth.

Chadron was a railroad town literally built in a day. When the Fremont, Elkhorn, and Missouri Valley Railroad selected Chadron for a terminal, the nearby settlement called O'Linn moved to Chadron on August 1, 1885 in a single day. "Wheel and skis (placed) under the makeshift stores hauled them along the trail, the merchandise riding on the shelves, ready for sale. Legend has it that a man, riding a horse along side the shop of B. F. Lowenthal, clothier, made the purchase of a pair of trousers with neither the buyer nor seller pausing enroute."[15]

Chadron is only a few miles south of the Pine Ridge Indian Reservation, established in 1868, known as the place where more than three hundred Indians were massacred in the battle of Wounded Knee in 1890. Fort Robinson, the site where in 1877 the Sioux Chief Crazy Horse surrendered, was also nearby. In 1879, a major battle ensued at Fort Robinson with the Cheyenne Chief Dull Knife. Fort Robinson also was the regimental headquarters for the African-American Buffalo Soldiers. Some of Leta's earliest memories were of Sioux Indians who lived in the area, though there is no record of whether she ever encountered the Buffalo Soldiers or ever met any Indian chiefs.

Chadron and Valentine were raucous places with many more saloons than churches, undisciplined vigilantes, unfettered prostitution, periodic murders, and lynchings. A reporter described an evening in Chadron as "interesting for the 'tender-foot' no more than for the old timer in wondering whether the next crack of some cowboy's 'forty-five' would send a bullet whistling by or into one's head... .We had...a sheriff who knew no such word as fear, but he did not feel called upon to make a corpse of himself by too strict police regulations."[16]

The population of Chadron was about six hundred; the town of Valentine was only slightly larger. An 1885 U.S. census counted just seven hundred people living in Valentine. The same census contained a list of Valentine's businesses, and the "Stetter Bros. Meat Market" is one of them.[17] Leta's father was one of the brothers in that business.

The roughness of daily life in such a small frontier town can only be imagined. One edition of the local paper, the Valentine Reporter, warned: "the promiscuous shooting upon our streets must be stopped if we want a prosperous town."[18] In 1887, an African-American male named Jerry White was charged with raping a white woman. He was jailed in a nearby town (Long Pine) and was later lynched by a group of vigilantes alleged to be from Long Pine or Valentine.

As late as 1894, settlers were receiving letters warning them not to break the sod and homestead. Three homesteaders were murdered. Some Valentine citizens suggested that the land office be relocated from Valentine to Ainsworth because it was "absolutely unsafe for a man to visit Valentine, that he is liable to be knocked down or shot."[19]

THE STETTER FAMILY

Leta's father, Johnny Stetter, was the youngest of four brothers who came to Nebraska from Virginia in the 1870s. This man, whom Leta called "Papa," lived a long life (1855-1943) and became something of a legend in northwestern Nebraska. On the one hand, he was charming and extroverted, but on the other hand, he was extremely irresponsible. Of the four brothers, he seemed the one least able to make either personal or financial commitments.

The four Stetter brothers—Henry, John, Jacob, and William— were the sons of German immigrants who had originally settled in Richmond, Virginia. John Stetter, Sr. opened a butcher business, and his sons joined the trade. In the 1870s, the brothers migrated to Nebraska, hoping to make their fortunes. With their parents deceased and their home burned to the ground by the Union Army, the Reconstructed South held no promise for them. Henry, the oldest, was the first to move west in the late 1870s. According to his daughter Helen, "Papa blazed the trail to come out here to make a place for the brothers. We housed them all until they got on their feet."[20] The brothers engaged in a variety of entrepreneurial pursuits, but the most successful was their butcher business, which had a contract with the United States Army to sell provisions to the frontier forts, including nearby Fort Niobrara, which had been built in 1879 to watch over the Sioux Indians on the Rosebud reservation just to the north.

Johnny Stetter is described in various places as an ambulance driver, a sheriff, a saloon owner, a prospector, a song and dance man, and finally, a Democrat.[21] From all accounts, the youngest Stetter brother was less interested in the responsibilities of business than he was in socializing and entertaining people. According to one friend, "Johnny Stetter was the only man I ever knew who could tell the same story a thousand times and the last time would be just as funny as the first time he told it!"[22] Another Nebraskan reported, "Give Johnny Stetter a good cigar and a half Nelson on your time and he will keep you interested for many hours."[23] An uninhibited extrovert, Johnny was renowned for his caustic wit, his reputation as a raconteur, and his pervasive charm. He was also notorious for being irresponsible. Leta's first cousin Helen Stetter, at the great age of 101, described him to the author as "just a big kid."[24]

Margaret Chase Tatroe, his granddaughter, found Johnny fascinating.

> Though he was an adventurer at heart, he did many good deeds in his…life…. He was what he was, and you either liked him or you didn't. He lived, as he wanted to live—for the moment—and I'll wager he enjoyed his life more than anyone I have ever known. To those who saw him only on the surface, he appeared irresponsible, childish, and shabby…. His many ventures included being a teamster, a cowboy, an absentee farmer…a land owner, a strolling minstrel player, at different times he ran bars, barber shops an dance halls. He was a natural born comedian and mimic…. He could sing and play the banjo in a style all his own, and he would do so at any time or place that the mood happened to strike him.[25]

Margaret's assessment was that you either accepted him or you did not. Johnny was gregarious, bright, and funny, but apparently he was also quite exasperating. Leta's family, the Danleys, detested Johnny. Leta's husband, Harry Hollingworth, found Johnny abhorrent and believed that he suffered from alcoholism, or "dipsomania" as it was called then. Nonetheless, Leta tried to be a good daughter to a rather inadequate father. He was the bane of Leta Stetter

Hollingworth's existence, and he remained a constant source of anxiety to her throughout her life.

THE DANLEY FAMILY

Unlike the Stetters, who were entrepreneurs and speculators, the Danleys were laborers and farmers. Leta's maternal grandfather, Samuel, born in 1833, was a deeply religious man. One of seven children, he had hoped to become a minister until his poor eyesight caused him to leave the seminary. Leta's grandmother, Mary Blair Danley, married Samuel in 1859 when she was twenty-one years old. They had two children, Margaret Elinor, Leta's mother, who was called Maggie, and William. Samuel had a great sense of responsibility. When several of his brothers could not pay on a loan borrowed in their father's name, Samuel paid it off over an eight-year period and was left impoverished. The Samuel Danley family then began an itinerant existence. In his autobiography, Will Danley later recalled:

> We lived several years on a farm 3 miles S.W. of Danvers [Illinois] afterwards buying and building a new home one mile North of Danvers. In 1873, we moved to Carthage Mo. where we lived one year then going back to Danvers and lived one year on the Old Danley Homestead. We then moved to Princeton where Maggie and I attended the High School and in 1879, we came to Niobrara, Nebraska, there until 1882. We then spent two years in camps grading the R.R. from O'Neill to Valentine Nebraska.[26]

During the two years that Samuel and his son William worked for the railroad, Mary and Maggie tended to their home—a canvas tent. They moved the tent from labor camp to labor camp, following the railroad line construction. The Danleys then moved to Valentine for a short time and finally purchased a 160-acre homestead on the White River just north of Chadron in 1885, one year before Leta's birth.

Leta's mother, Margaret Danley (1862-1890), called Maggie, was by all accounts a talented and lovely person. According to anyone who knew her, she was a small, dainty woman with a gentle, religious spirit who enjoyed her children, her many friends, her church activities, her parents, and her husband Johnny's brothers and their families. She played the organ for the Congregational Church in Chadron every Sunday and spent many hours during the week in sewing and embroidering, which she did beautifully.[27] She also conducted the first Sabbath School in Dawes County.[28] A high school graduate, Maggie was unusually literate for a woman of her times.

Maggie Danley and Johnny Stetter were a most unlikely couple. Johnny was a son of the Confederacy, and she was the daughter and granddaughter of Abolitionists. Johnny was crude; Maggie was refined. He was short, swarthy, and had a stocky build. She was petite, small boned, and fair. How and where they met is not known. That they fell madly in love seems sure.

> The thing that always amazed everyone, and for which no one ever found a satisfactory answer, was why my grandmother married him... . What she saw in Johnny was a mystery. He had never been inside a church, never said a prayer, and was the exact opposite from Maggie in every respect. It nearly broke her parents' hearts when she decided to marry him.[29]

Contrary to the wishes of her parents and in an uncharacteristically rebellious act, the demure Maggie Danley eloped with Johnny Stetter in 1885. And although Johnny survived his wife by more than fifty years, she remained his great love. The newlyweds moved into the tiny prairie dugout home of Mary and Samuel Danley. Life must have been difficult. One year after their marriage, Leta Ann Stetter was born.

CHILDHOOD: 1886-1896

Leta Stetter was born in Chadron on May 26, 1886. Although her parents lived with the Danleys in their dugout, Leta's mother decided that it was more prudent to deliver her children in town rather than in such an isolated area. The midwife who assisted at Leta's birth was Fannie O'Linn, a woman of many talents and a frontier legend.[30] This midwife was also a frontier lawyer and a strong advocate for women's rights. She became an important role model in later years to the young Leta.

When she was an adult, Leta discovered a bound, red, leather diary written by her mother that recalled events in Leta's life from birth to age one. Written with grace and wit and from the infant child's viewpoint, it is clear that Maggie Stetter was talented, sensitive, and creative. This document provides evidence of baby Leta's rapid developmental progress, as well as insight into Maggie and Johnny's relationship. Her mother's diary, in fact, informs us that Leta was a highly gifted, precocious child, and that Maggie Stetter was a loving, gentle, and nurturing mother with a wonderful sense of humor. We also learn that Johnny was an absentee father, coming and going as he pleased, and that when he was with the family, he was often more entertaining than paternal. One diary entry reports that before she was a year old, Johnny had Leta "mounted on the back of a bronco."[31] His interactions with Leta were exciting, enthralling, and sometimes terrifying—the beginning of many such occurrences.

This pattern of paternal abandonment, sweet reunion, playfulness, and irresponsibility continued throughout Leta's life, and it was no doubt very confusing and frustrating for her. The father-daughter relationship did not begin well. Johnny was not present at Leta's birth—his first child—and when he finally did appear, he expressed displeasure. The diary notes:

> As soon as I saw Mamma I knew I would like her and we would have a nice time together. She was so glad that I was a girl instead of a boy.... I heard Mamma tell grandpa to send a telegram to my Papa to come and see his little baby girl.... Now it was Friday [she'd been born three days prior] and I had not seen my Papa yet. I was beginning to think I had no Papa or he was not very anxious to see his little girl. Uncle Willie sent him another telegram (Your daughter is crying for her pa).... Then I

heard the door open—a man came in, walked up to the bed, kissed Mamma, then took me up in his arms, sat down on a chair by the side of the bed and took a good look at me—laughed—and said, "It's the prettiest baby I ever saw." I was looking at him too—I had been waiting eight days to see him and now I was wondering how well we would like each other. I had just about made up my mind that I was going to love him a great deal, when he said, "I'd give a thousand dollars if it was a boy." That made me so mad but I could not talk and tell Papa what I thought of him just then. It made Mamma angry too I think, because she said, "I would not give her for a half dozen boys... ." I did not like Papa very well yet because he had said he wished I had been a boy.[32]

Subsequently, according to Maggie's diary, Johnny visited his young wife and baby girl only about once a month.

Leta was baptized December 5, 1886 at her "Aunt" Fannie O'Linn's home, and according to Maggie's diary, it was a joyous occasion. "Maggie played the organ, so I sat on Aunt Fannie's lap all the time and I was real good and listened to Mr. Powell [the minister] talk and helped sing the songs as well I could and everybody laughed at me because I tried to sing. Papa and I had lots of fun playing dog, peek-a-boo." Mention is often made of "Aunt Fannie" in Maggie's diary. She was a frequent visitor to the Danley home and clearly a central figure in Maggie's life.

According to her mother's recollections, Leta showed precocious development both verbally and physically. She laughed, smiled, sat up, imitated, and talked much earlier than most children do. In her paper *Facts about Bright Children* (1929), the then-Dr. Leta Hollingworth herself observed, "although early talking (and other uses of words as symbols) is one of the most reliable signs of brightness in a baby, almost any tendency to develop faster than average is likely to be significant."[33] Long before she started school, Leta taught herself to read. Her own early precocity was a sign of things to come. Gifted children usually do mature into gifted adults.

In 1888, Leta's sister Ruth was born. And two years after that, when Leta was three and one-half years old, her mother gave birth to a third daughter, Margaret Carley. But simultaneously, a catastrophic event—not uncommon in those days—occurred. The child Margaret was born, but the mother Margaret died. Maggie Danley Stetter passed away February 9, 1890, one day after giving birth. She must have known that she was dying, because her last words were, "My poor children." It was a prescient statement.[34] Leta, Ruth, and Margaret Stetter's lives would no doubt have been very different had their mother survived to love and nurture them. Maggie adored her children, and they responded in kind.

Although Leta was just three years old chronologically, she was far older by many other measures. The toll Maggie's death must have exacted upon young Leta is incalculable, given her intensity and sensitivity—today sometimes called "overexcitabilities." In *Motherless Daughters: The Legacy of Loss*, Hope Edelman suggests:

> Unlike the adult, who experiences parent loss with a relatively intact personality, a girl who loses her mother during childhood or adolescence co-opts the loss into her emerging personality, where it then becomes a defining characteristic of her identity. From learning at early age that close relationships can be impermanent, security ephemeral, and family capable of being redefined, the motherless daughter develops an adult insight while still a child but has only juvenile resources to help her cope.[35]

Emotional scars left by her mother's death were made even deeper and more excruciating by Johnny Stetter's subsequent behavior.

After Maggie died, Johnny essentially abandoned his three little girls, leaving them to their grandparents, Samuel and Margaret Danley, to raise. No one knew where he went. In the ensuing years, he returned to visit his daughters so infrequently that they referred to him as "the candyman."

The pain of losing her mother from complications of childbirth and her father from whatever psychological forces resulted in this paternal neglect remained with Leta throughout her life. While she tried mightily to put the pain in some kind of adult perspective, it nonetheless remained a source of enormous anguish. Her highly sensitive, gifted personality structure only deepened her hurt. As the eminent educator Annemarie Roeper notes, "the Self of the gifted child is structured differently. Their depth of awareness is different. The center of their inner life is different. Their view of the world is more complex in a fundamental way."[36]

In a letter written to her father dated November 11, 1934, when she was forty-eight years old, we see that Leta had attempted to learn more about her mother: "Many thanks for the typewritten account you sent about early days. If you remember any more about the dug-out, and the sod-house, let me know.... I remember a great deal about the beginning when I was about three years old, but not much previous to three years of age."[37] She was still a child in search of her mother.

Leta's poignant concerns with her childhood remembrances are evident in her poem "When I Was a Child."

When I Was a Child

When I was a child I can remember how
The fairies came and taught me their plays,
And led me forth into the golden ways
Where they went, and they told me magic words,
And made me understand the song of birds,—
I have forgotten now.

And how the sweet-faced women gently smiled
And held me in their arms and every one
Was good and happy. When the day was done
My mother kept me safely on her knee
And softly sang a little prayer for me,—
When I was a child.[38]

Leta Stetter's mother had kept her safely on her knee for a mere three years—those years when Leta apparently still felt like a child. The segment of the poem, "The fairies came and taught me their plays,/And led me forth into the golden ways/ Where they went, and they told me magic words" is evocative of a gifted child's imaginational sensitivity.

Another poem, "Papoose," was written when she was either in high school or a freshman in college. It is an early example of her intense spirituality.

The Papoose

Close your eyes, dear little child.
Hear! The coyotes call afar
Where the Day Chief's tepees are,
And the west wind breathes so mild
Through the gold beam of the star.

Pale-face women showed to me
As I sat here yesteryear
The picture of a child away
Underneath a star, and he
Is a God-child, so they say.
Close your eyes, dear little child.
Little dark child with dark hair.
The God-child's face was spirit fair
Like the white man's—but he smiled
Like the little babe I bare.[39]

The "God-child" is, of course, the infant Jesus. While it is not known whether Leta as an adult was a churchgoer or even a church member, she did maintain a very deep, personal Christian belief throughout her life.[40]

Like most orphans, the Stetter sisters clung to one another. Because they had no mother and Johnny was an absent father, the girls trusted and needed others far less than they trusted and needed one another. Gradually, Mary and Samuel Danley became surrogate parents to their grandchildren, and the girls referred to these gentle and pious individuals as "Grandma Ma" and "Grandpa Pa." The sisters particularly enjoyed their grandmother's blackberry brandy cordials, which allegedly cured all illnesses.[41]

On the Danley homestead in Chadron, Leta, Ruth, and Maggie probably behaved like siblings everywhere. They played together, they squabbled, and they formed forever-shifting alliances, two against the other. The 160-acre homestead with its open grasslands by the White River undoubtedly provided them with many opportunities for exploration and adventure. As Maggie and Ruth grew older, their relationships began to change. Leta withdrew from the alliances, choosing instead to spend more time alone, thinking, observing, and reading as many books as she possibly could. The intensities of a profoundly gifted person were becoming more apparent. In one of her letters, Leta remembered:

> Before I was seven, I still recall the sobs that used to overcome me when the sweetness of a birds' singing or the silence of evening laid their message on my inarticulate, childish soul. The pain of my own experience is yet very clear to me. It was pain because there was no means or outlet for its expression, for it gripped me too young. Before I knew the medium of sentences or of written words that can make a sunset burn or a flower bloom forever.[42]

Leta was "gripped too young" by thoughts that she could not yet express in writing because she did not know how to write. This is a prime example of the asynchronous nature of a gifted child's development.

Among Leta's most vivid childhood memories were "Texas Longhorns, Sioux Indians, blizzards, sod-houses, our log-house, and the one-room log schoolhouse, where I attended from six to ten years of age."[43] An observer from an early age, Leta's experiences in this one-room school gave her insights about effective teaching methods, which she used subsequently. The class was multi-age out of necessity rather than design. Each child learned in her own way, in her own time. The outdoors was the science laboratory. So effective was this prairie pedagogy that Leta later transposed many of the teaching strategies to gifted education.

A TERRIBLE YEAR

The summer of 1896 was traumatic for the three sisters and their grandparents. First, Samuel Danley was forced to foreclose on the homestead in order to pay his debts. One of the most severe droughts in Nebraska history had claimed another victim. Leta learned a painful lesson: failure was possible, no matter how one persevered.

Homesteading in Nebraska was never easy. Crops—and thus a family's survival—were subject to wind and rain and pestilence, and the mid-1890s were particularly harsh years. So Grandma Ma and Grandpa Pa moved with their three young granddaughters from the homestead into the town of Chadron.

But more trauma was to come. On May 20 of that same year, Leta's father, John G. Stetter, married Fanny Berling, a dressmaker in Valentine who had immigrated to the United States from England. He probably thought he had found a new mother for his daughters. He could not have been more mistaken.

The third family tragedy that year occurred by fire. On September 3, 1896, a suspicious fire occurred at the Chadron home of Leta's Uncle, Will Danley—a fire that killed Leta's two young cousins—Marie, age four, and Irene, age one. Leta's Aunt Jenny was found unconscious on the bed but was resuscitated. Marie was dead; Irene was unconscious but could not be revived. Kerosene was found on some of Will's clothes, under his bed, and near a window. The local newspaper, *The Dawes County Journal*, reported that two days before the conflagration, "Mr. Danley purchased a large bottle of gasoline…to clean some clothes."[44] It appeared that no windows or screens were tampered with, and the doors were locked. A sprinkling can with milk at the bottom and kerosene in the spout was found in the Danley basement, and Will suggested that the girls may have been playing with the oil. Neither Will nor Jennie had any memory of the catastrophe. *The Dawes County Journal* reported that upon learning of the death of her children, Jennie Danley said, "They are all right; they are resting in Jesus' arms."[45]

Others, however, thought the fire might not have been accidental. A Coroner's Jury met the following day "from 9 o'clock Friday morning until 11 o'clock the same night" and concluded "that Marie and Irene Danley came to their death by suffocation caused by fire in the residence on Eagan Street…said fire being started with murderous intent, by party or parties unknown to this jury."[46] The *Dawes County Journal* headlined the story the following week:

Failed to Find Firebug
Coroner's Inquest Proves to be of Little Avail
No New Facts are Developed
Origin of the Danley Fire as Mysterious as Ever
May be Investigated Farther

The arsonist, if there was one, was never charged. Initially, Jennie Danley was suspected by some townspeople because she was a Christian Scientist and was thus considered by some to be quite strange, if not insane. A Chadron resident was outraged at the suggestion, noting that "persons not holding the tenets of Christian Scientists become insane" and that some of those very persons were Chadron wives.[47] Although Will Danley was never tried, he remained a prime suspect and was no doubt viewed unfavorably by some in the small town of Chadron.

The impact of her cousins' death by fire upon ten-year-old Leta had to be enormous. She had little enough trust in adults before the incident. Now, not only were her cousins dead, but some thought that her uncle or aunt might have killed their own children.

Within a one-year span Leta had lost her prairie home and had moved to town, learned that her father had re-married, and experienced the death of two cousins. It was almost more than this sensitive ten-year-old gifted young girl could bear.

At about this time, Leta seems to have made an incredible decision. She quite consciously and deliberately ended her childhood, as she described many years later in a letter to her future husband, Harry Hollingworth.

> It seems uncanny to me now, noting many children, that when I was less than ten years old I had taken a look at life and decided that in order to be competitive some period of it must be left out. I had read in some book that man's life is divided into stages and this put the uncanny idea of omitting one of them into my head. I should be frightened if any ten year old child should say such things to me now, but then I never opened my mouth on the subject, so nobody but you knows or ever knew of that solemnly kept compact with life—that if I left out part of childhood I should be granted other values which seemed more to be desired. I decided to grow up then and there, solemnly renouncing the rest of childhood. Nor has life failed thus far to keep the compact.[48]

Her decision is consistent with Leta Stetter's gifted self. By renouncing childhood and entering adulthood, she reclaimed her internal locus of control. A child decides not to be a child. Only she knew it. Leta kept secrets. It was the only way she felt safe. Negative external forces cascaded all around her. Psychologically, she was painfully progressing toward self-actualization even as a ten-year-old adult.

Perhaps because the town of Chadron now had such sad memories for them or perhaps for better opportunities, Grandma Ma and Grandpa Pa decided again to head west. They moved to Rocky Ford, Colorado, a small farming town on the Arkansas River, seventy miles east of Pueblo. They lived there for two years. And when it appeared that things could not possibly get worse, they did get worse—much worse.

STILL MORE LOSSES

Whatever emotional security the Stetter sisters may have regained through the nine years of their grandparents' nurturance and love in Nebraska and later in Colorado was again shattered in 1898. Their father, Johnny, insisted that his daughters move from Colorado to Valentine, Nebraska, to live with him and his new wife. Leta was now twelve, Ruth eleven, and Maggie nine years old, and they would be moving for the third time in three years, leaving the only family stability they had ever known.

Though they might have had some hope for happiness at first, their life in Valentine with Leta's new stepmother, Fanny Berling Stetter, turned out to be a nightmare that did not end at daybreak. Maggie Stetter later referred to Fanny as the devil. Helen Stetter, Leta's first cousin, angrily described Fanny as a "mental case." As for Leta, she felt as though she was living day by day in a "fiery furnace."

All of the cleaning and washing was assigned to the three girls. It had to be completed perfectly before they left for school in the morning. When they returned home, more chores awaited. The girls were exhausted and frightened all the time. Having been raised on a farm, they were accustomed to hard work. However, Leta and her sisters were utterly unprepared for the verbal and emotional abuse that, according to several sources, was heaped upon them day after day.

During this period, Johnny continued his long absences, supervising his out-of-town businesses, and the children were alone with Fanny most of the time. When their father did come home, he and Fanny fought violently over her treatment of the girls. Leta recoiled from these arguments, which often went on for hours. Fanny apparently behaved with some restraint if Johnny was present, but her abuse resumed as soon as he went away. Leta was often accused of and then punished for acts she did not commit. Her stepmother's sense of right and wrong was arbitrary, and Leta never understood what would trigger Fanny's anger. A heightened sense of justice is part of a gifted child's psyche, and this unjustifiable anger must have seemed particularly reprehensible. Still, Leta had no recourse but to obey this mentally unstable woman and remain silent in order to protect her younger sisters. Years later, she wrote her fiancé, Harry Hollingworth: "They ought not to have expected mere children to bear their burdens, yet many and many a night I have gone to bed, and so have my sisters, wearily wondering what a day would bring forth in the way of strife and turmoil"[49]

The following year, in 1899, Leta's beloved grandfather, Samuel Danley, died in Colorado, and her grandmother, Mary, returned to Chadron. The girls must have looked forward to having their Grandma Ma closer to them in their childhood town only 120 miles away. But Fanny compounded Leta's misery with her cruelest act of all. She adamantly refused to let the girls visit or see their grandmother, the one person they loved most in all the world. They could not see or write her, and she was forbidden to visit them. Even when Mary visited Valentine, her granddaughters had to ignore her. Mary stayed with Henry Stetter's family during visits to Valentine, and she paced back and forth on the sidewalk in front of the house, hoping to see her grandchildren walking down the street. Some ninety years later, Helen Stetter remembered this clearly and thought it "just pitiful" for a grandmother to be denied access to her grandchildren.

Leta felt guilty and cowardly about her inability to cross the street to see her Grandma Ma. But so terrified was she of Fanny's wrath that it was as if her legs would not carry her into the arms of her grandmother. In truth, she and her sisters were victims of child abuse—certainly emotional abuse, and possibly physical abuse as well. Years later, Leta wrote:

> More serious even in adverse effect than the unsuccessful contact with other children are the contact with dull, carping or otherwise unworthy adult "authorities." The very intelligent child, perceiving the illogical and unjust conduct of elders in charge of his affairs, may learn to hate all authority, and become incapable of taking a cooperative attitude towards commands. The great problem of learning to suffer fools gladly is one which many gifted persons never solve, as long as they live.[50]

Although Leta wrote these words as Professor Leta Hollingworth in 1931, she may well have been remembering her own difficult childhood. And she, herself, never did learn to tolerate fools gladly, or to tolerate them at all.

A second set of surrogate parents, Uncle Henry and Aunt Martha Stetter, probably saved Leta, Maggie, and Ruth from further emotional ruin. Their home in Valentine became a refuge. When she was in a state of uncontrolled fury, Fanny often banished the girls from their father's home. Henry and Martha and their four children—Anna, Frank, Helen, and Luther—frequently and generously took Leta and her sisters in. Leta never forgot the kindness and generosity of the Henry Stetter family. Although as an adult she refused to go back to visit Valentine, she corresponded regularly with her uncle Henry Stetter's family for almost forty years.

Fortunately, one other individual also emerged in the midst of Leta's emotional maelstrom who became a positive force in her sad life. It was Valentine School Superintendent Robert H. Watson, also her English teacher. He recognized Leta's special talents, and throughout high school, he was the first of several important mentors in Leta's life who would give her the support and recognition she did not receive from her own father.

According to Mihaly Csikszentmihalyi, "The mentor's main role is to validate the identify of the younger person and to encourage him or her to continue working in the domain."[51] At a time when Leta was probably most fragile, Robert Watson gave her some needed psychological support. "I tried to tell my old teacher," she wrote in 1906, "what he had done for me, and that his influence would go on as far as I went…but before I knew it, life had flowed tremendously back from those high, white walls, and choked utterances."[52] Leta survived Valentine in part because of this teacher/mentor who encouraged her to persist and endure. He believed in her, and she felt validated. But even though she managed to rise above them, her wounds and her pain from them were deep and long lasting.

From her childhood, Leta had wanted to be a writer. When she was in high school, the town newspaper, *The Valentine Democrat* hired her to write a weekly column even though she was only fifteen years old. Her job, which she held from October 10, 1901 through April 24, 1902, was to diligently record school news and gossip. Her column, entitled "The Education Department," was a page-one feature. The columns contain no hint of her troubles in the "fiery furnace" at home. Instead, her writings reflect wry humor, keen powers of observation, and crisp intelligence. There is even a hint of her evolving feminism.

> Mr. Growlen contends that there is a certain statement in Caesar which includes the expression, "Women, children and other household utensils." If such is the case, Caesar has lowered himself in the H. S. girls' estimation (October 17, 1901).

> An opinion is prevalent among the seniors that the man who made the geometry mixed his prefixes and that many so-called propositions are in reality impositions (November 7, 1901).

> In marching, the high school adheres strictly to the commandment, "Let not thy left foot know what thy right foot doeth" (November 14, 1901).

> Like Tennyson, the Seniors find a special charm in the words—"Far, far away"—where geometry is concerned (January 16, 1902).

> Who hath trouble and striving? Who worketh long and faithfully and receiveth no reward? Who hath woe? They that are on the program committee.... Yea, many are called but few are chosen, and there shall be diverging of opinion and talking and reading and shaking of heads. Verily, verily I say unto you, be not weary in

program making for in due season yet shall succeed if ye fail not (February 27, 1902).

Once upon a time, a great many years ago, there lived a student who always took class notes, kept his time card conscientiously and studied his spelling lesson. His species is now extinct. This fable teaches that overwork is always duly punished, and that the warning has not been in vain to others (March 13, 1902).

Examination was conducted throughout the school, Friday. It was the last high school exam that the seniors will ever experience and they felt that they had crossed the Red Sea and were nearly out of the wilderness (April 17, 1903).

These writings show some of Leta's specific writing talent, as well as her overall intelligence, wit, and humor. They are remarkable not only given her young age, but also in light of her personal circumstances.

Perhaps the most striking summary of Leta's psyche during her childhood years in Nebraska is reflected in her poem "The Lone Pine." It is one of the few instances in which young Leta's inner voice is loud and clear.

The Lone Pine (1898-1902)
High up, on the peak of the hill-top,
Where the tempests met in strife,
Thro' the night and the storm and the darkness
It stands like a lonesome life.

Beaten and scarred and crippled,
By the winds and rain made old,
While the pine trees down in the valley
Are sheltered from storm and cold.

From a barren rock on the summit
Of the hill it lifts its form,
Alike to the warm spring sunshine
And the fury of the storm.

Silent and uncomplaining,
Except when the sad winds moan
Tho' its broken and battered branches,
The tale of a life, alone.

High up where the world may see it,
Sharp outlined against the sky,
While its brothers down in the valley
Unnoticed are all passed by.

And the Lone Pine standing patient,
Where the wild winds wage their strife,
Beaten and scarred and crippled,
Like a broken, lonely life.

It is telling again the story,
As the winds thro' its branches moan,
Of a soul lifted high o'er its brothers,
That must bear the storm alone.[53]

Leta Setter identified with the lone pine in the poem. Unprotected, she endured Fanny's fury and beatings. Forced to be silent and uncomplaining, she survived the storm—alone.

We know from her letters that for many years, even as an adult, Leta was subject to upsetting flashbacks of her abuse at the hands of Fanny Berling Stetter. Neither time nor distance prevented these terrors from returning. She was suffering from what was then an unnamed psychiatric disorder, Post Traumatic Stress Syndrome.

While she idealized her mother, Leta was undoubtedly confused and dismayed by the behaviors of her father. As frustrating and difficult as it must have been to be Johnny Stetter's daughter, she modeled some of his same characteristics and behaviors. Father and daughter resembled each other physically; both were short and somewhat stocky with swarthy complexions. Johnny often teased Leta about their looks by insisting they came from Jewish ancestry in Germany, though there is no record of this being the case. It was not gentle teasing. It was a deliberate way to upset Leta.

There is ample evidence of some ugly strains of nativism, racism, and anti-Semitism inherent in the frontier prairie at that time. Such sentiments were part of Leta's cultural context, and she was not immune to their influence. Leta's youngest sister, Maggie, recalled Ruth and Leta once frightening her by telling her they saw a "big 'nigger' woman who was coming to get her. Maggie would be screaming hysterically by the time Grandma Danley could get outdoors to find out what happened."[54] There is even some suggestion, according to Maggie, that Leta was anti-Semitic.[55] Given her circumstances, locale, and time in history, it would not be totally surprising.

Though Leta was terribly disappointed in her father and even disliked him intensely at times, she also behaved like him in several significant ways. Johnny Stetter marched to his own drummer, and Leta did as well. Her father was unconventional and cared little about others' opinions of his actions. These characteristics were also exhibited by Leta throughout her life. Even Johnny's harshest critics would admit that he was kind and generous; so was Leta. And Johnny Stetter strongly encouraged his three daughters to go to college. Despite living in a time when few women attended college, Leta, Ruth, and Maggie not only attended college, they graduated. Leta always felt that she could and should accomplish great things. Her self-confidence was due in no small part to Johnny Stetter's belief in her.

Abraham Tannenbaum suggests that "giftedness requires social contexts that enable it to mature.... Human potential cannot flourish in an arid cultural climate. It needs nurturance, urgings, encouragement, and even pressures from a world that cares."[56] Despite the many hardships and tragedies that she endured as a child and young woman, Leta somehow managed to flourish intellectually. Though faced with much sorrow and hardship, she did have significant persons who formed the "world that cares." Notable among them were her mother Margaret Danley Stetter, Mary and Samuel Danley, the Henry Stetter family, Ruth and Maggie Stetter, her mother's friend Fannie O'Linn, and her teacher Robert Watson.

CHAPTER 3

The Girl In the Red Tam O'Shanter

Then, all of a sudden I knew!
That evening—the first that we
Kissed each other,—a little wind blew
Over us, long ago, in another place.[1]
—Leta Stetter Hollingworth, 1940

When Leta Stetter attended college, many educators and psychologists of the day argued that women were unable to withstand intellectual rigor.[2] Edward Lee Thorndike, a well-known psychologist in Leta's time, suggested that women were inferior intellectually.

> Of the hundred most gifted individuals in the country, not two would be women.... Thus, though women should capture the teaching profession, they would hardly fill its most eminent positions...[and] even should all women vote, they would play a small role in the senate.[3]

Ironically, Thorndike became Leta's professor and advisor at Columbia University during her graduate school years and later her mentor. It is interesting to speculate whether he believed that she was the one gifted woman of a hundred or whether her obvious high intelligence helped change his beliefs about women.

Some opponents of women attending college argued that higher education was so intense that it was likely to damage women's reproductive health and would ultimately create "race suicide." They feared that if educated women were barren, the undereducated population would soon out-populate the current American middle and upper class society. Dr. Edward Clark, a member of the Harvard Board of Overseers, believed that, "Given women's special mental and physical qualities…the campaign to open higher education to women could only have a destructive effect on American society."[4] Another prominent physician wondered, "Why should we spoil a good mother by making an ordinary grammarian?"[5]

A twentieth-century Harvard University historian, Barbara Solomon, notes:

> The process of women's entry into higher education has been integrally linked with economic and social factors that have shaped American life. Among these, the impact of industrialization, the significant decline in fertility rates, and the introduction of formal schooling for youth, have all contributed to the release of women from expected societal roles. For women more than men, education evoked opposition, because it gave women an identity outside the family. While the utility of educating women gradually gained acceptance, anxiety over their possible abandonment of traditional roles endured.[6]

Despite the reactionary views of so many professional men, women's attendance in institutions of higher education steadily increased. In 1870, only one percent of Americans were enrolled in college; of these, only one in five were female. By 1900, four percent of the American population attended college, and thirty-six percent of enrollees were women.[7] Typically encouraged to enter sex-segregated programs, these women often graduated with degrees in fields that were essentially extensions of domestic care—occupations such as social work, nursing, teaching, and library science.[8]

COLLEGE YEARS: 1902-1906

Leta recalled the day she arrived at the University of Nebraska for her freshman year. It was 1902, and she was sixteen years old.

> I shall never forget a certain immediate moment which touched the consciousness as the train took me into Lincoln for the first time.... An emotion of the irresistible swept over me, an impression of inevitable movement and destination.... And the thought flashed through me that my life must always be like that, and the thought bound itself up with the visual memory of red sun setting across farms. Then at last we alighted from the train and saw for the first time the buildings of the old University to the east. But I have always remembered the strange immediacy of that moment.[9]

Leta's sensory overexcitabilities are evident in moments like these: a train thunders, an emotion is irresistible, there is an inevitable movement. Her recollections are palpable. She was now far from Valentine; her new world was filled with promise and possibilities.

The University of Nebraska, founded by an act of the Nebraska Legislature in 1869, began with four faculty members and twenty students. Writing in the 1890s, Chancellor James H. Canfield declared, "Any young man or woman who has finished the course in a good country school may enter the University and find...a welcome... Higher education—a possible luxury to the rich, but a necessity to the poor!"[10]

The standard college preparatory studies curriculum recommended for high school included four years of Latin, four years of English, three years of mathematics, three years of science, and some study of German and history.[11] Despite the rural location, it appears that Leta received such a rigorous classical education. According to Harry Hollingworth, Leta graduated from Valentine High School with the following course credits:[12]

Algebra	3
Botany	1
English	4
Geometry (Plain)	2
Geometry (Solid)	1
German	2
General	1
History	3
Latin	7
Physiography	1
Physics	1
Civics	1
Physiology	1

The University of Nebraska in Lincoln was an exciting place in 1902. There were eleven buildings within the 420-acre university. The sheer size and variety of people must have been quite a stimulating experience for Leta in comparison to the small towns she came from. During the four-year period that Leta Stetter attended the University of Nebraska, enrollment increased from 2,560 to 2,914 students.[13] The student body of the University of Nebraska was almost four times the population of Chadron or Valentine, Nebraska or Rocky Ford, Colorado.

Despite the often male-dominated frontier aspects of Nebraska, Leta was not the only female in her class; in fact, her class was unusual. Although females constituted only about one-third of the college population in the United States, Leta's University of Nebraska class of 1906 had a majority of females and was the first University of Nebraska class to elect a female president.

Leta enjoyed her college years in Lincoln, more than two hundred miles from home. She felt liberated both intellectually and emotionally. She was soon an active participant in class committees and activities. During her sophomore year, she was present at a friendly altercation with the freshmen.

The year ended with a chapter which will be a "burning record" in the annals of the Varsity forever. The freshmen decided, contrary to all custom and precedence, to wear caps... . The caps came and the sophomores of course took charge of them, and one morning marched up in front of the campus, and, pouring a little coal oil upon the treasures, touched a match, and the chemists can tell you what became of them... . One cap was left, and this was raffled off, No. 190 being the lucky number... . Miss Leta Stetter drew the lucky number and now counts it among her heirlooms.[14]

Leta wrote several poems during her first two years at the University of Nebraska, some of which are included here.[15] They reflect her increasingly heightened sensitivities, as well as her religiosity. The intensity of feeling in the writer is almost palpable.

Crying in the Wilderness (1902-1903)

Out in God's wilderness, the creepers run
And mind their own wild will. The untaught trees
Stand glorious in earthly pride. The sun
At setting throws its long thin jets of light
Like crimson fountain on the wayward world.
And seldom man has broke that silence, for
The finger of awe lies heavy on his lips
When he steps there.

But this thought leaps up in me like a joy;
If any man should raise his voice out there—
Out in the waiting wilderness should cry
Aloud with faith in a thundering prophecy—
How long and grandly down that infinite
A crying voice might tremble all the leaves,
And echo and thrill.

A Philosopher (1902-1903)

Gray are these walls of Oxford and they wear
That dimness that old th'ots and musings cast
Over a city, reared in the long past
For heark'ning to God's Word, and for the care
Of that strange dream, that mystically, somewhere,
God's voice must speak to comfort man, at last.
Now from the cloisters quick, new murmurs fast
Break forth,—no echo of a dull word-prayer
Nor of a lip-worn ritual wearisome.
Now all the altars are left void and lone.
From list'ning for God's voice that still is dumb,
Thro' all the ages silent as the stone,
Man turns his soul, and sees young science come,
Free, open eyed, to claim all for her own.

John the Baptist (1902-1903)

And he said, "I am the voice of one
Crying in the wilderness." No Rabbi he;
He was born to preach his blessed Lord,
Jesus, the Saviour, and asked no reward
Except the knowledge of his duty done
And that the people all might turn and see
The heavenly kingdom waiting there at hand,
And follow Jesus in his ministry.

He must decrease; the people must forget
The humble hermit when the Saviour came;
All this he knew, and meekly did accept
His fate, and in his stern, strong heart he kept
The lamp of loyalty forever set
Burning and burning like a holy flame.
Yet in his wanderings thro' Judah's land,
Bearing the tidings in the Christ's pure name.

No woman ministered unto his need,
Sternness and strength ungraced by any touch
Of lovely things,—this was his way of life;
No heart was his; no home, no child, no wife,
Nothing of these, for these are but for such
As bear no burden of great word and deed.
And so he said, "I am the voice,
The voice in the wildness, crying that all may hear."

The Hermit (1902-1903)

I am a hermit. Let the sad world roll
On with its burdens and its pain and strife.
I look to a better and higher life,
For I shall chasten and preserve my soul.
From all the world's wild cares I make me free,
And naught have I to do with human pain,
Nor have I fear of loss nor greed of gain,
And yet I heard them say they pitied me.

A Widow (1902-1903)

Make not your glance so brief!
Do you not understand?
This dim blue gown, with cornflowers down
The breast, and its yellow band,
Instead of the gown of grief?
Make not your glance so brief!
Can you not understand?
Oh, he loved dim blue, and the cornflower's hue!
He would love this gown with its band
Instead of the gown of grief.

The Listener (1902-1903)

The song of great, harmonious winds that blow
Around a canyon at the close of day
Made yearning in the world. And far away
The sundown, like a sacrifice burn low,
Flared red and flamed. Old, solitary, slow,

The hour passed, brooding, staring on its way,
A prophet among hours,—as on whom lay
The burden and necessity to know
And cry God's word. There quick my listening mind
Harked to old dreams, and trembling—eager caught
A sudden faith up. Here perhaps to find
The Burning Bush!
Bust listening, I heard naught
For God has never spoken since mankind
Let go fair, flashing fancy and seized thought.

Twilight (1902-1903)

Twilight creeping over the world;
The noises of night in the quiet land;
Wavelets lapping the level sand,
Where the shore and the water meet and part;
Twilight lying calm on the heart
Like a brooding dove, with its soft wings furled.

The March from Faust (1902-1903)

Let not your faith be abated!
Onward! Onward! marching along.
Men, have courage and be strong!
What if the petty rage and fret,
What if the weakling hearts forget?
Stand by life and with a calm repose,
Have faith in the task,—God surely knows
Why his world was created.

Ruskin (1902-1903)

"Blessed are the pure in heart for they shall see
God,"—it is the promise of the Christ
Made on the mount…Ruskin, that spirit-man
Who knew the truth about what life could mean,
And rose up calmly to reposeful deeds
Of self-renunciation, and lived on
Still meek and pure in heart,—he saw his God

In human faces and in flow'rs and thoughts,
And gave to us the vision that he saw.

The Junior Class book, *The Sombrero* (1905), describes Leta this way:

> This accomplished little "Navajo" was born in Chadron in 1886 and a graduate from the Valentine high school in 1902. She is an associate editor of *The Sombrero*, belongs to the English Club, was on the Junior Prom committee, and at one time literary editor of the *Daily Nebraskan* staff.[16]

The Senior Book (1906) gives a more expansive listing of Leta's impressive and diverse activities during her four years at the University of Nebraska: "Leta Stetter, Associate Editor, Chi Omega, English Club, Psychological Club, Phi Beta Kappa, Silver Serpent, Junior Prom, Literary Editor *Daily Nebraskan*, Assistant in English Literature."[17] Leta included the following quotation from Edmund Burke to accompany her *Senior Book* picture and list of accomplishments: "I had indeed the folly to write it, but, oh, that I had the wit to keep it to myself."[18]

At that time, planning to become a writer, Leta majored in English literature and writing. Her professors and peers recognized her literary gifts. Hired as a theme reader by the English Department when she was just a sophomore, professors encouraged her to submit several of her short stories and poems for publication. She did so, but they were rejected.

"Miss Leta Setter" first appears on the masthead of the *Daily Nebraskan* as literary editor on September 28, 1904, the beginning of her junior year. Also in her junior year, she was elected to the English Club, whose membership was "based on proficiency in writing, originality, knowledge of the mother tongue, the language and the literature, and adequate scholarship."[19]

The Class of 1906 selected Leta Stetter as its Class Poet. She also contributed two of her short stories to *The Senior Book*: "An

Incident at Devlin's" and "The Skull." The former tells the sad tale of a naïve gambler and an experienced card shark. Growing up in Chadron and Valentine, where her father and uncle owned saloons, Leta was able to set the scene:

> Devlin's place was at its best tonight. Huge arc lights illumined shelling hall with brilliant white light and cast a peculiar shimmer on the green topped table which stretched down either side of the room. There was a confusion of sounds, low and rumbling, broken now and then by a ringing laugh or a curse. From the far end came the clack of billiard balls. In the center of the room a crowd of men were gathered about the roulette wheel, watching with staring eyes the spinning arrow as it whirred and clicked, while another group was watching a little ball as it started on its downed course among the pegs, as it glanced-and spun—and rolled—and teetered— and finally stopped. Still others were gathered about round tables playing cards and nervously fingering large stacks of chips.[20]

Her story "The Skull" is a Gothic tale of love and rejection in which a young woman, Kittie, agrees to pose for a young artist, Ben. Her demanding nature quickly rises to the surface. She insists upon wearing a dress Ben considers too decorative; then the odor of oil paint distresses her, so Ben does the portrait in crayon. He acquiesces because he has fallen in love with her. When the portrait is complete, Kittie is ready for her first glimpse of the work. Ben pulls the curtain back. "When he turned to look at his companion's face, he was startled…her cheeks were bright with anger, and her eyes flashed resentment as they met his own." The beautiful portrait of Kittie had mysteriously metamorphosed into a skull. "In tracing the picture of the girl, his unconscious fingers had at the same time been busily shaping the form of this horrid thing." Kittie rushes out of the studio, and Ben does not attempt to stop her. "The skull has saved me, he said to himself, not bitterly, but as one who has reached a conclusion."[21]

It is interesting that in this story, the coquettish and vacuous Kittie is the villain, while the talented and patient Ben is the hero. Kittie seems the antithesis of Leta's idea of a strong, intelligent, and loving young woman. But Ben's attributes are similar to those of a man who would later be very important in Leta's life—Harry L. Hollingworth.

On April 11, 1906, the *Daily Nebraskan* announced the names of eighteen new members elected to Phi Beta Kappa. Leta Stetter and H.L. Hollingworth were among the fourteen women and four men honored. When the seniors were inducted into the organization a month later, Leta Stetter gave the class response. She also sat on stage with the class president and two other senior men to deliver the Class Poem during the traditional Ivy Day commemorative Senior Class activity. The Ivy Day orator presented his address, and the Seniors loudly sang the Class Song. Then, Leta read the class poem she had composed, entitled "Always and Forever Roses Die."

Always and Forever Roses Die (May 24, 1906)

One thinks when some dear, gladsome time is done,
"What if thro' all the rounds and rounds of years,
The heart should lose it!" and the sudden tears
Spring hurting to the eyes. Well, this is one
Of all those times of which an end must be;
How shall its life be kept for you and me?
Oh, never weep with him of bitter heart
I saw once pausing where white roses die
And hide the earth in fragrance where they lie.
With darkened eyes he looked, then turned apart,
And murmuring "hopeless" to himself he said,
"The thorns still sharpen when the flowers are dead."

Another came and stood within the place—
Where softly breathing lay the living snow,
And looked upon the waste and bending low,
Stooped as he loved it. Then I saw his face!
He gathered all the petals at his feet
And thro' his life they gave him fragrance sweet.

So we may know what wisdom is, we read
Its mighty meaning in the brow and eyes
Of him who knows to keep his paradise
In fragrance when the living thing is dead.
He looked so calm, for tho' his eyes were wet
His face was placid and without regret.

This story runs in sweet and tender ways,
For always and forever roses die
And all about us fragrant petals lie;
The remnants of the precious, perfect days
Which come and pass. But mem'ry still may lend
A fragrance sweet to gladden to the end.[22]

Her poem was judged "...a very pretty piece" by a campus critic.[23] Was Leta coming to terms with her personal losses when she wrote, "But mem'ry still may lend/A fragrance sweet to gladden till the end"?

It was during her sophomore year that Leta began to know Harry Hollingworth. In an unpublished manuscript, Harry vividly recalled the first time he laid eyes upon Leta.

There entered the stack room of the library, where Kiesselbach [a friend] and I made ourselves at home because of the nearness of the book shelves, a small dark haired girl wearing a scarlet Tam-O-Shanter. I had already seen her on the campus and was struck by a certain pensive quality of her features and a characteristic animation in her activity. It was, however, surprising to see one of her youth (she was only 17) and liveliness interested in this remote room where the heavier tomes were kept, and where resorted mainly the few graduate students and sober philosophy majors on the trail of the "concrete universal." How clearly I can see Kisselbach stretching up on tiptoe to peer over and through the book shelves when I warned him to leave her alone because she was my discovery. I did not yet know her name, but she became one of the few people who could frequently be seen retreating to this book filled stack room in the library.[24]

Harry had seen Leta, but she had not seen him. Not yet. In time, they would get to know one another and would graduate, teach in Nebraska, and later marry.

"HOLLY"

Harry Levi Hollingworth (1880-1954) became the singularly most important person in Leta's life. He was her lover, her husband, her friend, and her mentor. Given the nickname "Holly" as a child, he remained "Holly" to family and friends until his death. Starting out as college sweethearts, their lives were entwined for thirty-six years. Leta and Holly both earned Ph.D. degrees from Columbia University and both became distinguished professors. For many years, they walked to work together, graded papers together in the late afternoon through the early evening (in what is now the Milbank Memorial Library at Teachers College, Columbia University), and walked home together. Friends viewed them as one entity and referred to the couple as "the Hollys." In the 1920s, after many years of marriage, they began to develop separate interests and separate circles of friends. Long-standing relationships are complex, and their relationship was no exception. But Holly's writings after her death showed that he had a deep love for her even then.

What attracted them to each other when Leta was only seventeen years old and he was twenty-three? They had many things in common. Both suffered lifelong fears of abandonment because of childhood traumas. Both had fathers who were very difficult men to live with. Both had maternal grandmothers who raised and nurtured them, but there were long periods of time when both Leta and Holly were deprived of love. The Hollingworths, Stetters, and Danleys were all often impoverished. Because the adults in their lives could not be trusted to provide consistent physical and emotional support, Leta and Holly may both have learned as young children to keep a safe psychological distance from certain family members as a way of maintaining their own emotional stability. Yet when illness or financial setbacks occurred back home, both selflessly assisted their Nebraska relatives.

Holly's paternal grandfather, Henry Hollingworth, was an English immigrant who initially settled in Racine County, Wisconsin. He married Mary Wild, and the marriage produced nine children. Thomas Hollingworth (1852-1890), Holly's father, was the second oldest child. In the 1870s, the family left Wisconsin to homestead in Gage County, Nebraska. When the homestead failed, the Hollingworth family relocated to Dewitt, a small town thirty miles south of Lincoln, where Henry and his sons started a construction business.

Family lore suggests that Holly's maternal grandmother, Margaret, was born in a covered wagon as her family trekked to Illinois. When Margaret married William Andrews, they had two children—Lizzie (1859-1882), who was Holly's mother, and John. Widowed in 1861, Margaret then married Levi Spencer and within a short time bore two more children—Ella and Mattie. In 1878, the Spencer family moved to Dewitt, Nebraska. Lizzie Andrews Spencer and Thomas Hollingworth met shortly after Lizzie arrived in Nebraska. They married in 1879, and Harry Levi Hollingworth, called Holly, was born May 26, 1880.

Unfortunately, Holly's mother died when he was only was sixteen months old. She had lived only twenty-three years. Six decades after his mother's death, Holly found a cigar box filled with items from his infancy. On the inside of the lid, in his mother's handwriting, he found the inscription, "Harry L. Hollingworth. Was born May the 26, 1880./He is a darling little blue-eyed beauty, as handsome as a rose. He is mama's little Treasure, her own sweet boy. Harry, May you always be happy/May you always be gay/and when sorrow and trouble comes/Try to cast them away,/Is your mother's wish."[25] Just as Leta had found her mother's diary, so, too, had Holly found a precious cigar box containing words written by his mother.

Holly's father, Thomas, decided to marry again, and events quickly transpired that closely resembled Leta's traumatic childhood. When Holly was eighteen months old, he was kidnapped by his Grandmother Margaret and taken to her farm. When Thomas took her to court, she was ordered to return the boy to his father and new stepmother, Mittie. The judge ruled further that Margaret Andrews could neither visit nor communicate with Holly in any way. If the Andrews' grandparents appeared near his home, he was quickly hidden from view by Thomas and Mittie. The kidnapping incident created a family feud with wounds that never healed. And incredibly, Holly's father burned an "H" into the palm of his son's right hand as an "infallible means of identification." Holly was branded for life, the mark still visible when he was in his sixties. He wrote, "It served as a constant reminder of a troubled infancy. It was also a genuine token of early concerns and attitudes from which I probably never wholly escaped."[26]

Holly was not told the truth about his mother's death until he was eighteen years old. Instead, he was expected to believe the fabrication that Mittie was his biological mother. At around the age of six or seven, however, he figured out that his parents had been married fewer years than he had been alive. In addition, townspeople hinted at the truth.

> From time to time I drew various conclusions—that I had been stolen from somewhere, that I was an Indian child, that I was another Jesus. Keeping my counsel, by the age of 11 I had learned the general facts but did not yet know my maternal relatives, although they lived a few miles out of town.[27]

His father and stepmother's deception, though well-intentioned, alienated Holly from his family for years. However, his stepmother, Mittie Gunder Hollingworth, "could not have been more kind and loyal had she been my real parent," he acknowledged.[28] Holly managed to find something positive from his experience with rotating mothers. He later wrote of Lizzie Andrews, Margaret Spencer, and Mittie Hollingworth:

There is one advantage that motherless children have over others: they may look back upon their youth with memories of more mothers than other children have. It was that way with me...at least three women played the role of mother in my life.... I seem to regard their memories in each case with at least as much affection as most children have for their only mother.[29]

There were often difficult financial periods for the Hollingworth family. Thomas and Mittie had at least twelve children, and although only three of these lived to adulthood, there were always mouths to feed. Holly supplemented the family income when he "became a hustler for all the stray jobs about the town." For several years, he was a janitor for the Methodist and the Congregational Churches in Dewitt. He also tended the lawns of well-heeled townspeople, delivered newspapers, became a telegraph operator, and was a grocery clerk for two different employers.

Included in his autobiography, *Born in Nebraska*, is an interesting chapter entitled, "Jew and Gentiles" in which Holly recounts a "short experience in a general store, newly established by a soft-spoken Jew and his wife, the first members of this census-group our town has known." Comparing this clerking job with the same position he held at his uncle's store, Holly writes:

At Uncle Henry's I was trusted with free access to the cash drawer. At Frishman's when change was needed, I had to tap furtively on the counter with a coin and the proprietor would come running to take care of things.... Finally, when he objected to my melodious whistling, which as a matter of fact was never inflicted upon him when customers were in the store, the camel's back was broken. By that time I had secured a school, which was soon to begin, so I left his grocery department high and dry.... Anyway, my uncle's customers did not flock to the new grocery where they heard I was installed there, and it is just possible that this Jew's whole original design had been frustrated.[30]

In a later revision of Born in Nebraska, Holly softens his rhetoric to "I left the Hebrew high and dry."[31] Prairie ethnic prejudices were no doubt equally prevalent in Chadron and Valentine.

After graduating from public school at the age of sixteen, Holly spent the next seven years attempting to complete the entrance requirements to the University of Nebraska. This period was the most disappointing thus far in his life, and he described them as feeling ensnared in a trap. As was customary at the time, Holly graduated from the tenth grade and had to complete two additional years' work to qualify for college. He thought he might be eligible to teach in a country school but discovered that he was too young to receive teaching certification. For the next several years, he worked with his father as a carpenter and in the evenings tried to teach himself German, bookkeeping, and shorthand. He briefly returned to public school to review subjects for the teacher certification examination.

During 1898 and 1899, Holly taught in a one-room schoolhouse in the Vroom District, No. 73, unaware that the school was in the same area where his maternal grandmother and a step-aunt lived. Nor did he suspect that the director of the school board was his uncle, or that he was the board's second choice. Visiting this school for the first time, he noted:

> There appeared to be reasons enough why the elected teacher resigned. The building was a ramshackle structure, with holes not only in the roof but also straight through the side walls.... As for the roof, there was just nothing that the teacher could do about it. Aside from seats and blackboards, a box of chalk, an old eraser...and much used books for reading, grammar arithmetic, geography, and a dirty kindergarten chart bearing the alphabet and a few words and sentences illustrated by pictures, there was nothing educational in the room.[32]

His first day in the classroom was miserable. "Never having been in a district school, with one room and no grade organization, there was no way of knowing how or where to begin."[33] Enrollment was seasonally dependent, and the student population varied month to month. During planting and harvest times, the only children in school were those still too young to be of material assistance in farm work. "The day would drag on interminably and this was largely my fault.... . My reach was exceeding my grasp."[34]

Most children in Nebraska were educated in rural schools similar to the one in Vroom. It was common for country school teachers to lack a high school diploma and for women (or men) as young as fifteen to teach children who were sometimes older than they. The most important lesson Holly learned from the experience was that he was utterly unprepared to teach. In retrospect, he believed the year in Vroom was a moderate success, because he was able to manage even the most difficult and boisterous male students. When school was not in session, Holly continued to work with his father doing general contracting work.

In 1889, he accepted another teaching position just three miles from Dewitt in District 149. His teaching experience there, in a more prosperous community, was successful. The school building was solidly constructed, and there were excellent teaching supplies and materials. Most important, the top drawer in the teacher's desk contained detailed academic records of each pupil. He even found a teaching manual and curriculum guide.

Planning to use his hard-earned savings to attend college, Holly was disappointed when he was asked relinquish every penny he had earned to pay for his father to attend a program designed to aid stutterers. A self-described pessimist, Holly fully expected the program to fail, but he paid his father's tuition anyway. As he feared, the treatments were worthless. Thomas continued to stutter, and Holly returned to District 149 for another year as schoolmaster. Although he never viewed teaching in a prairie school as a likely career, he observed:

> The little school house of District 149 is one of the spots
> on earth for which I cherish a real fondness. It was there
> that I first began to see the way out of the trap of igno-
> rance and poverty and get my feet set on the glory road.[35]

However, perhaps due to the teaching and carpentry years, Holly never overcame his fear of poverty, no matter how well off he was financially.

In September of 1901, Holly was financially able to move to Lincoln, Nebraska to attend Wesleyan Academy, a preparatory school.[36] During his first year at the Academy, he studied botany, European history, English composition, and the history of English literature, which he described as the "best course of instruction ever given me in my life."[37] As the summer of 1902 approached, he was encouraged by his father to join him in Cheyenne, Wyoming to work in the railroad shops. There were no summer employment opportunities in Dewitt but plenty of jobs in Cheyenne. So when the semester ended, Holly "set out to ride 600 miles across the prairies of Nebraska to Cheyenne, Wyoming…looking for work," pedaling in the old covered wagon ruts that can still be seen today from outer space.[38] He even customized his bicycle with special tires so he could ride on the railroad tracks. The experience of traveling alone with only a backpack and a revolver must have been exhilarating. Holly worked his way west doing occasional work as a carpenter, grave-digger, cowboy, and handyman. He returned to do one more year of preparatory studies.

Finally, in September 1903, he was accepted into the University of Nebraska's sophomore class. Though he enjoyed the academics, he noted in his autobiography: "midway…there entered also a stream of affection. This at first thin current in time engulfed me in the profound depths of a partnership a devotion such as it can be the privilege of few men to know."[39] The stream of affection was his growing love for Leta Stetter.

Leta and Holly became acquainted academically before they ever met socially. Holly's English literature papers were often returned with comments in the margins from a theme reader who initialed her comments L.A.S. A year or so later, Holly worked as a reader for the psychology department. There, he evaluated Miss Stetter's papers and initialed his comments H.L.H. The two became even better acquainted during their junior year when both were members of a psychology class taught by Professor Thaddeus L. Bolton. Professor Bolton, who emphasized the psychology of imitation, conducted the class in a manner that was unusual in the 1900s—seminar-style around a large table in his laboratory, rather than in front of a room with formal lectures. Holly and Leta were also charter members of Tau Psi XI, the Psychology Club created by Bolton, one of the first such clubs in the country.

It was during the 1903-1904 semester that the two Nebraska students fell in love. Both were sophomores. "L.A.S. and H.L.H at once found that they had much in common by way of background, interest, information and values." Holly recalled, "around Chi Omega, I became a familiar figure." Chi Omega was a women's college fraternity that had been established in 1895 at the University of Arkansas; the University of Nebraska chapter was founded in 1903. Leta was one of its earliest members.

When writing his memoirs some thirty-seven years after first catching a glimpse of Leta in the University of Nebraska Library, Holly still referred to her affectionately as "my Chi Omega" and the "Scarlet Tam-o-Shanter girl."

A poem entitled "Remembering" was found in Leta Hollingworth's papers after her death. She had written it many years after their courtship, yet the moment it described still glowing.

Remembering

Last eve a wandering wind
Passed over the grass and me.
I marveled, but did not find
A reason why it should be
As though a kind hand stroked my face.
Yet my blood grew quick in me.

> *Then, all of a sudden I knew!*
> *That evening—the first that we*
> *Kissed each other,—a little wind blew*
> *Over us, long ago, in another place.*[40]

Holly was well aware of Leta's traumatic past. He wrote, "The flames of this furnace stretched so far that they threatened to scorch my own aspirations as well. I still tremble to remember how the bitter taste of discord and cruelty contributed a hesitant reluctance toward the initiation of domestic adventures on her own part."[41] He recalled, "early in that last year [1906] we agreed (I can still visualize so clearly the spot where this took place) that we belonged to each other, and that when it became humanly possible, we would pitch our tent together."[42] Leta was nineteen years old when she agreed to be Holly's wife, though they did not marry for two more years. In a letter to Holly, written in 1907, Leta revealed, "Sometimes I ponder and ponder to think any man could ever have made me love him trustingly enough to marry him."[43]

Leta Ann Stetter and Harry Levi Hollingworth both were awarded Bachelor of Arts degrees from the University of Nebraska in May 1906. Leta also obtained a State Teacher's Certificate in English and English literature.

The moment had arrived for Leta and Holly to put their college educations to work. She was well on her way to becoming an "adequate adult," a term she used years later when, as Dr. Leta Hollingworth, she was an acclaimed expert on the subject of adolescence. In 1928, the year her text, *The Psychology of the Adolescent*, was published, she stated that the ultimate goal of adolescence was to evolve into what she envisioned as the "adequate adult." In subsequent articles and public addresses, she returned to this concept. Her description of this "adequate adult" reveals much about herself, her childhood, and her tolerance or intolerance regarding others.

> What kind of person is it, then, who emerges successfully from the period of adolescence, with all of its major problems solved? Such a person will be an adequate

adult, fit to engage in the trials of maturity and of old age without "a nervous breakdown." The adequate adult is able, in the first place, to sustain himself or herself physically. This means economic competence.... It is in this fundamental respect that women have had and still have the greatest difficulty in meeting the conditions of adulthood. Because of their part in reproduction, women have been dependent on men for subsistence instead of being themselves in direct contact with the source of supply.... Intellectually, the adequate adult arrives at his own opinions and follows his own conclusions in handling life's difficulties.... [H]e is not dependent on constant advice or admonition.... [44]

According to Leta, adequate adults were also self-sufficient, "independent of coddling," and "could suffer without raising an ostentatious lamentation, and without draining the sympathy of others."[45] Leta exhibited many of these characteristics. Some enhanced her personality and work, but others did not. She had little patience for adults behaving like children, and she recalled telling a female colleague, also from the Great Plains, "What that man needs is a cactus in his foot." This was in reference to a professor who seemed to complain constantly.

When Leta became seriously ill with cancer in 1929, true to her own conception of adulthood, she raised no "ostentatious lamentation," nor did she drain "the sympathies of others." Consequently, she suffered alone.

In 1906, Leta was hired as a teacher and assistant principal of a small, rural K-12 school in Dewitt, Nebraska (Holly's hometown) and was paid the sum of sixty dollars per month. She was disappointed to learn that she was also expected to serve as the school janitor. The more experienced principal of the Dewitt School and the neophyte Leta taught the entire last several grades in the school. Besides teaching English, Leta was assigned to teach Latin, German, history, physiology, civics, and botany. This assignment would be daunting for even the most experienced and gifted teacher. An inexperienced instructor such as Leta, no matter how intelligent or well prepared, must have found the task nearly impossible.

In September 1906, Harry Hollingworth was appointed principal of Fremont High School, some one hundred miles north of Dewitt. In addition to fulfilling his administrative duties, he taught bookkeeping, agriculture, and general English literature. He was also track coach, director of the Glee Club, and was a substitute teacher in any subject whenever one was needed. Holly's tenure as principal lasted only six months, for he was soon to relocate to New York City.

On occasion, Holly wrote that he went to "Lincoln or elsewhere to hold communion with a young friend of mine who was assistant principal in my home town school. Very often I would meet her at the home of Mrs. Nellie Pickup who for long years maintained an almost maternal instinct in us." Mrs. Pickup, who preferred to be called "Ma" by the couple,[46] lived with her sister in Lincoln, and they became dear and lifelong friends of Leta and Holly.[47]

Midway through the school year, Professor James McKeen Cattell of Columbia University in New York offered Holly a graduate assistantship in psychology. Holly later wrote that "it was the opportunity of a lifetime and meant the possibility of realizing a deep seated ambition."[48] Thus it was that in March 1907, Holly left his position as principal at Fremont High School in Nebraska to pursue graduate study in psychology in New York City. Leta remained, for the time being, in Nebraska. Her Dewitt teaching experience lasted one year, after which she readily accepted a new teaching position 180 miles farther west in McCook, Nebraska that offered more money and a new school building.

While she was delighted with the new opportunity, she feared any uprooting, as she had been so often abruptly moved away from loved ones as a child. She began teaching at McCook High School in September 1907 and found the contrast between the two school districts quite striking. She taught two subjects, English literature and German, rather than seven; McCook High School was new, and the students appeared eager to learn. In Leta's estimation, the town of Dewitt was "hopelessly static," while McCook was "young, vigorous, adolescent, growing, dynamic in every way."[49]

Leta and Holly continued their relationship by correspondence. Holly was still a struggling Ph.D. student with no guarantee of a university position when he graduated. His situation was somewhat unpredictable. Nevertheless, by the spring of 1908, the couple decided that they had endured a long enough separation. They decided to get married. Under the headline "North Nebraska Wedding," *The Fremont Herald* reported:

> It is rumored among his large circle of friends in this city that H. L. Hollingworth, familiarly known as "Holly," has fallen victim to Cupid's wiles and will enter the blissful state of matrimony December 29. His bride is to be Miss Leta Stetter of Valentine. The wedding will be held in New York City where Mr. Hollingworth holds a position in...Columbia University....[50]

Leta Stetter was going to New York City! She must have hoped that the physical distance between New York City and Valentine, Nebraska would be sufficient to free her from memories of Fanny and Johnny. "Now I wash my hands of all their affairs forever. And thank the good Lord I am quit forever of that dreadful place. I feel that it would choke me ever to set foot upon its 'threshold' again; so terribly do I remember it."[51] She almost kept this vow. There are only two recorded instances when Leta, as an adult, returned to her childhood home. The first was in 1916, when she buried her sister Ruth in Chadron. The second time she returned was in 1938, when, at the age of fifty-two, she gathered enough courage to visit her Valentine relatives in northwestern Nebraska.

What a change it must have been to live in New York City! She no doubt saw the opportunities. She wondered:

> As for me...quite possibly I shall not fulfill the "promise" of my adolescence. Some kind of "promise" I conclude

there was or is to this external world, for I never had but one instructor who did not bring it verbally to my notice. It grew into a kind of little game, to see how long it would take them to say it."[52]

She was not immune to the pressures placed upon a gifted individual to succeed, and even more, to do great things. Yet she was optimistic. She and Holly were embarking upon an exciting new life. But first, she was in for a rude awakening; for a time, her feelings of "inevitable movement and destination" were to come to an abrupt halt.

CHAPTER 4

Making Lemon Pies

*To me there is nothing so sad as to look back on the
capable, intelligent, women I have known, and see
how they have been bound down hand and foot by
custom, and economic dependence.*[1]
—Leta Stetter Hollingworth, 1917

The seven-year period from 1909-1916 was a personal and professional watershed for Leta, both in positive and in negative ways. She painfully experienced for the first time overt and pernicious gender bias. She had not found gender bias or discrimination on the Nebraska frontier. Encountering bias against women in the university community, coupled with her profound giftedness, seems to have been the catalyst to ignite both her scholarship and her feminism.

She attacked gender misinformation and discrimination on many fronts. In the early 1910s, she became a charter member of two feminist organizations—the Heterodoxy Club and the Feminist Alliance—which were vehicles for social change. She was also active in the New York Woman Suffrage Party, a group devoted to earning the vote for women. Her later scientific work on sex differences was an outgrowth of these experiences, and her research results provided a rationale that supported many feminist causes. She attained the sobriquet "scientific pillar" of the woman's movement.[2]

LIFE IN THE CITY

Leta and Holly lived in New York City during particularly exciting times. Over one million immigrants entered New York in 1909, and almost one-fourth of them stayed in the city. A newly-completed "skyscraper," the Singer Building, was impressive at forty-seven stories, as were movies, autos, a new subway, and telephones. Fulton's Fish Market was just opened, the New York Stock Market was trading in a volatile fashion, and the Metropolitan Opera, Ziegfield Follies, and Vaudeville were underway.

Social change was rampant. A race riot had occurred in Harlem, women were marching for suffrage and against child labor practices, and workers were on strike to protest low wages and fifty to sixty hour workweeks. W.E.B. Dubois and William James were prominent figures, and Sigmund Freud and Carl Jung visited New York City on their way to Massachusetts' Clark University.

These years were the heyday of the Progressive Movement, whose political agenda served as a middle ground between socialism on the left and populism on the right. The essence of progressivism—of the progressive spirit—was eloquently expressed by Inez Irwin, a feminist, political activist, and friend of Leta's, who wrote: "Life was full of hope and freedom. Great movements were starting everywhere. In the United States, the loudest voice in the land was that of the liberal. Everyone was fighting for something. Everyone was sure of victory."[3]

Leta and Holly were neither socialists nor populists. Although she was active in the suffrage and women's rights movements of her time, Leta remained an unreconstructed social conservative. She and Holly both had particular disdain for governmentally funded social welfare programs. They believed in the importance of an individual's efforts. More to the right politically and socially than his wife, Holly truly believed that the good fortune he had in life occurred only during Republican administrations. He referred to Franklin Roosevelt's presidency as a "protracted reign."[4] Having great faith in the primacy of the individual, Holly (and Leta) felt it was within each person's power to rise from illiteracy and poverty to a successful and productive life. He wrote:

> I had never complained of my lot. "Naked came I into the world" and I accepted the challenge to clothe myself with my own hands. All I ever wanted was a chance to earn my own way, and I never did acquire any sickly tolerance for those, no poorer than I, who felt that society owed them anything. Whatever may be the case in the present generation, at that date I found that it was to achieve the life I most wanted...if I would only wait patiently and pay the price. Perhaps it is wrong to expect such patience and such price from others.... My sympathies and loyalties are limited and narrow.... I...have little or no interest in trying to change our institutions any more rapidly than they will change anyway. My primary concerns are not with the cosmos, nor even with the brotherhood of man, but with the more immediate fate of my personal friends, my very, very, local community, my closer associates, and the very few human beings for whom I have real affection. And so I am not a joiner.[5]

Holly was, in his own words, apolitical. His emotional and financial support of Leta's graduate education and her career may be interpreted by some as proof positive that he was a feminist. His belief that his wife (and other women) should not be constrained from achieving personal and professional goals was more likely an expression of his life-long frontier mentality concerning the central importance of the individual and the necessity to reward outstanding individual efforts.

Leta was more of a joiner, and she did attempt to change institutions when she felt that women or children were not receiving their fair share of the American dream. Writing to a Nebraska acquaintance in 1917, several years after moving to New York, she explained:

I've been interested in the progress of suffrage and all the
other interests of women out in the West. It's wonderful
how all of those things have developed in the last fifteen
years. But the West always has been ahead of the East in
most things pertaining to the advancement of women's
status.... . Fortunately for me, I married a Western man,
who wanted me to go ahead and make all I possibly
could out of myself, and who did not wish to restrain me
in any way within my "proper sphere" ("the home"). So I
have been more fortunate than most women have. But in
the course of my endeavors to "amount to something"
my eyes have been opened to the scores of obstacles that
keep women from living freely even in our democratic
land. To me there is nothing so sad as to look back on the
capable, intelligent, women I have known, and see how
they have been bound down hand and foot by custom,
and economic dependence.[6]

Leta understood these women. During her early years living in
New York City, it appears that she was one of these oppressed
women herself. She never forgot it.

CAUGHT IN A TRAP

On December 31, 1908, Holly met Leta's train at the Albany,
New York station, and together they traveled to New York City for
their marriage ceremony. Earlier, Holly had persuaded a New York
City License Bureau clerk to remain open as late as possible that
New Year's Eve. The clerk was waiting for them with the license.
One step remained—the marriage ceremony. The couple ate a lei-
surely dinner, visited the apartment Holly rented, and arrived at the
neighborhood Lutheran church as arranged. To their great surprise,
the Reverend Walker was not expecting them. He had been expecting to conduct the marriage ceremony the previous evening.

The groom, in his excitement, had hastily run through the
jingle verse that had hitherto been a sufficient guide, but

had apparently made it—"Thirty days hath December, April, June and November…" Tonight, at the late hour, he was not wholly ready for us. But he had our license in hand, and the next three days were holidays, and we wanted to go home (as) man and wife. So two satisfactory witnesses were found who had not yet retired for the night. Except for a little awkwardness arising from the failure to know that Lutherans expected both bride and groom to have rings, and to exchange them…the ceremony went off without a hitch. [7]

The newlyweds believed they had "crossed one of the long stretches we had foreseen, and we had not hesitated to recognize it for what it was. Our hoped for 'forty years together' were at least beginning, and thereafter our two lives were to be as one."[8]

The Hollingworths began their married life in an apartment on West 136th Street, nearly a mile—walking distance—from Columbia University, Teachers College, and Barnard College, which were in Morningside Heights, one of the intellectual centers of the city. They lived in Harlem, which was growing and beginning a renaissance. Holly recalled:

> Harlem, and especially 125th Street, was a busy up-town center…. There were good stores; theatres which showed the good plays after their initial run on Broadway; several famous variety shows. The bars usually offered a generous free lunch and some of them became favorite student resorts.[9]

New York City was also expensive. Leta and Holly were barely able to pay their bills. The stipend for a Psychology Assistant was a paltry $41.66 per month, hardly enough to buy food. Their second floor rear apartment was in a new building on West 136th Street; it consisted of a sitting room, dining room, bedroom, and bath. The furniture was second-hand and minimal. Leta's first cousin, Helen Stetter, remarked, "Leta said that when they were first married that he made their furniture. They had to rent a second class apartment, and they couldn't invite any of their friends to the house because they had furniture made out of boxes they would save at the store for Holly."[10]

Compounding the dismal state of their finances was Leta's inability to secure a teaching position, despite her previous experience and her earlier awards and positions at the University of Nebraska. While "Miss Stetter" might be hired, "Mrs. Hollingworth" could not because the Board of Education of the City of New York had enacted a policy that prohibited hiring married women as teachers. If a single teacher married, she could retain her position, however. The policy stated further that if a female teacher became pregnant, she would be dismissed. Leta and Holly reacted to this state of affairs with disbelief. Her Phi Beta Kappa award and prior teaching experience seemed to be of little use. They had counted on Leta's teaching salary to help with living expenses. But the social climate in the city at that time did not support women working outside the home.

Such restrictive attitudes were even present among many leaders in education and psychology. The renowned Columbia University Professor James McKeen Cattell wrote in 1909:

> The vast horde of female teachers in the United States tends to subvert both the school and the family.... The ultimate results of letting the celibate female be the usual teacher has been such as to make it a question whether it would not be an advantage to the country if the whole school plant could be scrapped.[11]

Leta could not win. If she had remained single, Cattell and his fellow scientists would condemn her as unsuitable because she was celibate. She did marry but was then rejected precisely because she was married. This kind of convoluted reasoning infuriated and depressed Leta. The fact that Cattell was Holly's doctoral adviser must have galled her even more.

She tried selling her short stories to publishers but was unsuccessful. Without a job, she was doing the laundry, cooking, and sewing all her clothes and even some of Holly's. She even trimmed her hats. Helen Stetter commented, "She made her own hats and they sure looked it!"[12] On January 30, 1909, Leta wrote a letter to Emma Zanuch Fischer, her cousin Anna's mother-in-law, that tells much about how she tried to manage her state of mind.

> Your box reached me a few days ago, and when I opened it I said, "Why here is just what I'm needing!" For I had told Mr. Hollingworth only the day before that I must get a book, because I'd forgotten so many tricks of the trade. I've already made lemon pie, pancakes and dressing according to it and all were beautifully successful.... It scarcely seems possible that I have been married and in the City a month. One of Mr. Hollingworth's friends gave him a clock, and it has done nothing but strike off the hours and half hours since it came. Time goes too fast when one is busy and happy.[13]

Rather than teaching or publishing her stories, Leta Hollingworth was making lemon pies. One cannot help but notice her mention of the clock, which "has done nothing but strike off the hours and half hours since it came. Time goes too fast when one is busy and happy," was written in sadness and bitterness, for Leta was not happy. In his autobiography, Holly recalled those days:

> There were a few occasions...when L.S.H. would unaccountably burst into tears. In those days she was never quite able to tell me why. Later on she said it was because she could not bear being strong and able, with a good mind and a sound education, and yet being so unable to contribute materially toward our welfare. This was only part of it, I know well enough, for L.S.H. was "caught in a trap." This time the trap was not due to ignorance nor to misguided faith, but solely to poverty. She was as full

as I of the urge toward intellectual endeavor, but for these five years she had been condemned to forms of housework, which a woman could have done without any of her training. And it did not yet appear how soon, if ever, it was going to be her turn to get her feet on the glory road.[14]

Fortunately, Leta's stultifying circumstances lasted only a few months. When Holly began to augment his income by teaching evening classes and grading exams for other professors, it became financially possible for Leta to take some graduate courses. At first, she randomly selected literature courses, but she soon decided that she wanted to enroll as a full-time graduate student. Planning to focus her studies on the relationship of schools to social maladjustment in children, Leta applied for financial aid from Columbia University. After all, Holly and she had the same academic credentials, and he had received an assistantship with the eminent Professor Cattell. Her application was rejected. Once again, Leta was denied a steady intellectual activity that would at least allow her to leave their tiny, dark apartment. What she could not have known was that each year, Columbia University offered only twelve fellowships (valued at $650) and thirty-two scholarships (valued at $150). Women were ineligible for any of the fellowships and all but four of the scholarships.[15]

Six years later, Leta had conducted several studies on sex differences. After attending a talk by Leta on this topic, Rheta Childe Dorr, a member of the Heterodoxy Club, was inspired to write an article titled "Is Woman Biologically Barred from Success?" that appeared in the September 19, 1915 edition of *The New York Times Magazine*. Based on extensive interviews with Leta, the article reveals Leta's thoughts and emotions during her very difficult early years in New York City.

> Now, by all the accepted laws of society, and of the fiction writers, she should have been perfectly happy. She had love, a cozy little home and a husband whose career she

was helping to advance. But she was not happy... . He was in line for a professorship in a department as familiar to her as it was to him. She was doing the same work as the janitor's wife downstairs.... Why were all women expected to like a domestic life? Why were men permitted to have both love and a career, while women were asked to choose between the two? Were women's lives thus conditioned because they occupy an inferior position in society, and if they do, why is it so?[16]

There is little question that Leta Hollingworth suffered from periodic depression when she could not find a meaningful life-role for herself. She felt unworthy, and the tears that Holly described show that her emotions were intense and quick to change. She later referred to this period in her life as "Staying at home eating a lone pork chop."[17] For she was again emotionally and physically trapped—not in the "fiery furnace" of her stepmother's home, but this time trapped by the bigotry against women that was blatant and acceptable in the 1910s. As a married woman, Leta Hollingworth was now in a more untenable position than she had been as a single woman. Her education and abilities, valued by so many others before her marriage, appeared valueless now. She had not changed—yet her status had diminished.

Holly did his utmost to improve his wife's spirits. "When morning came, the first one to awake would call out, 'Come on: Got to pull on our pants and get great!,' and this was our mutual slogan for a long time thereafter. We had no special longing to be 'great' as such; what we meant was that only by becoming 'known' could we finally reach a place where the things we were both wanting for both of us could be realized."[18]

At Columbia University in 1909, Harry Hollingworth was awarded a Ph.D. degree, but he chose not to attend the commencement exercises. His priorities were with his wife and friends. Holly and Leta spent that day with their old friend and mentor from the University of Nebraska, Thaddeus L. Bolton. Dr. Harry L. Hollingworth was twenty-nine years old and a newly appointed instructor at Barnard College, a four-year women's college that had been in existence since 1889, where he later founded the Psychology Department. Since Barnard was just across Broadway Avenue from Columbia University and was closely affiliated with it, it was relatively easy for Holly to maintain connections with his colleagues there.

For Leta, however, things were not progressing as well. She was twenty-three years old and unemployed. But Leta Hollingworth would soon be far too busy to make lemon pies. Thanks to Holly and the Coca-Cola Company, her life was about to change.

THE CAFFEINE STUDY

Federal agents, in 1909, seized a shipment of forty barrels and twenty kegs of Coca-Cola syrup. Under the Pure Food and Drug Act of 1906, it was illegal to market a product that contained any additive harmful to human health. The government maintained that the caffeine in Coca-Cola was increased to compensate for the decrease in coca extract and that caffeine was a harmful ingredient. The Coca Cola Company was thus charged with violating the Pure Food and Drug Act.

Early in 1911, the defendants decided to hire a psychologist to conduct a formal study on the behavioral effects of caffeine upon humans. Professor James McKeen Cattell was recommended to direct the study but declined. Harry Hollingworth received the grant instead. Despite the negative attitude of many in the scientific community because funding for the study would be coming from the subjects of the lawsuit, Holly reasoned:

> No such experiments on such a scale as seemed necessary for conclusive results had even been staged in the history of experimental psychology.... . With me there was a double motive at work. I needed money, and here was a chance to accept employment at work for which I had been trained, with not only the cost of the investigation met, but with a very satisfactory retaining fee and stipend

for my own time and services. I believed I could consciously conduct such an investigation, without prejudice to the results, and secure information of a valuable scientific character as well as answer the practice questions raised by the sponsor of the study.[19]

But since Holly was working full-time at Barnard College, he could not personally oversee the experiment. So he hired Leta to be Assistant Director and gave her full command of the laboratory. Her scientific career was thus underway.

The experimental design was impressively intricate and elegant. It contained both blind and double-blind procedures; not only were the subjects unaware as to whether or not they were receiving caffeine, but the experimenters were also kept unaware. The variability of taste was eliminated because the subjects ingested gelatin capsules containing either caffeine or a milk and sugar placebo.

> In order to reduce to a minimum distracts and disturbances…and to provide for the greatest convenience of the experimenters and the comfort of the subjects, a well lighted and ventilated six-room apartment on the ground floor of a building a quiet part of the city was equipped as a special laboratory. Sixteen subjects, ten men and six women, were engaged for full time for a period of 40 days, and were required to appear at the laboratory at stated times during the day or to remain there permanently…and subject themselves to a series of mental and motor tests.[20]

The subjects were paid a set fee for their participation. Most were moderate caffeine users.

Three separate studies were conducted under Leta Hollingworth's guidance. The first was the longest and most complex. Between February 5 and March 3, 1911, the subjects were tested daily for five days in five areas—simple association, discrimination and judgment, motor speed and coordination, susceptibility to illusion, and typewriting. Six trained assistants and a physician worked with Leta to test the subjects.

The subjects in this first study were divided into four groups. The first subjects, in the control group named Squad 1, were given no caffeine at all throughout the experiment. Squad 2 was given caffeine on three days and the milk and sugar placebo on the following three days at 10:30 am. The third group was administered caffeine and milk and sugar on alternate days at the lunch hour. Squad 4 took caffeine and milk and sugar on alternate days from two and one-half to three hours after lunch. Each subject kept a daily journal, recording items relating to health and disposition.[21]

The second study lasted seven days and was designed to determine if the ingestion of caffeine impaired sleep. The four squads were given either Coca-Cola or a placebo at lunch and dinner and then tested "across a range of post-drug intervals."[22] The third study, a week in duration, compared the effects of caffeinated Coca-Cola with de-caffeinated Coca-Cola when each was taken with food.

Long after the subjects went home, a group of assistants recorded and assessed the daily data, and then, because of what Holly termed his "catastrophobia," duplicate records were made and placed in another location.

The studies were rigorous and time-intensive. The Hollingworths suffered emotionally and physically from the stress of the unrelenting testing and work schedule. Both Holly and Leta suffered persistent insomnia during this time; Holly lost weight and suffered from twitches in his fingers. Ever the scientists, they began keeping joint records of their own sleep patterns, and Holly later published an article titled "The Psychology of Drowsiness" based upon their findings.

The conclusions of the caffeine study were based on more than seventy-six thousand measurements and more than eight hundred efficiency curves.[23] The findings suggested that caffeine acted as a mild stimulant, particularly when the subjects were fatigued. Effects were lessened if the caffeine was taken on a full stomach. The influence of caffeine on motor processes was rapid and temporary, but effects were more prolonged on mental processes. Doses from one to four grains did not impair sleep, whereas six or more grains did affect sleep patterns. Women were influenced by smaller doses of caffeine than were males.[24]

In March 1911, the Hollingworths traveled to Chattanooga, Tennessee for the trial. When they discovered that their hotel was owned by Coca-Cola Company, they insisted that they stay at another lodging.[25] In his testimony, Holly presented quantitative data concluding that caffeine was not harmful to human mental or motor performance. The Coca-Cola Company introduced a dismissal motion on grounds that caffeine was not added to the beverage but was instead an inherent ingredient. Judge Edward T. Stanford upheld their motion, and the jury was directed to find in favor of Coca-Cola. Three years later, the verdict was upheld by the Appeals Court in Cincinnati.

In 1916, the case reached the United States Supreme Court, which ruled that caffeine was indeed added, and therefore the case had to be retried in the Chattanooga District Court. Coca-Cola modified its formula and reduced the amount of caffeine by fifty percent. The company then argued that it could not be tried based on a previous formula. The case was finally dismissed, and the issue was never brought to court again.

The caffeine study was important for Leta and Harry in several ways, not the least of which that it was one of the first scientific studies to apply psychology research to a social or industrial concern. It also was a substantial help to Harry and Leta financially. Writing in 1940, Harry Hollingworth noted:

> I have always been glad that we took on this project, which in the beginning appeared to all concerned to be a somewhat dubious undertaking. It did yield results of scientific value and they have stood the test of time and of such repetition as has been accorded them. It yielded... much valuable information in the form of record and measurements that could be used for the investigation of

questions remote from those originally raised. It yielded me a reputation for work of that character... . The investigation, and its report, did I believe its bit to break down some of the taboos then prevalent and to encourage cooperative investigation in which science provided the insight and technique and industry offers the problems and the means. Last, but far from least so far as L.S.H. and H.L.H. were concerned, it was one of the various things that canceled the deficit... .[26]

In a letter to her cousin "Kutzie" and her husband Frank just after the study had been completed, Leta summed up the Coca-Cola caffeine study very succinctly: "We did a big experiment for the Coca-Cola [C]ompany; and made quite a 'wad' of money."[27] That wad of money was used to send Leta Stetter Hollingworth to graduate school full time at Columbia University and Teachers College where she did a double major in psychology and sociology.

GRADUATE STUDENT YEARS

Columbia University, Teachers College, and Barnard College were central to Leta and Holly's lives for many decades.[28] At the time when Leta and Holly were graduate students, the Columbia University and Teachers College faculty included such luminaries as James McKeen Cattell, Robert Woodworth, Edward Thorndike, Naomi Norsworthy, John Dewey, William Heard Kilpatrick, and Patti Hill Smith. The learning environment was ideal for Leta. It was characterized by "the absence of dictatorship in research or in systematic thinking about the field of psychology. Students were always encouraged there...to stand on their own feet, to find their own problems if possible, and to make the most of them, even if they appeared quite irrelevant to the current interests of the professors."[29]

Several professors were influential to Leta's intellectual development—some directly, as her instructors, and others indirectly through their contributions to the study of psychology and education. Many of these were the same persons who influenced Holly.

When Holly accepted a graduate fellowship with Professor James McKeen Cattell in 1907, he did so with the knowledge that he would be studying with a man who was a pioneer in the new science of psychology. Professor Cattell had been a student of the philosopher and psychologist Wilhelm Wundt, who had established the first psychology laboratory in Leipzig, Germany, and Cattell (1860-1944) was among the first to study individual differences. He introduced the term "mental tests" and was a proponent of the new concept of psychometrics—measurements of mental processes, including intelligence.

Cattell recognized the importance of environment as well as heredity in their effect upon intelligence. In an unpublished autobiographical sketch written at the age of seventy-six, James McKeen Cattell wrote, "what a man can do is prescribed by heredity; what he does is determined by circumstance... . Chance is the guide that leads us all."[30] Though she did not directly work with Cattell, Leta Hollingworth concurred in such beliefs. Inherited abilities reflect what one can do, but environment influences what one actually does with those innate abilities. Her subsequent philosophy about gifted children did not arise from thin air. She was taught, she learned, she synthesized, and then she constructed her theories and practices.

Perhaps Cattell's greatest accomplishment at Columbia was as an advocate for experimental studies of human behavior. It was no doubt exciting and challenging to be an early student of Professor Cattell. Certainly, it was a great opportunity for Holly to work under the tutelage and aura of a man who had been named Professor of Psychology by Columbia University in 1888, the first person in the world to have such a title. Immensely influential in the teaching of psychology, Cattell was also an editor of many scientific and educational journals, such as *American Men of Science* and *A Directory of American Scholars*, and he was the founder of the journals *Science* and *School and Society.*

Leta's primary mentor was Professor Edward Lee Thorndike (1874-1949), who, himself, had received his doctorate degree in psychology under the tutelage of Professor Cattell at Columbia University and was the successor to Cattell's prominence in educational psychology there. Of all the faculty members Leta Hollingworth encountered in her graduate studies, Thorndike was the most influential to her intellectual and philosophical evolution as a scientist and a teacher.

A graduate of Wesleyan University in Middletown, Connecticut in 1895, Thorndike had attended Harvard and studied with William James while receiving his master of arts degree in 1897. He was awarded a doctorate from Columbia University in 1898. He was immediately hired to teach psychology at the College for Women of Western Reserve University in Cleveland, Ohio. The Dean of Teachers College, James Earl Russell, traveled to Ohio, observed Thorndike teaching, and although he found him "dealing with the investigations of mice and monkeys," he was "satisfied that he was worth trying out on humans."[31] Russell had little trouble convincing Thorndike to return to New York City. Teachers College gave him a one-year contract to teach psychology and child study. Within five years, Thorndike was promoted to the rank of full professor, appointed Chair of the Psychology Department, and remained on the faculty for forty years.

Thorndike's teaching method, like that of his model and mentor Cattell, was far different than the pedagogical norm. Instead of straight lecturing, the professor was a facilitator of learning, giving his graduate students great academic liberties. Years later, this refreshing academic climate was noted by Heidbreder, who wrote, "Cattell tradition at Columbia stands for a certain independence...and latitudinarianism in dealing with psychological material."[32] This favorable climate enabled Harry and Leta Hollingworth to do their work unhampered by prevailing dogma.

Long before such terms as "multiple intelligences" entered educational jargon, Thorndike understood the multidimensional nature of intelligence. His son, Robert, recalled his father speaking about abstract, mechanical, and social or executive intelligence.[33] It was Thorndike who transformed G. Stanley Hall's child-study philosophies into educational psychology.[34] He "accepted the biological framework Hall had brought to the study of child nature, and injected into it methodological sophistication and systematic concern for the learning process itself... ."[35]

Thorndike's passionate concern with measurement permeated his work, and it laid the groundwork for the Hollingworths' later studies on individual differences. In the *1918 National Society for the Study of Education Yearbook*, Thorndike issued his often-quoted statement that "Whatever exists, exists in some amount. To know it thoroughly involves knowing its quantity as well as its quality."[36] His concern with measurement was not limited, however, to a university laboratory. He viewed the school itself as a laboratory and devoted his professional life to seeking out the quantitative in classroom practices.

> When he became interested in education...he immediately sought to discover just what and how much was accomplished by the attempt to educate. Even before intelligence tests came into vogue, Thorndike had adopted the practice of measurement in education and had taken his problem into the laboratory.... Instead of the minute introspection of a few trained observers, he studied the performances of large numbers of subjects, obtaining results that could be tabulated and treated statistically by the experimenter.[37]

"Like all pioneers. Thorndike inspired innumerable disciples and leaders to carry on his revolutionary work in education. Many of them became his colleagues on the Faculty of Teachers College, among them Leta S. Hollingworth, renowned for her work with exceptional and gifted children...," wrote Lawrence Cremin, President of Teachers College.[38]

Another influential educator at Columbia University and Teachers College during this time was John Dewey. "Thorndike and Dewey," according to Cremin, "supplied the two great formative influences of twentieth-century educational theory and together established the frame of reference in which their contemporaries and successors were to work."[39] It was John Dewey who stressed over and over again the importance of teaching students *how* to think rather than *what* to think.[40] It is unclear how much direct interaction Leta and Harry Hollingworth had with Professor Dewey, but his influence was certainly present nonetheless.[41]

NAOMI NORSWORTHY

The sex stereotypes and discrimination that Leta encountered when she first tried to get a teaching job in New York City also prevailed in the graduate school at Teachers College. The prevailing attitude was summarized by one male faculty member who wrote:

> In most cases the women make good students...but on the whole, I think a smaller proportion of them than of the men are capable, either by natural endowment of opportunity, of undertaking really advanced or original work, and the proportion of them who reach the doctorate is almost pathetically small.[42]

Fortunately, Leta Hollingworth had a predecessor at Teachers College—Naomi Norsworthy. Professor Norsworthy (1877-1916) was one of the "pathetically small" number of women referred to above who prevailed and had earned her doctoral degree, and her background was similar to Leta's. She had been a precocious child who had completed her elementary school studies in only seven years. She never attended high school, and at the age of fifteen entered the New Jersey State Normal School in Trenton, New Jersey. Upon certification, she taught third grade in Morristown. When she was financially able, she enrolled at Columbia University Teachers College in 1899, earning a bachelor of science degree in 1901. The following year, she became the first woman graduate student admitted to Teachers College to work toward a Ph.D. in psychology. Much to his credit, and probably amid much controversy, Professor Thorndike appointed her to be his graduate assistant and later asked her to remain on the faculty as an instructor.[43]

James Russell, as Dean in charge, agreed, and Norsworthy was promoted to the rank of instructor in 1904 without further controversy. Three years later, however, when Thorndike proposed Norsworthy's promotion to Assistant Professor, Professor Cattell was incensed, even though he was not a member of the Teachers College faculty. Thorndike responded:

> Teachers College is in part a graduate school and in part a professional school. The most gifted people for training teachers in certain lines...are at present and will for a long time be women. We shall for a long time have women in leading positions on our staff. Dr. Norsworthy is beyond question enormously successful in training teachers.... She does exactly what is required of a teacher in an undergraduate professional school. I should be sacrificing the interests of Teachers College to do anything that helps withhold from her the promotion that a man equally competent would be sure to have had.[44]

Cattell did not relent in his criticism, but was overruled by Dean James Russell who not only fired off a memorandum to Cattell saying, "...I cannot assent to your plan to check promotions in Teacher College because of your inability to make similar promotions elsewhere,"[45] but also sent a letter to Teachers College President Nicholas Murray Butler supporting the promotion of Naomi Norsworthy.

> She is a good scholar...a superb teacher and the mainstay of our department. Her influence not only with the students of psychology but to all students of the institution is phenomenal.... We have no woman on our professorial staff who has earned the right to promotion through scholarship and teaching ability. With so many students and the necessity of promotion to professorships women of exceptional technical ability as chief claims to their rank, I feel we should offer some encouragement to younger women along scholarly lines.[46]

The accomplishment of Naomi Norsworthy's promotion at Teachers College in 1907 paved the way for Leta, both as an entering graduate student in 1911 and as a faculty member at Teachers College beginning in 1916. It did not, of course, resolve the sex-role stereotyping and sex discrimination rampant within higher education. Although women were being awarded doctorates in increasing numbers, it was very difficult for female scientists to find positions in academia, and these women often encountered an unpleasant atmosphere even when they did. For example, Norsworthy, the consummate faculty member, often had to substitute for Edward Thorndike. She recalled that she was very nervous in doing so because of certain things she experienced, such as walking into Professor Thorndike's class and overhearing a student remark, "Where is the professor today? and who is this in his place? I, for one, did not come to Teachers College to be taught by a chit of a girl." Even though at the end of class this same young man complimented her on her teaching, she disliked teaching men because of their hostility—so much so that she said:

> I wish I could creep into some little backwoods village and be lost so I wouldn't have to teach graduate classes with men in them that don't want to be taught by women.... I wish I could be a rural school teacher in the deepest of the Wilds for just a bit of time![47]

Undoubtedly, Leta Hollingworth encountered similar experiences and was faced with similar reactions. Naomi Norsworthy was promoted to the rank of Professor of Educational Psychology on February 16, 1912. After a long struggle with cancer, she died in 1916, the year that Leta joined the Teachers College faculty. When Norsworthy became ill, the faculty position opened. Leta Hollingworth, it was decided, would be a worthy successor, displaying a similar devotion and sensitivity to students, a high degree of professionalism, and excellence in teaching.

Thus, from 1916 until her death in 1939, Leta was a member of the Teachers College faculty. Harry Hollingworth taught at Barnard

College from 1909 until his retirement in 1946. Although the Hollingworths never taught in the same college, they both were considered Columbia University professors.

A photograph of the oaken doors of Schermerhorn Hall, which housed the psychology department at Columbia University, later was framed by Leta and hung in a prominent place in the Hollingworth home. "Those ponderous doors have shadowed us from the beginning of our life together to the very end of our companionship.... To our friends the picture means little enough. To us it was always a tiny symbol of the things we jointly held most precious."[48] The doors may have been ponderous, but they also opened onto an exciting lifelong path for the Hollingworths. Both Leta and Harry passionately enjoyed and were dedicated to the study of psychology.

EDUCATION IN AMERICAN SCHOOLS

American education was in the midst of a sea of change, and Columbia University was very involved. In 1910, the *Journal of Educational Psychology* was begun, with Professor Edward Thorndike of Teachers College, Columbia University espousing the potential contributions of psychology to education. In 1916, John Dewey, also of Columbia University, published his seminal book, *Democracy and Education: An Introduction to the Philosophy of Education*, which further changed how educators viewed schools and themselves. Patty Smith Hill and William Heard Kilpatrick, members of the Teachers College faculty, were also eminent in their specialties within education and influenced Leta in her attitudes toward childhood education in the schools.

William Heard Kilpatrick was perhaps the single most prominent interpreter of John Dewey's philosophy. In 1918, Kilpatrick articulated his "Projects Methods" hypothesis. Building upon his mentor John Dewey's work, Kilpatrick argued that:

> Education should encompass not only the intellectual but the aesthetic and the social.... This assumption was predicated on the idea that children could not be adequately prepared for an unknowable future through a

static curriculum.... The ideal was to involve the student actively in the process of education and to emphasize the experiences and knowledge the child might bring to the subject matter, rather than solely what the subject matter brought to the child.[49]

Kilpatrick had come to Teachers College in 1907 after a career in public schools and at Mercer College in Georgia. He was one of the most controversial figures on campus, but also perhaps the most popular instructor. When she was a graduate student, Leta Hollingworth studied under him and later was his colleague throughout her tenure at Teachers College—though it was not always a collegial relationship. Although they co-taught a course in the 1930s, a profound difference in their philosophy of education evolved.

Patty Smith Hill integrated the new science of educational psychology with early childhood education. A former student of both John Dewey and G. Stanley Hall, she was first a guest lecturer and then a faculty member at Teachers College. A leader in the liberal kindergarten movement, she, like Dewey, believed that children learn by actively participating in the classroom and that they learn best by doing authentic activities. Patty Smith Hill incorporated the projects method into early childhood education, believing that "the...project method with its emphasis upon the child's ability and right to plan, as well as execute, the plans of the teacher, the ability and the right of children to learn from and to help each other, has given us the socialized kindergarten of today."[50]

When Leta Hollingworth later experimented with her "Evolution of Common Things" curriculum in gifted education, she was doing so in the spirit of the child-study and project-approach pedagogy. If it is true that an innovator stands on the shoulders of her predecessors, Leta was bolstered by John Dewey, William Heard Kilpatrick, Edward Lee Thorndike, Patti Smith Hill, and Naomi Norsworthy.

THE BINET-SIMON INTELLIGENCE SCALE

By 1913, Leta had received her master's degree and soon after was offered a temporary position as a part-time clinical psychologist at The Clearing House for Mental Defectives. Her job was to administer the new Binet-Simon mental tests to clients referred to the Clearing House by the courts. Though unfamiliar with the tests and the procedures for giving them, Hollingworth could not pass up such a fine opportunity. So she taught herself how to administer and score the Binet mental tests.

In the early years of the twentieth century, Theodore Simon and Alfred Binet were appointed by the Minister of Instruction in Paris to develop an intelligence test that would identify children of subnormal intelligence in order to place them special schools. The two men constructed a battery of thirty tasks with the tasks assembled in a series so that each new task was more difficult than the previous one. In this initial Binet-Simon Scale (1905), the criterion for passing each test was somewhat arbitrary. Nonetheless, it was the first practical intelligence test, and it allowed Binet and Simon to diagnose various degrees of mental retardation.

The Binet-Simon scale was later modified by grouping the tests into average mental levels for various age groups—or mental age categories—and in 1908, the first age-grade scale was published. Each task "came to have a certain objective value, expressible in terms of the average intelligence of children of a given birthday age."[51] It was Binet's belief that when the below-normal students were identified, they could then be segregated into special classes, remediated, and eventually "catch-up" to normal children.

The excitement concerning this new test quickly crossed the Atlantic, and in 1906, Henry Goddard, of the newly established Psychological Research Laboratory at the Vineland Training School in New Jersey, began the translation to introduce the 1905 Binet-Simon test to America. By 1908, Goddard had administered his translated test to two thousand students at the Vineland Training School as a way of obtaining standardized norms. The Binet-Simon was subsequently employed widely in the United States as a means to identify children who were thought to be uneducable in the regular classroom. Goddard's work caught the attention of Lewis Terman at Stanford University. Terman recognized the great potential value of this test and suggested several additional tasks that could be used to supplement the original thirty.

In 1912, the German psychologist Wilhelm Stern first coined the term "mental quotient" (later renamed "Intelligence Quotient" or "IQ" by Terman), as a figure derived from the ratio of the child's mental age score to the child's chronological age, a concept quickly adopted by Terman. Then, in 1916, under Terman's guidance, the Binet-Simon was modified, producing "the grandfather of all American intelligence tests, the Stanford-Binet Intelligence Scale."[52]

Terman's book, *The Measurement of Intelligence* (1916), was dedicated "to the memory of Alfred Binet, patient researcher, creative thinker, unpretentious scholar, inspiring and fruitful devotee of inductive and dynamic psychology."[53] The revised test was named the *Stanford Revision of the Binet* and informally called the Stanford-Binet.

In the first one-third of the twentieth century, there were very few psychological practitioners and even fewer established psychological service facilities. In the 1910s, psychologists like Leta were primarily psychometricians, or mental testers. The excitement over the new and various mental measurements of intelligence and other mental abilities led to the construction of group tests, particularly in the 1910-1920 decade, so that large numbers of children could be tested simultaneously. Leta Hollingworth never trusted the accuracy of group intelligence test scores, always preferring individualized assessment.

The cases presented to psychologists for evaluation often originated in the courts and dealt with mentally retarded and/or educationally maladjusted individuals. These were the types of cases that were referred to The Clearing House for Mental Defectives for Leta Hollingworth's assessment. Founded in 1913, The Clearing House was a branch of the Department of Public Charities. Its mission was "to examine mentally, physically, and socially all cases of suspected mental defect that are brought to its clinic, and to record and file the histories thus obtained, together with all available information concerning the individual examined."[54] Recommendations for either treatment or incarceration of the individuals then followed.

Initially hired as a substitute for Emily T. Burr, one of the earliest psychologists in the field of mental testing, Leta Hollingworth was retained after Burr returned from her sabbatical. Leta remained at the Clearing House for two years. The Clearing House director, Dr. Max Schlapp, became one of Leta's mentors. She later wrote, "I, who had prepared for work in schools, found myself working in a hospital, a great surprise to me!"[55]

When psychological examiners became subject to Civil Service Examinations in 1914, Leta placed highest on the list and was appointed as the first psychologist under the Civil Service in the City of New York. She was then transferred to the Psychopathic Service at Bellevue Hospital in 1915 where she discovered that the director, psychiatrist Dr. Menas S. Gregory, did not know how a psychologist ought to function because the field was so new. Gregory later became both a friend and a mentor to Leta.

The Clearing House and Bellevue Hospital cases provided a rich database for Leta's early psychological investigations of sex differences. Several questions guided her studies. She wondered whether males and females were referred for examination in equal numbers. Were they committed to institutions in equal numbers? If there was a difference in the frequency with which males and females were committed based on extremely low intelligence, could inferences be drawn?

It was in part through her Clearing House research studies that Leta was able to scientifically prove that theories of male superiority based upon Darwin's theory of variation from the norm were wrong. She later extended her research of sex differences among the cognitively challenged to their psychology and education. It was only later that she became intrigued with the intellectually superior child.

PSYCHOLOGY OF WOMEN BASED ON TRUTH

In actuality, Leta Hollingworth's intense focus on sex discrimination had begun in graduate school. Her scholarly work as a graduate student had one paramount objective—she was going to use science as her weapon of choice to dismantle unsubstantiated theories that denigrated women. Most of her published writings between 1913 and 1916 relate to sex differences. Holly explained:

> L.S.H. had long been strongly interested in the social and educational barriers encountered by women, and especially married women, who wanted to depart from the conventional domestic mode of life and exercise their gifts and talents in professional ways. Examining the literature concerning the achievement of women, she had been impressed especially by the dogmatic and unsupported character of the statement there found. It was clear enough that the historical achievements in the arts, sciences, and professions, were mainly accredited to men. But why? Two dogmas cropped up constantly among the arm-chair observations about women (chiefly written by men) that, it seemed to L.S.H., could be put to experimental tests. One was the handicap that women are supposed to suffer because of their menstrual rhythm. The other was the assertion that women as a species were less variable, among themselves, than were males.[56]

Her studies of variability and sexual (i.e., menstrual) periodicity would make it very difficult for proponents of sex differences to use "science" to justify their bigotry. In both her writings and her speeches, Leta emphasized the difference between the "literature of opinion" and the "literature of fact." She wrote:

> The literature of opinion includes all written statements, made by scientific men and others, not based on experimental evidence. The literature of opinion on the subject of sex differences and mental traits is voluminous. It

appears in the writings of Nietzche, Schopenhauer, Mill, Mobius, and others. By the literature of fact is meant those written statements based on experimental data, which have been obtained under carefully controlled conditions, and which may be verified by anyone competent to understand and criticize them... . Before experimental data were sought, the hypothesis was accepted that human females are, by original nature, different from and inferior to human males, intellectually. The factor of sex determined everything; the way to discover whether a given individual was capable of any given intellectual task was not to let the individual undertake the task and to judge by the result, but to indicate the sex of the person in question.[57]

When she listed the name of "Mobius" in the previous statement, she was referring to German scientist J. P Mobius, whose statements in "The Psychological Mental Weakness of Woman" served as an example of the misogynistic opinions regarded as truth in Leta's era. For example, Mobius wrote:

Physically, irrespective of the sexual characteristics, woman is an intermediate between child and man and mentally also in many respects at least.... They are strictly conservative and loath innovations.... Like animals they always do the same thing, hence the human race would have remained in its primitive state if there were only women. All progress is due to man. Therefore the woman is like a dead weight on him.... That the sciences strictly have not received nor can expect any advancement from woman is self-evident.... [T]he incapacity of the female mind for combination, the want of independent thought is encountered daily....[58]

The first theory discredited by Leta Hollingworth was the variability hypothesis, which was supposedly the "incorporation of evolutionary theory into the practice of psychology."[59] According to Charles Darwin, variability (variation from the norm) within a species correlated with adaptation and, therefore, enhanced the species' evolutionary progress. Darwin found more anomalies in male animals. Scientists later argued that human males varied more than human females in most characteristics. This was proof, in their view, that males were superior to females.

The variability hypothesis was based upon several assumptions: (1) genius is almost exclusively a male attribute; male geniuses by their very nature "gravitate to positions of power and prestige by virtue of talent" and become eminent in their fields; (2) women should not be expected to attain such high ability levels; and (3) "the education of women should, therefore, be consonant with their special talents and special place in society as wives and mothers."[60]

James McKeen Cattell and Edward Lee Thorndike both subscribed to the variability theory. Cattell was responsible for perpetuating many of the sex difference theories and dogmas that contributed to the subjugation of women. "A Statistical Study of Eminent Men" appeared in *Popular Science Monthly* in 1903, and in that article, Cattell postulated that men were obviously superior to women because there were so few eminent women. His method for deciding which one thousand individuals belonged on the eminence list was to study six dictionaries or encyclopedias (two were English, two French, one German, and one American) and to determine which persons were listed there. He then narrowed the list of six thousand men to sixteen hundred by eliminating those not mentioned in at least three of these reference books. The final one thousand eminent men were determined by average space allotment. Cattell, in the same article, also had the audacity to suggest that women had the same opportunity as men to gain recognition.

Edward L. Thorndike, who only one year later would be Leta's professor and advisor, said:

> Women may and doubtless will be scientists and engineers, but the Joseph Henry, the Rowland, and the Edison of the future will be men; even should all women vote,

they would play a small part in the Senate.... The education of women for such professions as administration,
statesmanship, philosophy, or scientific research, where
a very few gifted individuals are what society requires, is
far less needed than education for such professions as
nursing, teaching, medicine, or architecture, where the
average level is essential.... Postgraduate instruction, to
which women are flocking in large numbers is, at least in
its higher reaches, a far more remunerative investment
in the case of men.[61]

Leta was well aware that many of the psychology professors at
Columbia University and Teachers College supported the variability
theory. Fortunately, this did not deter her from finding factual
evidence that invalidated it. Nor did it inhibit her from accusing her
very eminent professors of very poor science, and from doing so publicly in respected academic journals.

Advocates of male superiority based their argument in part
upon the alleged fact that males displayed greater variance in intelligence. In her article "The Frequency of Amentia Related to Sex"
(1913), Hollingworth asserted that the reason more males than females
were housed in institutions for the mentally disabled was that subnormal females remained in society longer. She argued, "if our social
habit and organization ever changes so that sex as such is no longer
of commercial and economic value to women, and so that women
become mentally competitive to the same extent as men, the number
of females in institutions for the feebleminded will be materially
increased."[62] In a later publication, she elaborated upon the hypothesis that it was sociology rather than biology that was the cause of
supposed male variability:

They [women] are at the mercy of the vilest and most
unscrupulous elements in society, helpless before suggestion, easily coerced into anything. Our data on the matter
of economic status reveal that society finds a use for
mentally defective females; they are to be found in the

kitchens of cheap hotels, as chambermaids in boarding houses, as prostitutes on the streets, as the support of the cadet, as underpaid or unpaid nursegirls, as scrub women in hospitals, office buildings or institutions. Thus unsegregated and at liberty, they are exposed to all those dangers and undesirable contingencies which bring them initially into grave conflict with society and at last to the Clearing House... . Our data here reveal that illegitimacy, attempted murder, theft, forgery, arson, prostitution, drunkenness, destitution, and disease are salient features of the social careers of these incompetents.[63]

Leta Hollingworth directly questioned the science of her two eminent Professors, Cattell and Thorndike, in her publication "Variability as Related to Sex Differences in Achievement."

All the influences of social pressure, religious precept, and even of the legal restriction of knowledge have been brought to bear on women.... Physiological facts...made it well nigh imperative, that women should contribute to the care of these numerous children by housekeeping.... In this century the cases of women who have found a way to vary from the modal occupation and status, and yet procreate, are rare indeed... . But men, except slave men, could always procreate and at the same time be as diverse in occupation, trade, and inclination as possible."[64]

And she also took dead aim at Cattell's 1903 "Statistical Study of Eminent Men."

No one knows, for instance, who at present is the best housekeeper in America, nor who has borne and reared the largest and finest family of children... . Eminent housekeepers and eminent mothers as such do exist. Yet to say that women of great intellectual gifts have not thus expended their energies is to affirm either (1) that there are no women of intellectual gifts, an affirmation now passé in the scientific world, (2) that intellect is unattractive to men, and that thus the most intelligent women are left unmarried, (3) that the most intelligent women will not marry, or (4) that bearing and rearing of children, and the performance of household tasks at present constitutes no handicap to the highest attainment in the fields where eminence is possible... . Men of science, seeking the cause of woman's failure, have not sufficiently recognized these facts and consequences, or else they have deemed it unpedagogical to announce them.[65]

Leta wrote these papers as a Ph.D. candidate. Clearly she was a student with a strong sense of self and the confidence in her abilities to challenge her eminent mentor Thorndike and his equally widely known mentor Cattell. One wonders how these men reacted. Leta was a rare individual indeed.

The most significant article refuting variability was written by Leta Hollingworth and her friend, pediatrician Helen Montague. Published in the *American Journal of Sociology*, "The Comparative Variability of the Sexes at Birth" (1914) addressed the question, "Are male human beings inherently more variable in anatomical traits than female human beings?"[66] Twenty thousand measurements of infants at the time of birth provided the data of the study. All babies born at the New York Infirmary for Women and Children were routinely given ten anatomical measurements practically at the moment of birth. There were two thousand subjects for the study—one thousand female infants and one thousand male infants. The researchers transcribed their data from records in the Infirmary dating back three and one-half years. Twins, premature babies, and syphilitic infants were excluded from the study. The subjects were heterogeneous in respect to race and national origin but were homogenous in respect to economic status; most were not from the upper class.

The results of their study demonstrated that male infants were, on the average, a bit larger, but the difference was not statistically significant. The authors concluded:

In view of the fact that the most accurate and comprehensive studies so far made of comparative anatomical variability of the sexes fail to reveal any sign of greater male variability, and since there is no experimental or statistical data extant which prove the greater mental variability of males, it would seem necessary to abandon greater male variability as the ingenious explanation of sex differences in achievement.[67]

The second major theory of the time that Leta Hollingworth disproved was the long-held belief that women were incapacitated when they menstruated. This supposedly handicapping condition was known as "functional periodicity." "No dogma about women's nature enjoyed wider acceptance among doctors and psychologists, from Edward Clarke to Havelock Ellis, than the idea that women suffered periodic incapacity from menstruation," wrote Barnard History Professor Rosalind Rosenberg.[68] The objections that men had to women attending institutions of higher education or concerning women preparing for professions were based in part upon acceptance of the functional periodicity idea. Rheta Childe Dorr, a journalist and activist of that era, noted that the periodicity argument "was used with great effect against woman suffrage, for it was a well known fact that on the first Tuesday after the first Monday in November millions of women would be physically and emotionally unfit to vote."[69]

Leta's doctoral dissertation, entitled "Functional Periodicity, An Experimental Study of the Mental and Motor Abilities of Women During Menstruation," was an extension of her master's thesis. Functional periodicity detailed the testing of the motor abilities of women during their menstrual period, as well as when they were not menstruating. She found no "feminine cycle impairment."[70] Ironically, Professor Edward Thorndike was the chair of Leta's dissertation committee. There must have been some very interesting discussions between these two persons.

In the introduction to her dissertation, Leta explained, "the present study concerns itself with the mental and motor abilities of women during menstruation, a question of special interest in the United States, where co-education and the higher education of women are well established."[71] Leta cited Henry Maudsley's 1874 opinion of functional periodicity as an example of prevailing attitudes toward menstruation.

> This is a matter of physiology, not a matter of sentiment; it is not a mere question of larger or smaller muscles, but of the energy and power of endurance, of the nerve force which drives the intellectual and muscular machinery; not a question of two bodies and minds that are in equal physical condition, but of one body and mind capable of sustained and regular hard labor, and of another body and mind which for one quarter of each month, during the best years of life, is more or less sick and unfit for hard work.[72]

Leta wondered why only some women were supposedly incapacitated twenty percent of the month, because women who had to work, particularly women in menial jobs, were in fact expected to work one hundred percent of the time. She believed that her study represented "an effort to treat objectively this phenomena concerning which such a remarkable variety of folk-lore and superstition has survived among civilized peoples from the days of savagery and magic."[73]

For her dissertation, she conducted two separate experiments. In the first, six women and two men were tested daily at the same hour by the same tester in the same order. The tests extended over four months. In the second study, seventeen women were monitored every third day for a period of thirty days. When the data were analyzed, Leta found that women were not adversely affected during menstruation. She concluded:

> Thus, in time, may be written a psychology of women based on truth, not on opinion; on precise, not on anecdotal evidence; on accurate data rather than on remnants

of magic. Thus may scientific light be cast upon the question so widely discussed at present for several decades past,—whether women may at last contribute their best intellectual effort toward human progress, or whether it will be expedient for them to remain in the future as they have remained in the past, the matrix from which proceed the dynamic agents of society.[74]

CHAPTER 5

A Somewhat More Agitated Woman

For there is no subtler pleasure
Than to know minds capable—
Of performing the complete act of thought.
There is no keener joy than to see
Clear-cut human faces—Faces like those men choose
For coins, and cameos.[1]

Concurrent with her graduate studies and research on sex differences, Leta Hollingworth immersed herself in feminist political causes. In *Leta Stetter Hollingworth, A Biography*, Holly attempts to distinguish his wife from other feminists in New York City: "In her own quiet way, Leta S. Hollingworth took her stand with this group of liberal although somewhat more agitated women"[2] He was wrong. She was an activist for women's rights, and she was every bit as agitated as her radical friends and acquaintances.

Hollingworth's awareness of women's issues undoubtedly began at an early age. Her first role model was probably Fanny O'Linn, her mother's closest friend and the midwife at Leta's birth. Postmistress, journalist, and notary public, as well as midwife, Fanny was also the first woman lawyer on the Nebraska prairie. O'Linn was the only witness to Johnny and Maggie Stetter's wedding ceremony, Leta was baptized in Fanny's home, and O'Linn was a frequent visitor to the

Danley-Stetter homestead. It was none other than William Jennings Bryan who formally introduced attorney O'Linn to members of the United States Supreme Court. An unabashed suffragist, it was O'Linn who first raised Leta's feminist consciousness.

During the Progressive Era of the late 1800s and early 1900s, women reformers attempted to redefine the very relationship between the home and the community. Blackstone's old English common law stated: "The husband and wife are one, and that one is the husband,"[3] and for much of United States history, this was indeed the case. Women could not own property, make contracts, or even be guardians of their children. They were denied the franchise. Providing virtuous and knowledgeable citizen-sons was the one way a woman was encouraged to participate in the new United States democracy. The very limited political roles of women traditionally occurred in a sphere separate from that of men, and this "woman's sphere" was centered upon the home and the family. Women (white women) were expected to marry, have children, and conform to the norms of submissiveness, piety, and purity. After the Civil War, and perhaps because of the heightened level of involvement by women during the war, women gradually expanded their political agenda from the private sector into the public sphere by forming associations and organizations.

Between roughly 1880-1920 women further expanded their political sphere to the national arena, mostly in the area of social reform. In the late nineteenth century and early twentieth century, the Temperance Movement against alcohol and the Settlement House Movement to aid the poor within city slums were two powerful expressions of women's reform efforts. But it was the struggle for women's suffrage that was the catalyst that united diverse groups of women activists. While the fight for the ballot had begun in the 1830s, it was the progressive generation that achieved ratification of the Nineteenth Amendment ninety years later. Leta was a member of the New York Women Suffrage Party. She and Holly marched in several suffrage parades, and in one instance, Holly recalled that the noted educator John Dewey was among the marchers.

THE WOMEN OF HETERODOXY

One of the most significant events in Leta Hollingworth's life occurred in 1912 when she and twenty-four other women founded the Heterodoxy Club. The Club held luncheon meetings every other week for twenty-eight years.[4] As this was an era of women's associations and clubs, the formation of another woman's club was not at all unusual; what was significant was that the membership of the Heterodoxy Club consisted of some of the most radical and boldly intellectual women of the time. All were highly educated women, either with formal education in colleges and graduate school or through informal education in labor or socialist movements. Each valued her independence, and the result was—by their purpose—a diverse group.

Although many of the names are no longer familiar today, the Club roster reads like a Who's Who of the women's movement at the time. Four of Leta's sister Heterodites were prominent and influential Greenwich Village feminists:

- Vassar graduate Crystal Eastman, socialist and lawyer who with her brother, Max Eastman, edited and published *The Masses* (a radical periodical).

- Henrietta Rodman, organizer of the Liberal Club and founder of the Feminist Alliance.

- Ida Rauh, a lawyer, socialist, and sculptor who in 1911 married author Max Eastman.

- Socialist and 1930 Pulitzer Prize-winning author and playwright Susan Glaspell, a graduate of Drake University in Iowa who co-founded the Provincetown Players, a troupe featuring such luminaries as Eugene O'Neill and Edna St. Vincent Millay.[5]

These Heterodites were well known to Harry and Leta, as were many of other members of the Club. Among these others were:

- Rose Pastor Stokes, founder of the American Communist Party.

- Charlotte Perkins Gilman, feminist author and lecturer.

- Mary Ware Dennett, co-founder (with Margaret Sanger) of the National Birth Control League.

- Rheta Childe Dorr, a fellow Nebraskan who was journalist for the *New York Evening Post*, socialist, and author of *What Eight Million Women Want*.

- Fola Lafollette, labor activist and daughter of Wisconsin presidential candidate Robert LaFollette.

- Elisabeth Irwin, progressive educator and disciple of John Dewey.

- Inez Milholland, Vassar graduate, suffragist, and labor activist.

- Elsie Crews Parsons, anthropologist, sociologist, president of the American Anthropological Association, and professor of sociology at Columbia University.

- Ruth Pinchot Pickering, a journalist and editor.

- Mary Field Parton, a close friend of Clarence Darrow and a colleague of Jane Addams at Hull House who edited the *Autobiography of Mother Jones*.

- Elizabeth Gurley Flynn, the "Rebel Girl" labor organizer for the Industrial Workers of the World.

- Neith Boyce, avant guarde writer, playwright, and novelist.

- Zona Gayle, socialist, author, playwright, and winner of the Pulitzer Prize for Drama in 1921.[6]

If one is judged by the company she keeps, Leta Hollingworth was ready to do battle. The Heterodoxy Club was vital to Leta's social and intellectual life, as well as her causes. In twenty-five years, she rarely missed a meeting, participating in discussions, presenting her research, and listening and learning. The guest book Holly and Leta kept in their Montrose, New York home contains the names of many Heterodites, and Leta was a frequent guest at their homes as well. While Leta had many friends in college, in New York City, this was initially not the case. A profoundly gifted person can often have difficulty making close friends. "The more intelligent a person is, regardless of age, the less often can he find a truly congenial companion," she wrote in *Children above 180 IQ*.[7] This described her own situation as well.

Her isolation, frustration, and lowered self-esteem when she could not find a teaching job nor publish her work were not atypical responses for such a highly intelligent person. The Heterodoxy Club became a haven for Leta; there, she found a lifelong circle of friends, as well as an outlet for her intellectualism. She discovered other gifted and eminent women and was never as lonely as she was before Heterodoxy. Her sister Heterodites understood what it meant to be a gifted woman in the 1910s.

"The only quality demanded of a member was that she should not be orthodox in her opinions. The club was, therefore, called Heterodoxy. The annual dues were two dollars," recalled Inez Hayes Irwin.[8] Another Heterodite, Mabel Dodge Luhan, defined unorthodox women as those "who did things and did them openly. Women who worked."[9] The Heterodites were unorthodox in their lifestyles as well. Some women were in traditional marriages, some were single, some were in same-sex relationships, some were married with lovers, and some were bisexual. Leta was a social conservative in many areas, but a strain of unorthodoxy ran through her.

Perhaps because so many members were journalists, all of the discussions and speeches were strictly off the record. The women could, and did, speak freely, and the discussions were often heated. Inez Hayes Irwin recalled:

> What did Heterodoxy talk about? The group talked about everything. Heterodoxy members came from many states of the Union. Most of them had traveled extensively. Among them were Democrats, Republicans,

Prohibitionists, socialists, anarchists, liberals, and radicals of all opinions. They possessed minds startlingly free of prejudice. They were at home with ideas. All could talk; all could argue; all could listen. The roster included many publicists; newspaperwomen; war correspondents; audio-commentators. There were dramatists, novelists and poets; painters and musicians; our occupations and preoccupations ranged the world. Many of our members were working for various reforms. A sizable proportion were always somewhere else. During the First World War, when no Americans were supposed to enter Russia, always at least two members of Heterodoxy were there writing articles.

Sprinkled among meetings came a series of what we called "background" talks. A member told whatever she chose to reveal about her childhood, girlhood and young womanhood. They ranged in atmosphere from the middle-western farm on which Leta Hollingworth's childhood was spent, where all her dresses were made from flour bags which had the manufacturer name printed on them, through a life of inherited rebelliousness like that of Charlotte Perkins Gilman.[10]

Like Edna Kenton, like Katharine Anthony, Leta was a wise woman. One of the most interesting talks she ever gave to Heterodoxy was an account of a class of high IQ children whose careers she managed to follow for twenty years. Once, for her special information, the mothers of Heterodoxy gave talks on their children.... How Leta, in her greatness, drank those talks down! With what wisdom and wit she interpreted them![11]

Rheta Dorr recollected, "when sufficiently annoyed by any restriction on the group liberty of women, the Heterodites acted. We were heart and soul back of the equal pay for equal work crusade, and we took part both as a club and as individuals in the splendid fight the New York City teachers put up to be allowed to marry and have children, at the same time keeping their jobs." This issue was spearheaded by Heterodite Henrietta Rodman, who was also the founder of the Feminist Alliance.[12]

During World War I, the Heterodites kept their meeting places secret. Because so many members were pacifists, the Heterodoxy Club was under government surveillance. Heterodite Sara Josephine Baker wrote of the war years:

> Perhaps it was the name that alarmed the spy-chasers.... [W]e really did have to shift our meeting-place every week to keep from being watched.... My colleagues in treason were not sloe-eyed countesses with small pearl-handled revolvers in their pocketbooks, but people like Crystal Eastman, Fannie Hurt, Rose Pastor Stokes, Inez Haynes Irwin, Fola LaFollette, and Mabel Dodge Luhan."[13]

And, she might have added, Leta Stetter Hollingworth.

On Christmas Day, 1920, Marie Jenny Howe, the founder of Heterodoxy, was given a photograph album, "Heterodoxy to Marie." It contained sixty photographs of members, and many Heterodites wrote a line or two or included a poem with their pictures. Leta Hollingworth is photographed sitting on what appears to be a rock in a wooded area. Wearing a white blouse with long sleeves and a long dark skirt, a cane rests nearby on a jacket—her hat and her suit jacket are on her other side. Her hair is in its usual style, parted in the middle and pulled back into a bun. The picture is not dated, but Leta is probably in her early thirties. Under her picture is a handwritten and signed poem, which follows.[14]

Salutation

Heterodites, yuletide greetings!
At this season of gifts.
Shall I tell you the gifts you bestow on me?
As we sit at the long tables
And the years slip along?
Gifts intangible and imponderable
Yet bright with reality?

For there is no subtler pleasure
Than to know minds capable—
Of performing the complete act of thought.
There is no keener joy than to see
Clear-cut human faces—
Faces like those men choose
For coins, and cameos.

"There is no subtler pleasure/Than to know minds capable/Of performing the complete act of thought." Leta was in her element.

Although Leta and Holly shared many social activities and events, Harry Hollingworth's political and social opinions were more traditional than his wife's. For example, in the 1910s, Leta, Holly, and their friends attended meetings of the Liberal Club, founded by the socialist reformer Upton Sinclair, just off of Washington Square area in Greenwich Village and around the corner from the Provincetown Playhouse. The area was teeming with dissident intellectuals, including such prominent persons as Max Eastman, attorney Clarence Darrow, and author Jack London. Holly later wrote:

> The aggregations of "rebels" in the dinner clubs of Greenwich Village were a new experience to both of the Nebraskans. We attended many of these with curiosity...came to know...such people as Henrietta Rodman, Rheta Childe Dorr, Florence Guy, Max Eastman, Henderson Deady, Adolph Elwin, Floyd Dell, Maurice Parmelee, Herman De Frem, J. George and Christine Frederick, Elizabeth Irwin, Katherine Anthony. On the whole we

found that much of the talk at these places, though warmly motivated and kindly in intention, was likely to be wild-eyed, and tended to overlook what we had both come to regard as the fundamental facts of individual differences.... When *The Masses* [a radical periodical] was started with great hurrah, I could not help, when opportunity offered, referring to it as "Them Asses."[15]

The fact that some of Leta's work was published in *The Masses* did not seem to cause Holly to change his outlook. While it is true that several of Leta's sister Heterodites appear in the Hollingworths' residence guest book, they were not the most radical of the Heterodoxy group. They were the scholars, educators, and writers, some of whom were same-sex couples.

THE FEMINIST ALLIANCE

In 1914, *The New York Times* reported:

Taking their inspiration from Charlotte Perkins Gilman, a number of men and women believers in feminism organized the Feminist Alliance at a meeting held yesterday at the home of Henrietta Rodman.... A plan of action for at least two years was definitely mapped out by the Alliance, and it includes a new apartment house to be built and run on model feminist lines.

The first move in this plan calls for verbal and legal assaults upon the exclusiveness of all institutions of learning from which women are now de-barred. Columbia University will be asked why it does not admit women to its law schools. Bellevue Hospital will be made the subject of unremitting attention until it decides that women interns are as welcome as men.... .[16]

Leta Hollingworth was present at this organizational meeting of the Feminist Alliance and was promptly made Chair of the Committee on the Biologic Status of Women. The one other member of the committee was cultural anthropologist Robert H. Lowie, Associate Curator of Anthropology of the American Museum of Natural History, who had received his Ph.D. in 1908 from Columbia University, having studied under the eminent Professor Franz Boas. The charge to the Biologic Status of Women twosome was to "prepare arguments 'refuting the ancient slander that woman is essentially man's inferior.'"

In early April, 1914, the Alliance adopted the following statement:

> Feminism is a movement which demands the removal of all social, political, economic, and other discriminations which are based upon sex, and the award of all rights and duties in all fields on the basis of individual capacity alone.[17]

Alliance members also wrote a proposed amendment to the Constitution of the United States stating, "no civil or political right shall be refused to any woman on account of her sex."[18] The following week, the Executive Committee, to which Leta belonged, wrote a letter to President Wilson urging him to support an amendment ending discrimination based on sex.[19] Later that month, on April 22, 1914, the Feminist Alliance received the report from the Committee on the Biological Status of women responding to "the slander that woman is essentially man's inferior." Lowie and Hollingworth's thorough report about women concluded, simply, that "she was not [inferior]."[20]

The Feminist Alliance, under the leadership of Henrietta Rodman, a teacher who was pregnant at the time, successfully waged a fight to repeal a Board of Education ruling that did not allow teachers the right to return to their jobs after they had children. In such situations, a woman was twice penalized. As Leta knew from experience, in New York City only single women were "new hires" in teaching. If the woman then married, she could remain in her teaching position. But if she became pregnant, she had to resign.

Rheta Childe Dorr believed that the public tolerated this policy because it viewed women teachers as interchangeable and replaceable like pieces of machinery.[21] She also noted that many Heterodites attended protests and Board of Education meetings to demonstrate support both for Rodman and for the belief that pregnant teachers should be granted leaves of absence. It is unknown if Leta was among the demonstrators, but she most likely could not resist the opportunity to let the Board of Education know exactly how she felt about its policies. A compromise was forged; a pregnant teacher was permitted to leave her job in her fifth month of pregnancy and return to it when the child was a year and half old. Several years later, the maternity leave policy was further amended to allow women teachers to have a two-year maternity leave of absence.[22] It is perhaps noteworthy that Henrietta Rodman, the pregnant teacher who initiated the lawsuit, was later suspended from her high school teaching duties by the Board of Education on grounds of insubordination.[23]

The Feminist Alliance quietly disappeared when its leader, Henrietta Rodman, moved on to other more radical causes. It is significant, however, that Leta Hollingworth was one of the group organizers and supporters from its earliest days. In the *Blue Book of Nebraska Women* published in 1916, Hollingworth's membership in the Feminist Alliance and its advisory committee is noted. It is described as an "organization formed for the purpose of furthering the interests of women, and of fostering their advancement into full equality opportunity with men."[24]

In 1916, cultural anthropologist Robert Lowie, committee member from the Feminist Alliance, and Leta Hollingworth co-authored another report entitled "Science and Feminism," which was published in *Scientific Monthly*.[25] The purpose of the article was to "fill the long-felt want of a concise popular summary of the present state of knowledge in regard to the question of woman's supposed natural disabilities."[26] The first sentence set the tone: "Feminism demands the removal of restrictions imposed on woman's activity."[27] The authors attacked assumptions of alleged male superiority. They argued that sex dominance is culture dependent: "In different communities [there are] considerable differences in the apportionment of modes of employment between the sexes." If this is the case, then "proof" of male superiority "must be given on other than ethnological grounds."

Many scientists believed that male brains weighed more than female brains; this, to them, was irrefutable evidence of male intellectual superiority. Lowie and Hollingworth first demonstrated that the "absolute size of man's brain does not exceed that of woman" when "compared for cubic capacity rather than weight." Further, they suggested,

> ...It is equally true that the absolute size of an elephant's or whale's brains considerably exceed that of the male human brain. Hence it would seem rash to attach much importance to absolute brain size in comparing male and female intelligence.... While it is true that distinguished men often have a brain of more than average size, this is by no means uniformly the case. Noted scientists have been known to fall appreciably below the mean, while persons of moderate ability have turned out to possess an enormous brain.[28]

Lowie and Hollingworth concluded: "The verdict of present-day science is thus an uncompromisingly negative one: no rational grounds have yet to be established that should lead to artificial limitation of woman's activity on the of ground inferior efficiency."[29]

When Leta discovered in 1916 that Phi Beta Kappa was planning to impose a quota upon the number of women admitted to the organization, she became outraged. In a letter to the Board of Phi Beta Kappa, she angrily stated:

> The irony grows when one remembers that less than half a century ago one of the most insistent arguments against admitting women to higher education was that standards of scholarship would be lowered through the inability of women to keep pace with men.... Women will have to...be content forever with falling short of the best, unless, through force of thought and action, they

are able to bring about a change in the attitude of the academic world.... This women can do by modifying social customs gradually, so that they may both fulfil [*sic*] their intellectual promise and enjoy a normal domestic life.[30]

THE "WOMAN QUESTION"

Another indication of the evolving power women had over their lives was the increasing use of birth control—either contraception or abstinence—to prevent conception. Access to reproductive information and products was a paramount issue to women of Leta Hollingworth's era.

When Leta was a young wife, the Comstock Law, enacted in 1873, was still the law of the land regarding birth control. Under its provisions, selling, lending, or publishing information about birth control or abortion was a federal crime. Even private conversations about birth control or abortion were punishable in some states. In Connecticut, the practice of contraception was banned outright.[31] The birth control movement of the 1910-1920 period was linked to feminist and socialist causes because reproductive control was recognized as a means of liberation for all women regardless of social class. One of the most visible and famous advocates of birth control, Margaret Sanger, published a newspaper aptly titled *The Woman Rebel*. In the first editorial, Sanger explained her reason for the newspaper's name:

> I believe that deep down in woman's nature lies slumbering the spirit of revolt. Because I believe that woman is enslaved by the world machine, be it by sex conventions, by motherhood and its present necessary child-rearing, by wage-slavery, by middle-class morality, by customs, laws and supervision.[32]

As far as Leta Hollingworth was concerned, the central question about women was "how to reproduce the species, and at the same time work and win work's full reward, in accordance with individual ability."[33] Leta wrote many articles on the subject of women's role in society and was a strong advocate of family planning—for some populations.

Two dichotomous positions are evident in Hollingworth's published writings on the "woman question" over time. According to Leta, the major detriment to gender equality was the social expectation that women reproduce and then raise the children. However, she was concerned that if only middle and upper class women practiced birth control, the undereducated classes would then produce the majority of American children.

"Social Devices for Impelling Women to Bear and Rear Children" was written by Leta in 1916. Many of her arguments relating to the woman question are imbedded in this article, and these assertions reappear in subsequent Hollingworth publications over the years. She believed that the maternal instinct was not present universally in women. She also believed that social institutions were guilty of pressuring women to believe that their only duty in life was to propagate, and she identified public opinion, law, religion, education, and art as the social institutions responsible.

Public opinion was dominated by newspapers in Leta's day. She was particularly unforgiving of those publications that perpetuated fears that the population was deteriorating because of a low birth rate. Always the scientist, she observed that of the fifty-five articles written about the supposed low birth rate, fifty-four were written by male reporters.

Leta also viewed law as an institution intended to subjugate women, and she focused on laws that prevented women from owning property as among the most insidious. She also condemned statutes that permitted a man to divorce his wife if she was sterile, as well as laws, like the Comstock Law, that made it illegal to disseminate birth control information.

Many religious customs relating to women, in Leta's opinion, were negative influences as well. She noted that most people reasoned that, as children are believed to be gifts from God, "it follows that they may not be refused except at the peril of incurring God's displeasure."[34] The proliferation of Madonnas and paintings of mothers breastfeeding are cited by Hollingworth as examples of the mother-child theme so pervasive in religion and art that "one would not be led to suspect that society finds it necessary to make laws against contraception, infanticide, abortion, and infant desertion."[35]

Even the field of education was instrumental in compelling women to become mothers. Leta wrote:

> The education of women has always…been limited to
> such matters as would become a creature who could and
> should have no aspirations for a life of her own… . Not
> only have the "social guardians" used education as a neg-
> ative means of control, by failing to provide any real
> enlightenment for women, but education has been made
> a positive instrument for control. This was accomplished
> by drilling into the young and unformed mind, while yet
> it was too immature to reason independently, such facts
> and notions as would give the girl a conception of herself
> only as a future wife and mother.[36]

The societal taboos of that time were so great that they inhibited doctors from honestly discussing physical processes and dangers inherent in childbirth. Leta concluded, with a bit of derisive sarcasm:

> If these matters could be clearly raised to consciousness,
> so that this aspect of human life could be managed ratio-
> nally, instead of irrationally as at present, the social gain
> would be enormous—assuming always that the increased
> happiness and usefulness of women would…be regarded
> as social gain.[37]

In 1922, Leta reviewed two books for *The New Republic*, a prominent weekly progressive magazine—*The Pivot Generation* by Margaret Sanger, and *Birth Control* by Holliday G. Sutherland. Both books had been written on the subject of birth control, but from different viewpoints.

Some of us remember how, in the days when we were "too young to understand," mothers of the neighborhood gathered with their sewing on the front porch to exchange confidences. As we played about, we heard terrifying words—the same words they used when they found things in traps—spoken in a whisper, over and over. Evidently there was a snare that mothers couldn't escape. Try as you would, you couldn't find out its ways by experience. There it was, a vague but adroit menace! Of course we lived to learn that the terrifying words were vulgar—vulgar in the true sense of the term.[38]

In her review, Hollingworth summarized the points of view of both authors and then "having heard the debate...by both sides, we begin to think it over for ourselves." She dismissed Sutherland's contentions that contraception could cause fibroid tumors, sterility, and neuroses. And she disputed that famine and poverty do not correlate with overpopulation, and that women cannot really decide what they want. Margaret Sanger was accorded somewhat better, but not uncritical, treatment.

Mrs. Sanger, like a true propagandist, claims too much for birth control. Very large sections of the population, whom she most pities and plans to aid, will be unable to profit by knowledge because they lack that "intelligence, forethought, and responsibility," which Mrs. Sanger tells us are required to control conception by scientific methods. Human nature being what it is, education for birth control will not cure every ill from which we suffer in the body politic.

But one's thoughts keep going back to the mothers on the porch, "our conscripts," as William James called them. Why shouldn't Mrs. Sanger rest on that? Her equipment is unique for piercing clean through the smug fiction that all is beautiful in motherhood. She can alleviate the repressive taboo on mention of its agonies and fears. As an obstetrical nurse, she has seen scores of women undergo childbirth. She has heard what they say. She has herself repeatedly borne children. She has developed a power of speech to tell exactly what she has seen and heard, and she is brave enough to do it. Margaret Sanger's real contribution is that she proclaims aloud what women have been taught they must smother in whispers.[39]

EUGENICS

Ironically, it appears that Leta Hollingworth's sensitive concern with women's rights and with the rights and well-being of the individual led her to support eugenics[40]—the attempt to improve humanity by encouraging the ablest and healthiest people to have more children. Only a few decades had passed since Charles Darwin had written about "survival of the fittest," and the importance of genetics in breeding was widely recognized. Certainly, psychologists and physicians of that time recognized the importance of the environment; but the influence of heredity was emphasized as even more important. Eugenicists believed that a population or a society could be improved through selective breeding, and as a result, birth control was often a key part of eugenicist concerns.

Many family planning advocates worried that if only the educated classes practiced family planning, then the under-educated classes would soon outbreed and outnumber them. Negative eugenics—that is, restricting the births of the least able—was a natural extension of this philosophy. Compulsory and involuntary sterilization, restriction of immigration, and anti-miscegenation laws were enacted and supported by many individuals in America in the 1910s, 1920s, 1930s, and even later.

Though she fought for the individual women's right to choose not to become pregnant, Leta Hollingworth, in fact, favored involuntary sterilization for those who were mentally deficient. Her view was not particularly shocking for her day. Many leading physicians supported the practice, which was upheld by the U.S. Supreme

Court in 1927.[41] In her text *The Psychology of Subnormal Children* (1920), Leta asserted:

> The known fact that stands out most clearly in a consideration of the causes of mental deficiency is that it is hereditary…. . It follows that the prevention of mental deficiency in the population can be accomplished by preventing defective persons form procreating…. . In states where sterilization is legalized it is carried out with relative infrequency. The law will have to make sterilization mandatory, not permissive only, before such measures will become effectual…."[42]

Her support for sterilization was only a small part of her views on eugenics. In *Gifted Children: Their Nature and Nurture* (1926), she elaborated upon eugenics, which she called "the art of technique of being well born."[43]

By selective breeding, we might eventually have a world in which the chronic diseases that afflict mankind would be no more, in which murder and theft would be unknown, and in which every person could earn a good living and attain a college education. This plan, however, is recognized as Utopian, for the species is not socially or psychologically constituted to carry it through. Only the very intelligent and altruistic minority will understand such propositions as that the earth might be saved by rational means from overpopulation and that, through this process of limitation, it would ultimately reduce misery if the stupid, the criminal, and other mentally, physically, and morally deficient would refrain from reproduction.

> Popular legislation is…far more likely to multiply palliatives for misery and to preserve unfortunates for parenthood. Eugenicists…stress more and more of the positive side of eugenics, urging that "the best" members of the species should procreate freely, in order to counteract the unfortunately biological consequences of philanthropy…. The intellectually gifted are thus urged to have many

children. This appeal to the intelligent does not raise the birth-rate among them, however... . Gifted women, especially, are doubtless impelled to avoid child-bearing for reasons which will become clear to anyone able to give the matter serious and consecutive thought.[44]

Given Leta's sentiments about the need for bright people to procreate, it is interesting that the Hollingworths did not have any children. Certainly, she must have believed that two such bright people were bound to produce intelligent offspring. While there has been speculation among family members, both then and now, that Leta was physically unable to have children or that Holly feared he might transmit some unnamed inherited disease, the most likely reason for their remaining childless is that it was a conscious choice. Leta's mother died as result of childbirth, and this may have been a contributing factor to Leta not having children. Her many allusions to the pain and danger inherent in childbirth support this hypothesis. Certainly, Helen Stetter believed that the terrible childhood both Holly and Leta experienced made them reluctant to bring children into the world.[45] The Hollingworths' decision to remain childless appears to have been a conscious decision to practice birth control.

Several statements from Harry Hollingworth's unpublished autobiography support the idea that they did not want children:

> To think of bringing children of ours into the world under these circumstances was wholly out of the question; if nothing else had done it, the misery of our own life long poverty would have deterred us. So that this issue was immediately disposed of.

Later he writes:

> Having agreed that there should be no children at least until we had both had a full chance to try out our personal interests and achieve a reasonable breathing spell, we were free to run about together with no domestic cares.[46]

Holly alluded to Leta's article, "Social Devices for Impelling Women to Bear and Rear Children," as "a topic not unrelated to her own decision to postpone procreation until other urges had been given their due opportunity."[47]

So it is curious that on the one hand Leta believed that bright women should have children, but on the other hand she recognized the constraints that child-bearing placed upon the likelihood of a woman being able to obtain achievements. This apparent contradiction also posed problems for her conceptualizations regarding lesbian couples. One such puzzling incident for Leta involved a 1927 Heterodoxy meeting. A guest at the meeting sent a letter to fellow Heterodite Ruth Pinchot Pickering, asking her opinion of the encounter:

> One thing interested or rather bothered me terribly in that meeting. I wonder whether you noticed it—or whether it was all my imagination? It was the woman who sat two places to the left of Dr. Hollingworth. I think her name was Miss Hull. It seemed to me that something awfully cruel was done to her at that meeting.... When Dr. Hollingworth included in her definition of perfect feminist a woman happily married and with children, it shattered all Miss Hull's defense mechanisms. Did you notice how she turned to the other psychoanalyst with white hair...and to one or two others, and hoped they would back her up—and when they did not, did you see her face and notice that she never spoke again?[48]

Helen Hull, a member of Heterodoxy, and Mary Louise Robinson lived together for fifty years. Leta had attended graduate school with both women in the 1910s. It was common knowledge that Hull and Robinson were a lesbian couple. They had built a cottage near the Hollingworths' Montrose home and were guests at the Hollingworths' home on many occasions. If Leta did express such sentiments, Helen Hull must have been upset and hurt. Also, as Leta had no children, was she saying that *she* was not a feminist?

BELLEVUE HOSPITAL AND TEACHERS COLLEGE

In 1916, Dr. Leta Hollingworth received two job offers. Bellevue Hospital invited her to join the staff as full-time psychologist, and Teachers College asked her to serve as the principal of a new school for exceptional children and to join the faculty as an instructor in psychology. She decided to have it both ways. When she accepted the Teachers College position, she asked to continue working part time at Bellevue Hospital. She joined the Teachers College faculty, a position she retained until her death twenty-six years later; at Bellevue Hospital, she worked for several years until demands upon her time grew too great.

As supportive as Holly was of Leta's professional growth, he did not want Leta to continue working at Bellevue Hospital after she was appointed to the faculty of Teachers College. Helen Stetter recalled:

> When Margaret and I visited Leta, she took us to the slums one Sunday, and Leta just nearly floored Holly! He said, "I've told you not to go to the slums," and she said, well, she wasn't afraid.... You see they brought in the trash from the streets too, and Leta was a psychologist that examined the people that were brought in and he was afraid that she would be murdered...he didn't want her to go, but she wouldn't listen.[49]

It is not surprising that the slum neighborhoods of New York City or Bellevue Hospital's indigent patients failed to intimidate Leta. New York City was not least bit threatening to this daughter of the Nebraska frontier.

Much later, when she was a nationally and internationally acclaimed educational psychologist, Leta published her last article specifically relating to women's issues, "The New Woman in the Making" (1927). One statement is particularly revealing of her sentiments:

> Each woman...who sets out upon a way of life different from that of the dependent housewife, is still an explorer....

The New Woman of today is consciously experimenting with her own life to find out how women can best live... .Surely this requires a courage and a genius desiring something better than blame or jeers, deserving at least open-minded toleration and assistance."[50]

In her lifetime, Leta needed both courage and genius. Fortunately, these characteristics were in ample supply.

CHAPTER 6

The Nurturant Mother
of Gifted Education

*Can American public schools identify and recognize gifted
children and make provisions for their education?[1]*
—Leta Stetter Hollingworth, 1931

Shortly after joining the Teachers College faculty in 1916, Leta
Hollingworth's primary research agenda changed from the study
of the psychology and sociology of women to the "comprehension of
the extent, nature and origin of individual differences in mental caliber."[2] Although she continued writing about women's issues and sex
discrimination throughout her life, the focus of her writings was as
an educational psychologist. Initially, her studies were of children
with below normal intelligence and children with learning disabilities, but this work led directly to her seminal work with children
who were intellectually gifted, including the profoundly gifted.

EXCEPTIONAL CHILDREN

Leta Hollingworth's publications in the 1916-1922 period primarily centered upon children who were cognitively disabled. In
addition to her research on these children, she continued to teach
courses concerning less able children throughout her career at Teachers
College. One of first courses she developed was "Subnormal Children,"

a course she inherited when Naomi Norsworthy died in 1916. Leta's contributions to the field—a field now termed "Special Education"—were clearly significant. According to psychologist Miriam Pritchard, Leta Hollingworth

> …was among the first to begin the systematic accumulation of facts which led to an impersonal and sound knowledge and characteristics of subnormal children.… [H]er practical experiences in the early psychological clinics were of immeasurable value. It was…on the basis of former researches, firsthand experiences with the mentally deficient, and her own numerous research studies that she formulated her concepts of intellectual deficiency.[3]

The newly established School for Exceptional Children was a second part of Leta's responsibilities at Teacher's College. This school, designed to respond to the medical and educational needs of learning disabled children, was an early "pull-out" program. Specific children from Public School 192 in Manhattan were selected to attend special remediation classes in spelling and arithmetic that were taught at Teachers College.

The goals of this school project were to observe how these children learned over a three-year period and to develop performance-enhancing remediation measures. Leta planned the experiments and provided psychological analysis, but she did not teach these children. Her aim was to study the individual child and to assist that child to find success in school. In this experiment, and in subsequent studies conducted by Leta Hollingworth, the emphasis was upon the child rather than the group; her child-centered approach never changed.

Although this experimental school program was designed to last for three years, it was abandoned after only one. The school building did not meet fire law specifications, and financial support was lacking from Teachers College. Leta learned a very important lesson. No matter how valuable a project, if the funding was not institutionalized (i.e., made part of the operating budget), its longevity was tenuous.

Nevertheless, Leta collected valuable data. She had a particular concern that learning disabled students might incorrectly be identified as retarded because of poor testing procedures. In two of her early groundbreaking books, *The Psychology of Special Disability in Spelling* (1918) and *The Psychological Examination of Poor Spellers* (1919), she detailed results of children who were within a normal IQ range, but who had particular difficulties with either arithmetic or spelling. She suggested that a battery of tests be administered to pinpoint the cause of the learning disability. Tests of general intelligence, auditory and visual acuity, speech, motor skills, conceptual understanding, and temperamental traits were among those recommended. In addition, she suggested that the "direct examination of the individual be augmented by developmental, familial, and school history and also note[d] that poor spelling may be hereditary."[4] Once again, Hollingworth clearly was concerned with studying the whole child.

In an address delivered before the Section for Study of Retarded Children of the New York State Teachers Association at Albany, November 24, 1919, Leta presented a brief history of the origins of classes for children of subnormal ability and then spoke of the importance of mental testing to help identify children who functioned poorly in school but who were not retarded due to lack of intelligence:

> Now that psychology has furnished instruments of precision for detecting those whose general intelligence is sub normal, we...can enter upon adequate analysis of their difficulties. What percentage of retardation in the schools is due to the operation of such special disabilities we do not know. It is...true beyond a doubt that the most important single cause of retardation is mental deficiency as ordinarily understood—general lack of capacity of learning. Nevertheless there are many intelligent children who become retarded simply through special disability to grasp of the most fundamental tools of learning—reading, spelling or arithmetic—and who are lost to education for want of an adequate analysis of the difficulty.[5]

Not only had she made an important conceptual distinction concerning why some children do not learn, she also highlighted methods that allowed educators and psychologists to identify the reasons that children were not learning. Having great faith in the newly developed and refined tests of mental ability, Leta felt that there now existed an objective way to determine capacities for learning.

Leta was an early advocate of differentiated education, but not necessarily within a single classroom. On the one hand, she believed that each child should be taught as far as possible within the regular classroom setting and allowed to proceed at his/her own pace. However, she also argued that there was also a great need for specialized, homogenous classes for children with severe cognitive deficits, as well as specialized homogenous classes for children who were profoundly gifted. Neither population, she concluded, could attain its potential in the regular classroom setting.

When her text *The Psychology of Subnormal Children* (1920) was published, it quickly became the standard text in the field, and it set a tone for the emerging field of school psychology. The focus was upon the psychology of below normal children, but the text also contained significant information about identification and diagnostic procedures. Hollingworth advocated the importance of identifying exceptional children (those who deviated significantly from the norm in either direction) at the earliest age possible so that they could be educated and parented appropriately. She contended that cognitively disabled children "can learn the same things that other children learn, up to the limits of their capacity."[6] She believed that these children did not simply start out with average abilities and then reach of point of "arrested development"; rather, they began life with below average intelligence and then progressed from that point in a continuous, albeit always below normal, rate of mental growth. Later, she applied the same thinking to gifted children. They began life, she concluded, with above average intelligence and subsequently progressed at an above normal rate of mental development.

As is most often the case, Leta's new concepts and approaches did not evolve in a vacuum, but instead were influenced by her

Leta's maternal grand-
mother Mary Blair Stanley

Courtesy of Patricia Johnson

Leta's mother
Margaret Stanley Stetter

Courtesy of Patricia Johnson

Baby Leta
Courtesy of Patricia Johnson

Maggie and Leta
Courtesy of Patricia Johnson

Ruth and Leta
Courtesy of Patricia Johnson

Ruth, Maggie, and Leta
Courtesy of Patricia Johnson

Fanny and John Stetter
Courtesy of Virginia Florence

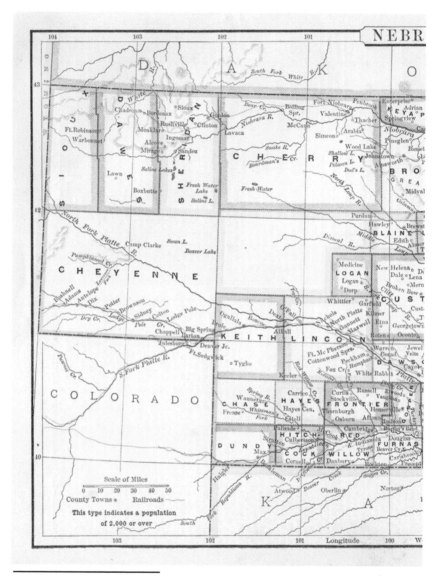

Nebraska, 1888
Courtesy of Atlas of United States

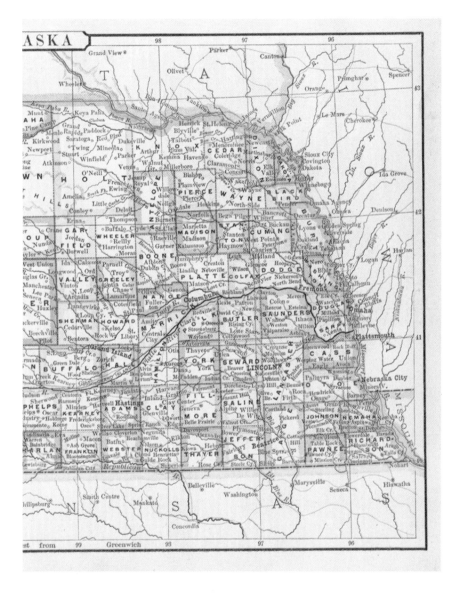

The Danleys and Ruth, Leta, and Maggie
Courtesy of Patricia Johnson

Fannie Berling Stetter, Maggie, Ruth, Leta
Courtesy of Patricia Johnson

Holly, 2 years
Courtesy of Virginia Florence

Holly, 1900, age 20
Courtesy of Virginia Florence

Leta's High School, 1901
Courtesy of Cherry Co. Historical Society

Leta in car at college, 1902-1906 (standing with bow on blouse)
Courtesy of Virginia Florence

Old University Hall
Courtesy of University of Nebraska

Leta in college, 1902-1906

Holly, 1906, age 26
Courtesy of Virginia Florence

Leta and Holly, early 1920s
Courtesy of Virginia Florence

Leta and Holly's family, DeWitt, Nebraska, mid-1910s
Courtesy of Virginia Florence

Holly and Leta, mid-1910s
Courtesy of Virginia Florence

Leta (right) and Ruth playing chess, early 1910s
Courtesy of Richard Fischer

Holly, 1916, 36 years
Courtesy of Virginia Florence

Leta, 1916-1920
Courtesy of Virginia Florence

Leta, ship to/from Europe, 1927-1928
Courtesy of Virginia Florence

Holly, WWI, 1918
Courtesy of Virginia Florence

Hollywyck, 1930
Courtesy of Virginia Florence

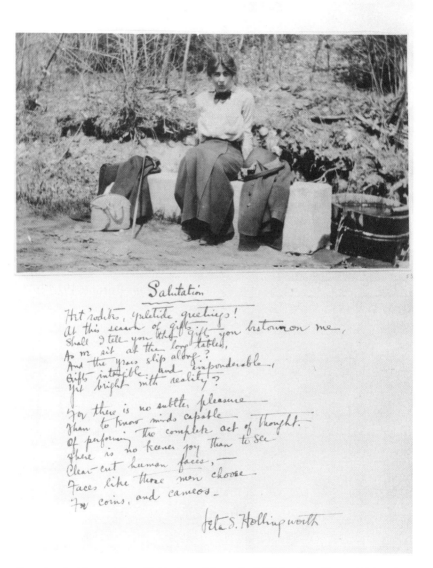

Salutation

Hit nodiks, Yuletide greetings!
At this season of gifts
Shall I tell you what gift you bestow on me,
As we sit at the long tables,
And the years slip along?
Gifts intangible, and imponderable,
Yet bright with reality?

For there is no subtler pleasure
Than to know minds capable
Of performing the complete act of thought.
There is no keener joy than to see
Clear-cut human faces,
Faces like those men choose
For coins, and cameos.

Leta S. Hollingworth

Reproduced with permission of Schlessinger Library, Radcliffe Institute, Harvard University

Ruth and Leta
Courtesy of Richard Fischer

Leta and her sisters
Courtesy of Richard Fischer

Leta and friend, 1905
Courtesy of Richard Fischer

Leta in her early 30s, 1920-1922
Courtesy of Virginia Florence

predecessors. Both in her work and in her writings, Leta was generous in recognizing how others had contributed to her keen insights. For example, she dedicated her book *The Psychology of Subnormal Children* to her good friend "Elizabeth E. Farrell, A Pioneer in the Educational Field of Which It Treats." Elizabeth Farrell had established the first special class in New York City in 1895, and because of Farrell's leadership, by 1920, there were more than 250 such classes within that school district.[7] And in the preface to *The Psychology of Subnormal Children*, Leta specifically acknowledged two other mentors: "As I formulated the book, I became increasingly conscious of what I owe to my years of professional association, first with Dr. M.G. Schlapp, Director of the Clearing House for Mental Defectives, the Post-Graduate Hospital, New York City, and Dr. Menas S. Gregory, Director of the Psychopathic and Alcoholic Services, Bellevue Hospital, New York City."

Leta's work with exceptional children was influenced by her previous research and experience in women's issues. In a 1922 publication, she reported yet another example of unequal treatment of females. Her article, which appeared in the *Journal of Abnormal and Social Psychology*, was titled "Differential Act Upon the Sexes of Forces Which Tend to Segregate the Feebleminded," and in that article, she documented that New York City's ungraded classes (the term used at that time for subnormal classes) contained a ratio of more than two boys to one girl. After extensive analysis of previous studies, she further found:

> Among public school children there are probably more
> feebleminded girls than boys.... Yet the registers of special
> classes for mentally deficient children show more boys
> than girls in such classes. Feebleminded girls will doubt-
> less continue to drift with the regular classes, unless selection
> for special classes is made in rigidly objective ways.[8]

The educational and social needs of below normal girls were obviously not being met. The unequal treatment of females at all levels in American society remained a deep and personal concern to Leta.

THE PUBLIC SCHOOL 165 EXPERIMENT IN GIFTED EDUCATION

Leta Hollingworth formally initiated the field of gifted education during the spring semester of the 1918-1919 academic year when she began teaching "Education 254," which she described as "the study of fortunate variants, the generally and specifically gifted." It was the first academic course in the field. Hollingworth's educational experiments with children from Public School 165 (1922-1925) and later with Speyer School (Public School 500), from 1936 until her death in 1939, would further illuminate educators, parents, and the public. At that time—now nearly a century ago—Leta Hollingworth identified four interrelated questions that she thought were the most crucial to the education of gifted children:

(1) Can American public schools identify and recognize gifted children and make provisions for their education?

(2) Should the problem of appropriate work be solved by acceleration at a rapid rate through school grades?

(3) Should the problem be solved by enrichment of the prescribed curriculum without acceleration and without segregation?

(4) Should gifted children be segregated in special schools or classes, and be educated by combining enrichment with a moderate degree of acceleration?[9]

Her findings concerning these questions evolved over two decades of study, and her conclusions have stood the test of time. The answer to all four questions was an emphatic "yes." Unfortunately, even today these same basic four elements of gifted education are only sparsely and randomly implemented by school districts, even with a long history of research since Leta's time showing them to be beneficial to gifted students.

PRECEDENTS IN GIFTED EDUCATION

When Leta Hollingworth conducted experiments with gifted children, she was guided by previous gifted programs from metropolitan areas such as Louisville, Kentucky; Urbana, Illinois; Columbus, Ohio; Appleton, Wisconsin; and New York City.[10] There had been sporadic attempts to provide specialized services to gifted children in the United States beginning in the late nineteenth century. By 1920, two-thirds of American cities had some type of program for gifted students. Before the Stanford-Binet IQ test was used as a primary way to identify high ability children, inclusion in gifted programs was determined by teachers' judgments and grades. Contrary to the popular notion of the period (and even today) that teachers are the most reliable sources of information about a student's intellectual capacities, Hollingworth argued that teachers were often the least reliable judges of giftedness. She found, for example, some children in gifted classes with IQs that were below 100.[11]

One gifted education program that was a precursor to Leta's work was that of New York City's Public School 64, a school for boys. Between 1916-1919, a three-year experimental project was conducted with special classes for the gifted (IQ 120+). Because the number of subjects was very small, the results of the study were not deemed generalizable; however, the processes employed to select, teach, and enrich the students helped guide Hollingworth to design her experiments in gifted education. In 1916, teachers and administrators in P.S. 64 believed that there was a need for a homogeneous class for the gifted when they encountered several students whose mental age exceeded their chronological age by at least two years. They reasoned:

> Special classes for defective children with a course of study adapted to their needs had been in existence for some time. Why not organize special classes for children at the other end of the scale composed of those showing the highest grade of intelligence? Surely these children, society's greatest assets, were entitled to progress at the

rate of speed that was desirable and normal for them. If defective children of ungraded classes were worthy of a course of study peculiarly adapted to their limitations, certainly an enriched curriculum must be provided with privileges to meet the needs of children whose capabilities extended to the highest possible degree of attainment.[12]

The first homogenous gifted class at P.S. 64 was named the Terman class, because

> ...to call it a class for superior or gifted children would tend to make its members unduly conceited, and to establish all sorts of undesirable attitudes. The name had to be short, one that required some explanation so that no prejudice might be aroused... (and) since the basis of selection was possible because of Dr. Louis Terman's revision and extension of the Binet-Terman scale for measuring intelligence, it might be called a Terman class.[13]

The selection of students was subsequently structured toward the goal of having an equal number of males and females in the class; female students were chosen from Public School 15, a nearby school for girls. Class size was held to a maximum of five students, and eventually there were three classes for children of exceptional ability with a median IQ of 137. The curriculum was enriched; in addition to the standard New York City Curriculum, student learning was through field trips to libraries, museums, Broadway plays, and flower shows. Supplementary reading lists were based upon suggestions from area librarians and professors. Students were even taken on a sightseeing cruise around Manhattan. A neighborhood settlement house provided physical education, domestic science, and drama facilities for the classes.

When a child displayed a particular talent, it was nourished. The P.S. 64 gifted children were permitted to advance at their own level, and some graduated from elementary school—at that time grade eight—when they were twelve years old. Like most other programs in

gifted education before Leta Hollingworth's time, grade acceleration was a primary strategy of choice. The median progress per term
was almost three grade levels, and all of the Terman class students
attended high school.

Many pedagogical strategies employed today in gifted education were in place at P.S. 64—homogeneous grouping for high ability
students; a modified, or differentiated, curriculum that emphasized
higher-level skills and complex concepts; individualized instruction;
independent projects; and grade and subject acceleration.[14] Subsequently, Leta Hollingworth's noteworthy experiments in gifted
education at Public School 165 (1922-1925) and at Public School 500,
also called the Speyer School (1936-1941), contained these educational
elements and more. They created a foundation for the education and
psychology of gifted children in years to come.

Leta's first experiment, conducted in Public School 165, New
York City, compared gifted children with highly gifted children
over a period of three years. This experiment began in 1922 when
Leta, along with several faculty members from Teachers College
and administrators and teachers from New York City Public School
165, initiated this three-year study of gifted children, with some students being studied for seven years. It had come to their attention
that "some unusually bright children who were very much younger
than the children of their grades...nevertheless found that the school
requirements presented very little challenge to their best efforts."[15]
This was the beginning of the realization that there is a large span of
intelligence within the territory called "gifted." The school/univer-
sity partners agreed upon some ground rules for this experiment:

> The register was to be not less than 25. The classes were
> to remain together for three years, at the end of which
> time the pupils were to have completed the require-
> ments of the 8-B elementary school course of study.
> There was to be enrichment beyond these requirements.
> There was to be no attempt at rapid progress since most
> of the children were already accelerated.

> The purpose was twofold: to provide enriched educational opportunities for very bright children; (and) to secure reliable data and knowledge as to their educational progress over an extended period of time.[16]

The intent was to find gifted and highly gifted children from area schools and to teach them in segregated classes,

> ...providing for them so far as possible the educational opportunities that should seem best adapted to their special needs... . The Special Opportunity Class was organized with the idea that within the district might be found enough such children of approximately the same chronological age to form a class, which would be relatively homogeneous, both socially and educationally.[17]

Thus, fifty gifted children were selected and enrolled in either the "Higher" (median IQ 165) or "Lower" (median IQ 146) class. Each class had twenty-five children. According to the school/university partners:

> The policy of instruction was to let each child learn at his own natural rate. Adjustments were made constantly according to individual advancement in any subject of study or project covering the prescribed curriculum, and also including in the daily program much unusual opportunity for education. French, social science, the history of civilization, music, biography, physical training, were all introduced to enrich the curriculum.... Under these conditions, the children learned as much as they would or could.[18]

One way the P.S. 165 project differed from earlier experiments with gifted children was that enrichment, rather than acceleration, was at the heart of the rapid learner curriculum. This remained a constant throughout Leta Hollingworth's writing and teaching about highly gifted children. She believed that, in an ideal world, highly gifted children would be taught in homogeneous classes and given an enriched curriculum in addition to the required curriculum. They were able to master a standard curriculum in half the time as unselected students. It made perfect sense then that the "other half" of the child's school day would consist of activities and assignments that went far beyond the regular course of study.

The P.S. 165 rapid learners were taught by the same two classroom teachers for three successive years and by six specialists assigned to teach enrichment subjects. Field trips to cultural attractions were an important part of the curriculum. The Museum of Natural History and the Metropolitan Museum of Art worked collaboratively with P.S. 165 teachers to provide special instruction. Believing that gifted children tend to be too sedentary, Saturday and after-school physical activities were provided by the school.

Leta Hollingworth herself taught the enrichment class on the genre of biography to both experimental classes. "We chose biography," she noted,

> ...because we believed it would tend to prepare young, very gifted children for the life of which they are capable, because at the age of 8 to 10 years they are intellectually ready to profit by it, because attitudes and ideals formed in childhood have great influence, and because biography is not offered elsewhere in the usual, established curriculum.[19]

Written expression was demanded and encouraged; students wrote daily letters, book reports, and journals of their field trips. Children with reading ability above the eighth-grade level were in charge of a small library, cataloging new acquisitions and checking them out when children took books home. Classroom resources included a typewriter, microscope, hand lenses, a carpenter bench, worktables, and a mimeograph machine.

As a result of the P.S. 165 three-year study, more than twenty papers were published in scholarly journals based upon the vast amount of data collected. Forty children remained with the class for the entire three-year period. In addition, researchers were able to conduct follow-up studies on fifty-four pupils who entered high school after they completed the elementary school course.[20] This made it possible to examine students' progress over a period of seven years, an unusually long period. The data were rich and, even more important, valid.[21]

Topics of inquiry about gifted children emerging from the experiment at P.S. 165 included motor coordination, neuromuscular capacity, personality development, emotional and social adjustment, sensitivity to music, interpersonal and intrapersonal relationships, and family patterns. Similarities and differences between the Higher and Lower gifted classes were studied and reported.

One study compared the achievement of children in the Special Opportunity classes with the achievement of gifted children attending public school heterogeneous classes. It found that gifted children in the regular classroom setting did not show lower accomplishments measured by the Stanford Achievement Test than the children in the Special Opportunity classes. Also, enrichment of the curriculum did not cause the Special Opportunity children to have lower scores in the traditionally prescribed subjects than gifted children who attended regular classes without enrichment.

Thus, those gifted children who spent half as much time studying the "regular" curriculum did just as well as gifted children who spent the entire day studying the prescribed subjects. The study showed that "homogeneous grouping of gifted children lie not so much in expectation of greater achievement in the tool subjects (reading, arithmetic, spelling) as in an enrichment of scholastic experience with additional intellectual opportunities."[22]

A study that compared the gifted and highly gifted students (the 146 IQ and 165 IQ clusters) indicated that those with higher IQs outperformed the others throughout the three-year period, even though both groups had the same opportunities. Leta concluded that the two groups would not have differed in achievement unless their measured intellect was the major determiner of such a difference. She reported that there was a "marked difference in achievement" between children with "very high" IQs and those with "still higher" IQs. "The achievements in which the two groups differed most are precisely the ones in which opportunity had been most indisputably equal…(namely) the world of word, sentence, and paragraph meaning… ."[23] It was the level of intelligence that accounted for the difference in achievement.

In a monograph detailing the constancy of mental development of the P.S. 165 group, Leta reported that in 1922, the fifty-six children had a mean IQ of 153; when the children were re-tested after a year, the mean IQ was 156; the following year, the mean IQ was 157. Not a single child in the top one percent at the time of selection fell below that percent during the three-year testing period. The IQ remained constant. Ten years after their initial testing, eighty-two percent of the subjects continued to remain in the top one percent of the population, and the remaining eighteen percent were only slightly lower. No one regressed to "average." Intellectually gifted children retained their intellectual status.

Leta also published a number of articles relating to the physique, strength, and motor abilities of children who test above 135 IQ.[24] In the "Tapping-Rate of Children Who Test above 135 IQ," Hollingworth and Monahan examined whether younger gifted children can keep up with older, less gifted children in motor capacity tasks. They concluded that motor skills were more like their age-mates than like their intellectual peers and that: "If graded with older people, whom they equal intellectually, children as young and as gifted as these will be well 'out of their depth' as respects size, strength and speed." Hollingworth and Monahan decided that despite these differences, gifted children could be academically advanced one or two years beyond age norms without a deficit either in motor capacity or size. However, intellectually, they were five years ahead of the average in their capacity to assimilate ideas. The solution was to either "compromise between intellect and sensori-motor mechanism in grading, or to segregate such children (where the population is dense) in special classes, so that appropriate provision can be made for the exercise of all capacities, without the necessity of compromise."[25]

The "Summary Report" of the P.S. 165 Special Opportunities Classes, presented to the Board of Education of the City of New York in 1929, included several suggestions:

> The emphasis should be on enrichment rather than on rapid progress.... The teacher selected should be particularly well informed, cultured, not forgetful of the need for developing fundamental skills, and familiar with the technique of projects, the socialized recitation.... Assurance must be given of a high degree of efficiency in fundamentals commensurate with their superior mental power.... A foreign language, geography, reading reports, may be introduced in the early years.... The physical aspects, play, outdoor recreation...need to be encouraged.... Abundant opportunity should be provided for cooperation with other classes and children, as well as in the activities of the rest of the school, to avoid the tendency to be self-centered.[26]

A predecessor for the modern educational emphasis on "multiple intelligences," Leta Hollingworth investigated abilities and disabilities in reading, spelling, arithmetic, drawing, and music in her text *Special Talents and Defects: Their Significance for Education* (1923). She concluded that while some special abilities correlated highly with the general factor of intelligence ("g"), other abilities had a very low correlation. Leta pointed out, for example, that all gifted children were not necessarily proficient in areas of special talents such as art and music. She noted that although they may not be above average in arithmetic, they usually would be exceptionally able in higher mathematics. She was one of the first psychologists to assert that one could be gifted in ways other than academically, and her concepts foreshadowed the modern notion in gifted education of "asynchronous development"—namely, that gifted children are often (and perhaps typically) uneven in the levels of ability within themselves.

Leta personally administered tests in musical sensitivities to all forty-nine students from the P.S. 165 Special Opportunity classes.

She did not find a positive correlation between high intelligence and musical sensitivity.

> Though they meet tests of intelligence as well as or better than average adults do, they meet tests of musical sensitivity only as well as average 10-year-olds can.[27]

She also examined drawing abilities, where drawings were classified according to a hierarchy that considered both technique and implied meaning—copying, representational, analytical, impressionistic, symbolic, and caricature. She noted that talent in drawing, like talent in music, required a combination of many elements, some of which seemed related to intelligence, but "a very stupid child may surpass a very bright child" in draftsmanship.[28] Yet "distinguished achievement in analytical, symbolic and interpretative art" was more likely compatible with high academic ability.[29]

Hollingworth expressed concern about the public schools' inattention to helping students with special talents cultivate their abilities:

> Instruction in music and in drawing, modeling, and painting has been given to all children alike, regardless…of the great individual differences in the distribution of ability. In music…all children must sing, the tone deaf along with those acutely sensitive to pitch.[30]

She recognized that it is not always easy to identify a special ability, in the same way that it can be difficult to identify a disability. "An intellectually gifted child may be deficient in music, in drawing, and in mechanical manipulation." However, when an intellectually gifted child also possesses a high degree of special talent, "there exists the basis for eminent achievement in the special field."[31]

She was hopeful that when mental testing became more sophisticated, and subsequently, when more children were assessed, children would be taught according to their abilities.

> In the United States, the theory was adopted that all men are created equal. All children must, therefore, be required to take the same education. Such a system violated

individuality even more painfully and wastefully than the despised caste system of the older countries does. As scientific psychology improves the methods of testing for individual differences in children, it will become possible to educate each one according to his capacity for learning. It will be possible to conserve and develop the special aptitudes of every child, regardless of race, sex, or circumstance. The humiliation and despair of chronic failure at prescribed tasks unsuited to capacity may be spared every child.[32]

THE "SPECIAL PERPLEXITIES" OF THE GIFTED

The first textbook in gifted education, *Gifted Children: Their Nature and Nurture* (1926), written by Leta Hollingworth, was derived in great part from studies and observations at P.S. 165. She dedicated the book "To the memory of my grandparents Samuel Thomas Danley and Mary Blair Danley," whom she must have felt nurtured her more than her father and stepmother. The contents of this important book were widespread and included:

- History of the Study of the Gifted
- The Modern Approach
- The Census of the Gifted
- Physique and Movement
- Character, Temperament, and Interests
- Development
- Family History
- Special Talents
- Children Who Test above 180 IQ (Stanford-Binet)
- Experimental Education and the Gifted
- Organization in Curriculum
- Social-Economic Implications

This book, *Gifted Children: Their Nature and Nurture*, became the definitive text on the cognitive, social, and emotional needs of gifted children for decades, and its contents are still relevant almost a century later.

In his review of Chapter IX, titled "Children Who Test above 180," Professor Lewis Terman wrote, "Here we find not merely descriptive case histories, but also measurements of numerous physical, intellectual, and personality traits. The results of such a clinical study give a fairly complete picture of the gifted child in terms that are objective and psychologically meaningful..."[33] Terman was at the time quite involved in his own longitudinal research of gifted students in California. Lewis Terman and Leta Hollingworth were certainly aware of each other's work, and Terman even visited with Leta and Harry Hollingworth in their New York home. Unfortunately, we know little more about their relationship.

Like so many of Leta Hollingworth's other texts, *Gifted Children: Their Nature and Nurture* was a compilation of class lectures, re-statements of findings from earlier publications, and new findings. In her subsequent writings about gifted children, she expanded upon several themes that were first articulated in earlier articles and then were subsequently refined and synthesized in this book. Five themes are particularly notable.

First, the nation's public schools were failing to serve their exceptional students. Leta railed against the "lock-step" approach in public education. The below normal child invariably fell behind the prescribed curriculum, while the above normal child was bored and uninspired by it. Children ought to be educated according to their capacities, she believed, and it was quite possible to determine these capacities because of the accuracy of mental tests.

Second, gifted children are those who test above 130 IQ, but gifted children are not necessarily all alike. There are significant differences between profoundly gifted children with IQs above 160 and gifted children with lower IQs.

Third, asynchrony is inherent within giftedness. Gifted children know more than they can do, and their abilities are not alike in all areas. Hollingworth wrote about the "wide discrepancies between desire and attainment.[34]

Fourth, although heredity plays the dominant role regarding the transmission of high IQ, the environment determines future attainments. We inherit genes that enable us to achieve, but whether or not we do so is largely up to the environment, with a little luck thrown in. Not all gifted children come from affluent families, although "to find most easily and quickly a group of gifted children, one should go to a private school, or to a public school in an excellent residential section of a city whose fathers are professionals."[35] Affluent families generally are more able to provide supportive environments for a child's inborn abilities.

Fifth, children of superior intelligence (130+ IQ) may have special problems with social adjustment, and the higher the gifted child's IQ, the more likely the problems will become apparent. She coined the phrase "special perplexities" to describe these difficulties. In an address given at the First International Congress on Mental Hygiene on May 8, 1930, she elaborated on these special perplexities. It was of immense importance to Leta that counselors and teachers helping gifted children understand them. One can't help thinking that she demonstrated many such characteristics in her own life and fully understood how difficult being gifted was, particularly if self-knowledge was limited. Leta's words in her writings poignantly describe the special perplexities for gifted children in the 1920s—as well as for gifted children today.

The Problem of Work

Where the gifted child drifts in the school unrecognized, held to the lock-step, which is determined by the capacities of the average, he has little to do. He receives daily practice in habits of idleness and daydreaming. His abilities are never genuinely challenged, and the situation is contrived to build in him expectations of an effortless existence. Children up to about 140 IQ tolerate the ordinary school routine quite well.... But above this status, children become increasingly bored with school work, if kept in or nearly in the lock-step. Children at or above

180 IQ, for instance, are likely to regard school with indifference, or with positive distaste, for they find nothing interesting to do there.

On the other hand, if the child is greatly accelerated in grade status...he will be misplaced in other important respects.[36]

The Problem of Adjustment to Classmates

The present writer knows of instances in which these young children have valiantly suffered at the hands of dull, bullying classmates, protecting themselves as best they might by agility and wit, since of course, they could not possibly compete in size and strength. The gross indignities and tortures thus suffered are directly a penalty of being gifted.... Segregation of pupils on the basis of mentality would go far to obviate such problems.... Gifted adults are free to segregate themselves from thugs and gangsters...but the American school forces the dull bully upon the gifted child, in daily contacts, out of which lasting problems of mental hygiene may arise.[37]

The Problem of Play

Reports by gifted children themselves show that they are, as a group, much interested in play, and that they have more "play knowledge" than has the average child... it appears that the gifted know more games of intellectual skill, such as bridge and chess.... and that gifted girls are far less interested in traditional girls' play, as with dolls and tea sets, than unselected girls.... But although they love play,... the play of the highly intelligent works out in practice as a somewhat difficult compromise among their various powers. They follow their intellectual interests as far as they can, but these are checked in many ways by age, by degree of physical immaturity, and by tradition.[38]

Special Problems of the Gifted Girl

Aside from their dissatisfaction with the play habits ordinarily associated with their sex, gifted girls have various other problems to face, which arise directly from the facts that they are able and that they are girls... . The intelligent girl begins very early to perceive that she is, so to speak, of the wrong sex. From a thousand tiny cues, she learns that she is not expected to entertain the same ambitions as her brother. Her problem is to adjust her ambitions to a sense of sex inferiority without, on the one hand losing self-respect and self-determination, and, on the other, without becoming morbidly aggressive... . The special problem of gifted girls is that they have strong references for activities that are hard to follow on account of their sex, which is inescapable.[39]

Until recently intellectual inferiority of girls was assumed, and public policy with regard to them fostered no expectation of intellectual performances on their part. Their social function was grounded in physique rather than in intellect, to produce the species, and to perform manual duties pertaining to and compatible with maternity... . Girls were assumed to be mentally inferior to boys, as a sex, and to resemble each other closely in intellectual caliber... . Is the implication of these facts that gifted girls should be given the same educational advantages as gifted boys?[40]

This solution will probably come through specialization of what is now known as women's work, so that the care of young children will be expertly undertaken; through knowledge of birth control with rational limitation and spacing of offspring; through the gradual evolution of public expectation favorable to the appointment of mothers in posts of conspicuous responsibility.[41]

Problems of Conformity

Certain problems of discipline do arise, which grow out of their intelligence. First, in the case of the schoolroom situation, almost the only respect in which it is especially troublesome to discipline these children is in the matter of orderly discussion, when they are together in special classes. It is hard for them to maintain silence when ideas press for utterance. The tendency is for many to speak at once, each striving to outspeak the other. To hold his tongue, to listen quietly and respectfully to others, to speak according to some order of procedure, and to restrain disappointment at failure to be heard at all— these habits seem especially difficult for gifted children to form.

Also, it has been noticed during the experiment education of the highly intelligent that they sometimes tend to slight routine drudgery in favor of more stimulating and more original products.

At home, a special problem of discipline may arise occasionally, due to the circumstances that a child, while still very immature in years, has come to exceed one parent or both in intelligent. For the best discipline, the parent must be more intelligent than the child must, or the child's respect for the opinions of the former will inevitably be lost.... Very readily, such a child perceives that in comparison with himself, his parent is slow-witted and poor in general information. Yet in self-control and experience of life, the child is still very immature.... Fortunately, in the vast majority of cases, at least one of the parents is a person of superior intelligence.

There is within intelligent children a stronger tendency to argue about what is required of them than is found with the average child.... To find a golden mean between arbitrary abolition of all argument, on the one

hand, and weak fostering of an intolerable habit of end-
less argumentation, on the other, is not always easy, but
is always worthwhile as a measure for retaining the
respect of the child.[42]

The Problems of Origin and of Destiny

Early interest in origins and in destinies is one of the conspicuous symptoms of intellectual acumen. "Where did the
moon come from?" "Who made the world?" "What is
the very end of autumn leaves?" "Where did I come
from?" What will become of me when I die?" Why did I
come into the world?"...

The higher the IQ, the earlier does the pressing
need for an explanation of the universe occur, (and) the
sooner does the demand for a concept of the origin and
destiny of the self appear.

In the cases of children who test above 180 IQ...
definite demand for a systematic philosophy of life and
death developed when they were but six or seven years
old.[43]

Despite her exciting formulations, her groundbreaking work,
and her numerous publications, Teachers College failed to provide
any financial support for Leta's studies of gifted children.[44] Disillu-
sioned by this lack of support, she had to be content to continue her
longitudinal research with the gifted students from the P.S. 165
three-year experiment, intending to eventually publish a book concerning children with IQs above 180.

She also continued teaching undergraduate courses and writing prolifically. She never anticipated that the New York City Board
of Education would collaborate with Teachers College to develop a
public school for children of exceptional abilities, although she prayed
about it for fifteen years.[45]

❧ CHAPTER 7 ❧

An "Unexpected Answer to Fifteen Years of Prayer"

The Speyer School (Public School 500) Experiment[1]

*For education most especially, there is no problem
more vital than that of determining the intellectual
capacity of the individual children who come to
school. To teach them without reference to the
ability of the learners is to involve the waste and
misery incidental to all irrational procedures.*[2]
—Leta Stetter Hollingworth, 1925

In 1934, nearly a decade after the completion of the P.S.165 experiment, Leta Hollingworth correctly sensed a possible positive change in Teachers College level of interest in gifted education. In a letter to colleagues, she suggested:

> I am disposed to come back to the development of this
> field at Teachers College, if "the times" have so changed
> that there is the slightest chance of administrative favor
> for it. As I have told you, my discouragement with the
> prospects for such development was made complete with
> the repeated failure to gain any administrative attention
> in the years between 1917-1922. At the end of those five

years of effort, I turned definitely away from the College as a medium of development for Special Classes, and went into Mr. Theobold's school (P.S. 165, Manhattan). With materials therein accumulated, I have been working ever since 1922; and I have plenty of work to do in developing these materials, as the subsequent history of our pupils there studied grows longer.

However, if the College now wishes to develop this field, there is a great opportunity for it. It looks to me as though all circumstances are favorable, just now. Dr. [Paul] Mort, as Director [Teachers College] understands this field (no one else in the past ever did); and Dr. [Harold G.] Campbell [Superintendent of the New York City Public Schools] has exceptional children in mind. Our connection with the Department of Ungraded Classes, of New York City, are of the friendliest.

I enclose a few reprints of studies made from the Special Classes at Mr. Theobold's school to exemplify the kinds of work that are possible with such classes, as concern the gifted. Altogether about twenty-five studies have been published from this project. We could go on with greatly increased effectiveness if the College would favor this work. There has never been any support for it, from the College, in the past.[3]

Leta had been waiting for the political and academic climate to change course, and she seized the opportunity to inform her colleagues at Teachers College of past indifference to her research agenda, while at the same time suggesting that the institution could make amends. Her patience was rewarded.

Leta Hollingworth's address to the Trustees and Faculty of Teachers College humorously recounts the beginning of the Speyer School experiment.[4] She told about having lunch one day in 1934 with Paul Mort, Director of Teachers College. Professor Mort asked her, "You know Speyer School Building is vacant now, and don't you think it's about time you started a school for exceptional children there to find out something about what we ought to teach such children?" She continued:

> Years ago, back in 1916, being then young and full of notions, I should have loved to hear of Speyer School being vacant. I wanted badly to start a school for exceptional children, but fate decreed otherwise. So in 1922, I went to the school of Mr. Jacob Theobald, Public School 165, Manhattan, and there we started classes for children above 135 IQ (Stanford-Binet)...and we wrought with diligence upon the eight and nine years old; and we wrought with diligence upon the whole children for three brief years; and then we watched them through high school, and then, fascinated with what we saw, we watched them through college; and just as Dr. Mort began to speak to me, these 56 youngsters were out of college, and I was fixing to observe them, and them only, for the rest of my life.... Dr. Mort and I finished our luncheons. I took a taxi to the Speyer School.[5]

On August 14, 1934, Paul Mort telephoned Leta, giving her formal permission to outline a plan for using the Speyer School as a school for exceptional children. She wrote him that "your phone call this afternoon seemed like the unexpected answer to fifteen years of prayer."[6]

During the summer of 1934, with the United States still gripped by the Great Depression, Leta Hollingworth developed an outline of her plans for the development of the Speyer School—a document that became the working framework for the project. The goal of the Speyer School experiment was to teach and study exceptional children—both above and below normal. She envisioned the student population as including:

> (1) those of low degree of intelligence (dull or feeble minded), (2) those with specialized deficiencies (poor in

TEACHERS COLLEGE
COLUMBIA UNIVERSITY
NEW YORK

August 14, 1934.

Prof. P. R. Mort,
Teachers College.

Dear Dr. Mort:

You 'phone call this afternoon seemed like the un-expected answer to fifteen years of prayer.

I have committed to paper the tentative outline, which I gave you orally, of plans for developing the Speyer School. I call the outline tentative, because it is subject to the counsel of Prof. Gates (who has not yet seen it on paper), and of the Committee on Special Classes, when and if appointed.

I attach herewith only a carbon copy of the outline, because I wish the signed copy, to be formally presented, to come through the hands of Prof. Gates. He and I have developed the idea together, and want approval from him, before submitting the plan. I hope to see him today.

In the meantime, I want a copy of what I am submitting to Prof. Gates to be in your hands, in view of our conversations of today.

I'm certain every element of the situation is at this moment favorable (since the Dean has approved the idea) for the building of a notable enterprise.

L.

reading, poor in arithmetic, etc.), (3) the left-handed, (4) sensory defectives (the hard of seeing, the hard of hearing), (5) speech defectives, (6) the intellectually gifted, (7) the specially talented.[7]

The plan specified that Teachers College would supply the building, the professors, and student-teacher assistance for teachers. The Board of Education would supply teachers, pupils, principal and assistant principal, furniture, school supplies, janitorial services, heat, and light. Each party had the right to approve personnel choices. The Guidance Laboratory of Teachers College would have opportunities to test and conduct case studies of exceptional children; facilities for instructing teachers majoring in the field of Special Classes would be provided as well. She suggested that the project begin in the spring semester of 1935.

Throughout the next weeks, Leta refined the outline and prepared a detailed memorandum, "A Plan for the Development of the Speyer School as a Joint Endeavor in the Education of Exceptional Children," for presentation to the Board of Superintendents of the Public Schools of New York. She informally met with New York City teachers and administrators to share the document and get their reactions to it. A copy of the memorandum was given to Teachers College Dean William Russell for his approval, and Leta requested that he then send it to the New York City Superintendent of Schools Harold Campbell. By the beginning of October, she wrote the Director of Teachers College, Dr. Paul R. Mort, saying, "I have already collected favorable unofficial reactions from all of those, both on our staff and in the public schools, whose good will would be indispensable. All are favorably disposed to the Speyer project." The potential collaborative partners were equally informed at this crucial germinal stage.[8]

In October 1934, Leta Hollingworth and Arthur Gates, Head of the Department of Educational Research at Teachers College, met with Harold Campbell, the Superintendent of Schools for the City of New York, and presented the Speyer School proposal.

Campbell agreed to establish a committee to study the merits of the plan and make recommendations to him. The issue of finances was raised, and as the New York City school budget had been cut, the Superintendent expressed concern with the costs of maintaining the school. The process to get the school up and running dragged on.

Nonetheless, Leta was selected by Teachers College Advanced School of Education as educational advisor to the Terman Classes. In May 1935, she noted that Teachers College would have to invest $6,500 in Speyer School furniture and physical improvements. Professor Gates supported this expenditure: "Unless I'm a bad guesser, the school could be organized to be of very great service to the Higher School [Teachers College], and could be operated in a way to bring us into very happy relationships with the city system."[9]

In the autumn of 1935, Leta Hollingworth personally interviewed and administered the *Stanford Revision of the Binet-Simon Measuring Scale for Intelligence* to hundreds of applicants.

> When it became publicly known…that it was the purpose of the Board of Education to found Public School 500, Manhattan, approximately six hundred applications were immediately received from all parts of the City, both orally and in writing, from parents, guardians, teachers, principals and even from children themselves, for admission to the classes for gifted children. Many parents came in person.… Nor did we depend on volunteered applicants, but went on our own initiative to principals…to seek out highly endowed pupils of the ages desired.[10]

When she realized that all nationality groups were not represented, Leta visited the schools and homes of underrepresented groups and explained the purpose of Speyer School. She must have been very persuasive, because when Speyer School opened in February 1936, children from twenty-three different national backgrounds were in attendance.

However, financial support was still inadequate, and again Leta's determination and ingenuity came into play. Harry Hollingworth noted:

> The chief impediment in the enterprise was that although experiments were to be undertaken, no personnel and no resources were provided for such activity. Taking the classes for rapid learners as her province, Leta S. Hollingworth inspired many volunteer helpers to undertake the researches. The resources she provided from her summer session earnings. She invited parents and friends to contribute bits of needed furniture, tools, books, and materials not in the standard lists. Necessities, evaded by both the founding institutions, such as partitions, seating changes, plumbing repairs, library shelves, she managed to have done by well-wishers with a mechanical bent but no union card.[11]

On January 28, 1936, Public School 500, Speyer School, was officially founded jointly by the New York City Board of Education and Teachers College, Columbia University. It opened February 3, 1936 with a population of 225 children divided into nine classes of twenty-five each. Seven classes of 175 students were devoted to pupils with IQs in the seventy-five to ninety (Stanford-Binet) range. Fifty gifted students with Stanford-Binet IQs of the 130 and above range were admitted, and the plan was to keep the fifty in Speyer School until the term nearest to their thirteenth birthday or until the experiment ended.[12] Selected teachers for the nine classes were all experienced teachers from the New York City school system. Children from fifty-six different elementary schools attended Speyer School during the experimental period—a broad constituency.

In the Reconstructionist tradition, the social philosophy of Speyer School was that the school should serve as an agent for positive social change.

> The first specification in the curriculum…was to give an abundance of opportunity for gifted pupils to develop

attitudes, understandings, appreciations, knowledges, and skills which would function in their lives as children. The second specification was to give them deeper insight into the significance of contemporary problems in order that they might become more effective citizens in a democratic society.[13]

One laudable component of the Speyer experiment for the rapid learners was that they would interact socially on a daily basis with the children from the Binet classes at the other end of the intelligence scale. Representatives from the seven Binet and two Terman classes thus jointly served on the student council, the school newspaper, a Girl Scout troop, and the boy's basketball team. In addition, the rapid learner children always had physical education and recess together with the Binet children. Tolerance and respect for individual differences were emphasized, taught, and practiced.[14]

The rapid learners progressed at their own pace academically, performing the prescribed curriculum on a contract basis that was developed by their teachers according to their performance on the Stanford Achievement Test. The curriculum was conceptualized as involving all activities—both in and out of school—over which the school has influence. The rapid learner curriculum was broadly inclusive rather than narrowly prescribed. Leta argued:

> The "top one per cent" can do all the rest can do, and some things that none of the rest can do. It is with the things which are restricted to these children that special education should busy itself.[15]

What Leta meant was this: while gifted children ought to be given a "wide horizon," she argued, "we must take responsibility for their intellectual training. We must decide what they should know." As part of this responsibility, Leta believed that appropriate education involved more than just the intellect, and that emotional education "may be even more important." Described as "their training in attitudes, emotions, and drives," she knew that gifted children had to be educated about the "special perplexities" of their emotional lives.[16]

The enrichment program for the rapid learners was constructed so that it was student-centered, interdisciplinary, and relevant to the pupils' lives.

> The education given should be such as will function specifically and uniquely in their lives. It should afford them a rich background of ideas, in terms of which they may perceive the significant features of their own times.... The education of the best thinkers should be an education for initiative and originality. Effective originality depends, first of all, upon sound and exhaustive knowledge of what the course of preceding events has been. To take their unique places in civilized society, it would seem, therefore, that the intellectually gifted need especially to know what the evolution of culture has been. And since at eight or nine years of age they are not yet ready for specialization, what they need to know is the evolution of culture, as it affected common things.[17]

Leta's curriculum and educational practices in 1934 were not all that different from practices advocated today by leaders in the field of gifted education. Student involvement in the curriculum was emphasized. Working together, the children, teachers, and advisors selected the areas of study; students then developed the units on a daily basis in consultation with classroom teachers and advisers.[18] Student-selected committees investigated segments of the larger topics and then presented findings to the class as a whole.[19] The culminating enrichment activity for each student was the preparation of an independent report detailing the entire unit; some reports written by students were more than one hundred pages long.[20]

Part of each school day was devoted to the traditional elementary school curriculum; however, the teachers had the flexibility "to select, rearrange, and adapt the content of these functional subjects to the mental caliber of the pupils they were teaching...."[21] Reading was not usually taught as a separate subject because most students learned to read before they entered school. The "drill-skill" method of teaching arithmetic and spelling was also used with the rapid learners, but for a much shorter period of time within the day; enrichment was kept separate from the basic subjects; homework was not required.

The study of French was included in the curriculum for the five-year period at the behest of Hollingworth, who believed that the earlier a language is learned, the earlier it can be mastered. She felt that children with high intellectual potential and the subsequent potential for leadership should be conversant in more than one language, and the acquisition of a foreign language when very young would facilitate the mastery of additional foreign languages when they were older.

Leta Hollingworth also taught the study of biography to rapid learner classes at Speyer School. The goal of her class was the same as it had been when she taught biography to the children at P.S. 165; students must learn that people, rather than things, were paramount to the development of humans. In addition, a unit on nutrition was extended throughout the experimental period. The fine arts—music, art, and drama—were taught by specialists from the New York City schools and integrated into each term's thematic units of study.

The focus on real-life relevance to the culture permeated the activities. The City of New York, with all its resources, was a primary source of enrichment. Hobby clubs, sport activities, trips to museums and the theater were among the "extra-curricular" activities made "intra-curricular" at Speyer School; that is, they were integrated into the school day. Leta understood the intricate relationship of motivation to learning, as well as the importance of connecting new content to prior knowledge.

During the first term alone, more than twenty field trips were taken to such sites as factories and museums to enhance the first of a new thematic curriculum endeavor called the "Evolution of Common Things" units. When Leta was on sabbatical in 1928, she spent six days in Germany visiting special schools for gifted children, as well as schools for cognitively challenged children. In her notebook of observations, one entry is particularly notable relative to her teaching approaches to gifted education, which later evolved into the "Evolution of Common Things" units.

Hamburg, March 1, 1928

Visited the Museum of Arts and Crafts, which is used in education. Went through the Museum with three different Wanderlungen [gifted children]—two from a boy's school and one from a girls' school The teacher explained the connections of the old things with contemporary life, and recited the history of the museum pieces.[22]

A decade later, Leta described a rationale to develop thematic units, which became the Speyer experiment's primary means of enriching the gifted children.

Between the ages of seven and thirteen years, the minds of these children are occupied primarily with exploration of the world in which they have recently arrived. They are full of questions of fact, not yet being distracted by the emotional and dynamic interests that come with adolescence and adulthood. This is the golden age of the intellect. Why? How? When? Who? Where? What? are constantly on their tongues, as any parent of a child in our classes will testify.[23]

She described the method for researching the "Evolution of Common Things" assignment:

The teachers did not discover and assemble the materials of instruction and "give them out." The children did this work.... When an area of knowledge had been circumscribed by the children as one chosen for study by class discussion, the teacher participating in the thinking but not leading it,...the pupils...divide themselves into "committees." These various groups of three to five children each bring special knowledge to class periods, and all share in the sum total of facts and ideas thus assembled.[24]

In twenty-first century jargon, Leta is describing cooperative learning strategies, where the teacher plays a facilitative rather than a directing role. During the five-year experiment at Speyer School (it continued two years after Leta died) more than fourteen separate "Evolution of Common Things" units were completed included. These included:

- The Evolution of Art, Literature and Music
- The History of Aviation
- The Story of Clothing
- The History of Communication
- The Development of Health and Sanitation Measures
- The History of Illumination
- The Evolution of Law and Order
- The Progress of Man's Efforts to Conserve Natural Resources
- The Story of Shelter
- The History of Trade and Money
- Time and Time-Keeping
- The Story of Toys and Games
- The Evolution of Transportation by Land
- The Evolution of Transportation by Water

The New York City Board of Education published Curriculum Bulletins with "Evolution of Common Things" instructional units that had been developed jointly by Teachers College professors, researchers, and Speyer School teachers. These were intended for use by other teachers within the New York City School System.

A report entitled "All the Children: The Thirty-Eighth Annual Report of the Superintendent of Schools City of New York for the 1935-1936 School Year" described the Rapid Learner classes. The section titled "Features of Program" delineates Leta Hollingworth's philosophical and psychological theories about gifted children. The list of features leaves no doubt that the whole child was to be considered in teaching, and the seven most essential guiding principles are listed as follows:

1. Each teacher has physical, mental, social, and environmental knowledge of each child, gained from one or more visits to each child's home and from a close contact with the home by the school nurse. A fine cooperation exists among the nurse, the teachers, and in many cases, the home, in a common desire to bring about the greatest good for the greatest number of children.

2. Diagnostic and remedial procedures are essential parts of the classroom situation.

3. The units of instruction include large areas of experience and learning; such education is continuous and active in view of the expanding knowledge of the pupils' interests and needs.

4. Education includes learning within and without the schools. Excursions, trips, or visits to museums, parks, farms, libraries, factories, galleries, and historical centers have been made almost daily. It is significant and interesting to note that while many of these trips are planned far in advance, many others are decided upon quickly, as the occasion arises and as the subjects investigated by the children bring new enthusiasms, new ideas, and new interests.

5. The printed page is not the only approach to learning. Visual-auditory learning, manual arts, and craft activities are naturally integrated with the large areas of experience.

6. Special abilities and interests of children are recognized and given the necessary educational guidance. Social misfits, maladjusted pupils, and children with personality and social problems are receiving therapeutic treatment in a natural environment.

7. The intra-curricular activities (Glee Club, Dramatic Club, Student Council, Art and Craft Club) have become part of the school living and have made effective a normal, satisfying, day-by-day group undertaking. It is possible to educate children according to their capacities because it is possible to quantify their capacities through mental testing.

Evaluation of student performance was based upon a variety of data. Teacher anecdotal records, standardized achievement tests, student self-assessment, and group assessment all played a role in determining how well a student was progressing. "I really believe," wrote Hollingworth, "that the experimental work being done at Speyer School, especially that being done to set up a curriculum for highly intelligent children, is one of the most significant to have been undertaken so far in the twentieth century. It might really make educational history."[25] To use a twentieth-century term, the assessment was "authentic."

Speyer School quickly became a news item in national popular media, as well as in educational publications. Even though seven of the nine classes were created for the education and study of the subnormal learner, the overwhelming majority of news coverage concerned the experiment with rapid learners and gifted education. Leta Hollingworth's duties expanded; she was responsible for "handling the reports, the feature writers, photographers, and visitors, who arrived in what seemed a steady stream."[26] She was proud of the interest in Speyer shown by the public, which she thought was both gratifying and amazing.

In February 1938, two years after Speyer School had opened, the Financial Office of Teachers College allocated funding for the purchase of larger seats for Speyer School students who by now had physically grown in size. Hollingworth was so grateful for the minimal Teachers College financial support that she wrote an effusive thank-you letter to Thad Hungate, the individual in the Teachers College Financial Office apparently responsible for allotting the funds. She alluded to the publicity that the school was receiving from the national media:

Since last November, *Time, The Literary Digest,* and the NEA Feature News Service have carried illustrated articles to millions of readers, the latter furnishing its write-up to over 800 newspapers here and abroad. *The Readers Digest* will carry the story from *The Literary Digest,* in April. On March 28, or a week later, *Life* will carry an illustrated article on the school. The metropolitan dailies have all carried news repeatedly, and syndicates have sent the story of the school to every small town in the U.S.A. We get clippings and letters from remote places, showing that the school has become known in such places. Such publicity brings scores of visitors from everywhere... .[27]

One such laudatory letter arrived from The Amsterdamsche Montessori-School, Amsterdam, Netherlands. Leta had had several articles about Speyer School translated into Dutch and sent to the correspondent. Although the letter is not from Dr. Montessori herself, it appears to be from one of her disciples. Dr. Maria Montessori by this time had relocated to Holland from Italy in 1936 to escape from Fascism. The reply to Leta's correspondence and articles is as follows:

2 July 1938

Dear Madam,

I am very grateful to you for your letter of June 21st and the trouble you took in sending me some printed matter on your school for exceptional children, which had my attention as well as that of the teachers of our school.

I am quite convinced that your experiment constitutes the greatest effort made for the amelioration of traditional educational methods since Dr. Montessori, and we are highly interested. We would be very grateful if you would keep our name on your mailing list, because

ERDAMSCHE MONTESSORI-SCHOOL,
DE LAIRESSESTRAAT 157 EN 159
ALBRECHT DÜRERSTRAAT 36.

AMSTERDAM-Z., 2nd July 195.8
Keizersgracht 484.

Mrs. Leta S. Hollingworth,
Teachers College,
Columbia University,
New York. U.S.A.

Dear Madam,

I am very grateful to you for your letter of June 21st and the trouble you took in sending me some printed matter on your school for exceptional children, which had my attention as well as that of the teachers of our school.

I am quite convinced that your experiment constitutes the greatest effort made for the amelioration of traditional educational methods since Dr. Montessori, and we are highly interested. We would be very grateful if you would keep our name on your mailing list, because we are making an inquiry to see if anything on the same lines could be got up here.

As the Montessori-method has already done away with the necessity for all pupils to work at the same thing at the same time or for that matter at the same speed, we are already acquainted with the great difference in absorbing capacity of different pupils in the same class. Therefor there was no difficulty in persuading our teachers of the exceptional possibilities of your experiment and we are keenly interested.

Yours very truly,

[handwritten annotations:] don't translated this for school, we are sure you will under Dutch. Will you please to the letter. correspondity. To the letter.

we are making an inquiry to see if anything on the same lines could be got up here.

As the Montessori-method has already done away with the necessity for all pupils to work at the same thing at the same time or for that matter at the same speed, we are already acquainted with the great differences in absorbing capacity of different pupils with the same class. Therefor [*sic*] there was no difficulty in persuading your teachers of the exceptional possibilities of your experiment and we are keenly interested.

Yours truly,
[Signature undecipherable][28]

Journalists writing about the Speyer School experiment reported on the success of the rapid learner classes. They interviewed Leta Hollingworth, who did not hesitate to talk about her beliefs regarding eugenics and heredity—beliefs that would, in a very few years, be sharply attacked by others. She particularly emphasized that basic differences existed among people relative to their innate capacity to develop intellectually and that the most intelligent were often also biologically superior to the less intelligent. The idea that intelligence was culturally dependent or that all children have an equal capacity to develop and learn were dismissed by her as scientifically unverifiable. She clearly believed that all children could learn, but that they would learn according to their capacity. She believed some individuals were particularly talented in art, music, and the like, but she did not believe that these talents were the same as intelligence. And she never modified her conviction that IQ remained constant throughout one's lifespan.

A sample of the media coverage of Leta's views are shown in the following two articles.

The New York Times, October 31, 1937

Bright children possess a finely developed sense of humor, and are above the average in personality, cheerfulness and good looks according to a study made public yesterday by Professor Leta S. Hollingworth, educational psychologist at Teachers College, Columbia University. Brains and beauty go together, she found. The old adage, "beautiful but dumb," is a superstitious saying without a grain of truth. Girls and for that matter, boys who wear Phi Beta Kappa keys are not serious-minded and homely. On the contrary, they are above the average in physical charm and rate high in personality tests. Rapid learners are found to be large for their age, well nourished and healthy looking. Their bodies, including their heads, are in excellent proportion while their appearance is found better than normal. Their faces are clean cut, heads beautifully molded, and their postures are firm and graceful. They have more delicately formed hands than average children have. Why good luck and intelligence should go together Professor Hollingworth did not know. One explanation offered was that frequently in science desirable traits are possibly correlated. It is just nature's way of concentrating her virtues.

The Literary Digest, February 19, 1938

The old belief that environment is all that prevents leaders from rising from the slums is simply not true. Dr. Hollingworth, in her thirteen years of study, has never found a superior child who came from inferior stock. The vast majority of bright children prove to have come from successful homes.... As Dr. Hollingworth put it, "the immemorial division of mankind into lower, middle, and upper classes economically speaking, rests on a biological foundation. It persists despite all efforts to abolish

it by artifice. Mediocre or dull parents can no more produce a brilliant child than a tomato plant can produce a
plum."[29]

Two examples of Leta Hollingworth's writings during the
Speyer School period similarly demonstrate her eugenicist and here-
ditarian philosophy. In her 1939 memorandum, "The Positive
Aspect of the Preservation of Hereditary Strength," she wrote:

> The biologically elite [are] composed of persons far above
> the average in respect to character, intelligence and stam-
> ina. Such persons are essentially and originally endowed
> by biological nature, but their development depends upon
> education. Education cannot create them, but education
> can develop them.
>
> Scientific studies of gifted children, made during
> the past two decades, show that there are in the United
> States large resources upon which to draw for an elite.
> One child in every hundred is as far above average in
> educability as the feeble-minded are below average. More-
> over, these children superior in power of learning are at
> the same time superior as a group in the other qualities
> necessary for development of the richest personalities. It
> is among highly intelligent children that the most ethical
> characteristics and the finest bodies are likely to be found.... .
> They mature into superior adults, maintaining their status
> constantly as they grow.... . [I]t is feasible to predict accu-
> rately who will be in adulthood the most capable thinkers
> among children at a given time in school.... . One element
> in development, pertaining especially to the maintenance
> of hereditary strength through reproduction of the able, is
> consideration of time saving in the long course of prepar-
> ing for the learned professions... . If it be arranged for
> them to save time in preparation...they can hope to enter
> upon their economic careers at a biologically appropriate
> and reasonable age, and can reproduce their kind.[30]

Also in 1939, she wrote an article for the *Teachers College Record* that she entitled "What We Know about the Early Selection and Training of Leaders":

> There is a strong probability that a child who rates as only one in a hundred of intelligence will also be endowed in superior degrees with "integrity, independence, origiaality, creative imagination, vitality, forcefulness, warmth, poise, and stability…I would… add to it audacity, capacity for nonconformity, the love of beauty, and cold courage, as traits to cherish in leaders, although these traits are often uncongenial to teachers in the elementary school, and possibly to other educators…. In the selection of any child testing far up in the top one percent…there is far more than an even chance of having thus automatically selected a tall, healthy, fine-looking, honest, and courageous child with great love of adventure and of beauty in his make-up….[31]

Leta also viewed high intelligence as a mixed blessing. In earlier works relating to leadership and the gifted, she suggested that a profoundly gifted child, for example, was less likely to be voted president of a class or a member of the Student Council than a child with a lower IQ. She believed that highly gifted individuals are sometimes viewed as odd by others not so endowed intellectually. She also knew that some of the personal characteristics of profoundly gifted children would not endear them to their age-peers.

And despite her statements emphasizing the importance of heredity, Leta certainly recognized the importance of environment. In many ways, her beliefs are quite similar to those held today. In a 1997 survey of the theories and research relating to the nature vs. nurture debate, three statements were identified as common points of agreement: "(1) Both heredity and environment contribute to intelligence; (2) heredity and environment interact in various ways; and (3) extremely poor as well as highly enriched environments can interfere with the realization of a person's intelligence, regardless of the person's heredity.[32] Leta Hollingworth would have concurred with all three statements.

SPEYER GRADUATES

Although she intended to write a longitudinal study of her P.S. 165 and Speyer School students as they progressed through adulthood, Leta did not live long enough to do so. However, other researchers did report upon the adult status of Speyer School graduates. A forty-year follow-up study of twenty of Speyer School's rapid learners found that Leta Hollingworth's great experiment in gifted education had indeed made a significantly positive difference in the lives of many of those gifted children, though a few of the students felt that the program did not specifically influence their adult success.

> They all…believed that their experience at Speyer School was instrumental in providing them with peer interaction for the first time, exposing them to competition, causing them to learn and like school for the first time, giving them a strong desire to excel, providing new exposures that were not possible in the other schools in New York City at that time, and having themselves recognized as being "special"… . The success of the… experiment leads to the inevitable conclusion that involvement in a special program can have a positive impact upon the lives of participants… . [F]orty years later, as adults, the participants still recall…the positive educational experiences of Speyer School. For some participants, these experiences changed their views of themselves and expanded their future options. For others, it directly affected their choice [of]…college and career. For some, Speyer School offered the first exposures to areas that later became their avocations.[33]

She would have been so pleased.

LETA'S LEGACY

What were Leta Hollingworth's responses to the four central questions of gifted education that she identified and then studied for two decades? It is interesting to consider how far our educational system has (or has not) progressed since Leta's time in implementing answers to her fundamental questions. In general, it appears that many school systems are still debating them and that the progress has been minimal.

Can American public schools identify and recognize gifted children and make provisions for their education? Leta's response was an unequivocal "yes." She believed that the individual (not the group) IQ test was the most accurate and valid measure of intelligence and that children in the top one percent of that population (IQ 130-180+) were gifted. She was the first gifted educator to use multiple criteria to identify the gifted child. In addition to IQ tests (individually administered), she also interviewed the parents and the child, reviewed teacher and principal nominations, and examined social and emotional maturity levels of the child. The school, she felt, had an obligation to make provisions for educating the gifted.

How should gifted children be grouped in schools? Leta believed that some degree of accelerated curriculum was appropriate for every gifted child. Aware of societal animosity toward specialized provisions for highly intelligent children, she nonetheless advocated for enriched homogeneous classes for the highest IQ rapid learners in elementary school (grades K-8) when it was feasible for the school district to provide such classes.

In the elementary grades, she envisioned a placement strategy combining segregation with acceleration. After the age of twelve, she thought rapid progress alone might suffice for the highly gifted student. Concerned that gifted students' classes should not be labeled by such terms as "Special Opportunity Classes for Superior Children," she agreed with some districts identifying the classes as simply "Special Opportunity" or "Terman" classes. She argued that fears that children in rapid learner classes would become elitist and subvert democratic principles were unfounded; intellectually alike adults, she noted, tended to associate primarily with one another, whether or not they were grouped homogeneously in elementary school. Without a specialized, differentiated, and enriched curriculum, rapid learners were not reaching their potential.

For the profoundly gifted (IQ 160+), she argued that homogeneous classes were as necessary for this population as they were for the extremely cognitively disabled. Through the P.S. 165 and Speyer School experiments in gifted education, Hollingworth forged a compromise between rapid progress and curriculum enrichment with attention to the needs and potentialities of individuals.

Leta argued that since human beings were not created intellectually equal, not all children should be educated in the same way. It came down to a fundamental aspect of all education—an appreciation of individual differences among learners. Her overriding objective was that all children have individualized curriculum that enriches them to the highest levels of their potentialities. She envisioned the day when the "school will be fitted to the child. Suicide of pupils, in despair at failure, will be unknown. Truancy will become outdated… The gifted will be selected for the extraordinary opportunity, which suits them by nature."[34]

A LOST LABOR OF LOVE

Despite her heartfelt commitment and hard work, Leta was not optimistic that the Speyer School experiment would be extended beyond the five-year school/college commitment. Angered by the reluctance of Teachers College and the New York City Board of Education to provide adequate funding for her efforts, Leta was prepared "to revert in February, 1941, to my former status of isolated research worker, in the continuation of friendly cooperating with administrators of the public schools as individuals, confident of the resumption of habitual contacts and long-time associations, in which professional interests will develop further."[35] That she viewed herself as an "isolated research worker" from 1917-1934 is illuminating. Although she was an eminent psychologist, she felt much like she had in her childhood—akin to that "Lone Pine" on a Valentine hill: "High up where the world may see it,/Sharp outlined against the sky,/While its brothers down in the valley/Unnoticed are all passed by./And the lone Pine standing patient,/Where the wild winds wage their strife,/Beaten and scarred and crippled,/Like a broken, lonely life,/Is telling again the story,/As the winds thro' its branches moan,/ Of a soul lifted high o'er its brothers/That must bear the storm alone."[36]

In 1941, a little more than a year after Leta Hollingworth died, Speyer School was closed. *The New York Times* reported:

> Leading spirit behind the movement was Professor Leta S. Hollingworth, noted psychologist, whose untimely passing a year ago filled the school, as well as her host of friends and colleagues, with sadness. She conceived a program that would provide an enriched, individualizing training for the mental giants of the younger generation....Last Friday the project came to an end.... The old weather-beaten doors are to be padlocked, the windows barred....[37]

Leta's great experiment in gifted education could not continue without its "leading spirit."

❧ CHAPTER 8 ❧
Loving and Working

For recreation I live in the country, talk to friends,
go to the theater, and play bridge when ever and
when I can; but I cannot yet afford enough
time to become a good player.[1]
—Leta Stetter Hollingworth, 1940

The Hollingworths' professional lives were very successful. Both were esteemed professors, received academic promotions, were in demand as consultants, presented papers at national professional meetings, and published prolifically—both individually and jointly. Harry Hollingworth's academic career was as noteworthy as Leta's. Chair of the Barnard College Psychology Department for many years, he was a pioneer in the area of applied psychology, and he helped involve women in the field of psychology generally. When he first began teaching psychology at Barnard College in 1909, it was not without controversy. Some colleagues and administrators thought that psychology was not a "fitting topic for young women."[2]

In 1917, Harry served as a member of the Council of Representatives of the American Psychological Association. In 1927, he was elected President of the American Psychological Association, an indication of the great respect in which he was held nationally by colleagues. "Holly made a tip-top presidential address. I almost took fire, glowing with pride," Leta wrote to her father.[3] During an illustrious career, Harry Levi Hollingworth published nineteen books, four monographs, and seventy-two articles. In addition to serving as the President of the American Psychological Association, he was awarded the prestigious Nicholas Murray Butler Medal of Columbia University.

When he died in 1956, the Barnard College Meeting made a resolution: "That the faculty of Barnard College express its sorrow at the death of Professor Harry L. Hollingworth."

> As an experimental psychologist he made fundamental contributions to a wide range of psychological problems, including learning (which he defined in terms of "reintegration"), thinking, character analysis, the functional neuroses, the forms of human judgment, and the effects on human behavior of caffeine and alcohol.... He also applied his clarifying theoretical acuity and experimental ingenuity to practical problems in the world of business, and published two books on the practice and principles of advertising.... Throughout his career, his interest was in ingenious experiments, yielding reliable objective results, which could be used in the construction of useful theories.... Professor Hollingworth's principal interest was always in the joy of seeking truth. In a letter a few years after his retirement he wrote... "But lots of times I could wish I was back in the laboratory, with my data spread out on the tables, calculating coefficients and drawing graphs of the results." He will be long remembered as an inspired researcher and wise friend.[4]

THE HOLLYS

Leta and Holly were a well-matched couple, and they managed well the complexities of nurturing their relationship while also engaging in myriad activities and achievements that made them both eminent professionals. Their marriage lasted thirty-one years. Like so many other long relationship, their years together consisted of periods of closeness as well as periods of some emotional distance.

Despite a self-imposed, grueling work schedule, Leta had a rich and rewarding personal life. Her professional accomplishments did not occur in a vacuum. Many places were home to Leta—the open Nebraska prairie, her various New York City apartments, her small Teachers College office, and her comfortable country home, "Hollywyck." With both the Hollingworths working as professors, their financial picture brightened considerably with each year. From their initial small, bare apartment, they moved several times within Morningside Heights. Each apartment was more spacious than its predecessor, reflecting their increasing ability to pay higher rent.

At last, theirs was a comfortable, upper middle class life. They traveled in the United States and in Europe in 1911 and again in 1928; they entertained friends, dined out in numerous New York City ethnic restaurants, attended lectures and meetings in Greenwich Village, explored art galleries and museums, enjoyed Coney Island, and marched in suffrage parades. According to Holly's recollections, the couple had an idyllic relationship for many years, particularly in the years before they both became eminent in their fields.

> The intimacies of our life and our close companionship of those days made for me the most beautiful thing I have ever known. I would gladly forfeit all our later years of professional achievement rather than lose the memory of the intense personal joy of those early years. Though gasping for breath, we were always together and completely "in with each other," with mutual faith and confidence, full of hope, and brimming over with energy.[5]

As young professors, Leta and Holly often worked together in the evenings at Milbank Hall on the Teachers College campus.

> With all the laboratory tables available, we could spread our data out before us and work until drowsiness finally drove us home. Then we would wander down the dark hallways, down the four dark flights of steps, out upon

Broadway and across to Amsterdam, near which we
always live in the city.... L.S.H. and H.L.H., by their
lonesome selves, working out their destiny on the bare
laboratory tables.... But it was never really lonesome
then, for her vivid spirit was there to quicken and illuminate our hours of work.[6]

Their evenings at Milbank working alone and yet together
gradually stopped when they moved to larger apartments and built
their country home. Housekeeping became less Leta's concern when,
in 1913, they hired their first live-in housekeeper, a Puerto Rican
immigrant named Francesca. She remained in their employ for
eleven years.

Although they maintained their apartment in Manhattan, the
couple purchased 2.5 acres of land in Westchester County, New
York in 1913. The "Montrose Colony," as it was called, consisted of
homes owned by several Columbia University professors and their
families. Drawing upon his skills as a carpenter and contractor,
Holly designed and built a summer cottage. It was ready for occu-
pancy in 1916, several weeks after Leta received her Ph.D.

Leta and Holly spent sixteen summers in Montrose, commut-
ing by train to Barnard College and Teachers College for summer
teaching. Holly described Leta in this period as:

...energetic as I, and she often took charge of one end of
a big cross cut saw after I had felled a huge dead chestnut
tree; together we would transform such logs into posts,
or wood for the huge fireplace. So jealous was L.S.H. of
all the branches and twigs, after her long years in the
sand hills of Nebraska, that she could not see them
burned as brush.[7]

When the home was renovated for year-round living in 1934, it
was formally named "Hollywyck." Leta loved nature and remained
deeply appreciative of the wooded acres in Montrose—having lived
so long on the "limitless" (and treeless) prairie. Among Harry

Hollingworth's prized belongings was a beautiful photograph, taken by Leta, of a dogwood tree.

World War I separated what appeared to be an inseparable couple. Many American soldiers suffering from what was then diagnosed as "shell-shock" were transferred from the European front lines to a special psychiatric hospital in Plattsburgh 320 miles away from New York City. Applied psychologists were suddenly in demand. Holly was asked by the Surgeon General's Office to direct the hospital as Chief of Educational and Psychological Services. In August 1917, Holly remembered walking sadly down a Montrose Colony road with Leta and then parting—he continuing to the railway station and she returning to their home "to carry on alone again." Leta later told him that after he "had disappeared down the hill, she ran up into the woods and cried her heart out."[8]

Leta did visit Plattsburgh on occasion and was permitted to share both Holly's bed and his right to eat at the Officer's Mess Hall. Service in the army was traumatic for Holly, so much so that upon his discharge, he developed a severe skin rash in which his "skin scaled off in great flakes and left a powdered wake behind…as if to shake off every possible vestige of the affair"[9]

Despite being apart and the hardships of the war years, all appeared well with the couple. "Yesterday was our thirteenth anniversary, you know," Leta wrote her cousin Anna (Kutzie) in 1922. "It doesn't seem possible that we've been married so many years. You'd be surprised to see the number of gray hairs in your cousin's head, I can tell you.… . Life in New York is always strenuous, in spite of all one can do. Each year we think we won't work so hard, and each year we work just as hard as ever. However, it seems to agree with us, for neither of us is ever sick."[10]

The major stress in Leta's life seemed to be with the housekeeper, Francesca.

> She [Francesca] had been saving her wages for many years, and had accumulated what would be a competence, in Puerto Rico.… . Ever since she had saved up to

the sum she had set for herself, she had been getting more and more indifferent to her other work, until activity practically ceased this autumn. I finally told her she could not have four hours in which to prepare a simple meal consisting of boiled chicken, potatoes, and peas (no dessert to it) and she took her final departure.[11]

In 1924, Francesca was succeeded by Josefine Weischer, a German immigrant, who arrived at the Hollingworths' with her six-year-old daughter Virginia.[12] Her demeanor contrasted sharply with that of the previous housekeeper.

> The changes in our ménage became conspicuous. Josefine, full of energy and exceptionally intelligent, with a cosmopolitan background, a passion for cleanliness, and fond of good things which she could make with skill to satisfy an epicure, at once took off the shoulders of L.S.H. the cares of marketing and planning. She and her work became the heart of our household, and she became famous for a variety of things that our friends knew they could enjoy if they came to visit "the Holly's."[13]

Josefine Weischer most certainly had a cosmopolitan background. Her father was professor of English at Bonn University; she had earned a university degree, and she was a certified high school teacher. However, opera was her great love. She must have been very talented musically because the renowned Italian composer Ottorino Resphigi had accepted her as a pupil, and she had studied with him in Italy.

While visiting New York as a tourist, Josefine met and married Ludwig Wiescher. In the great flu epidemic of 1918, Ludwig died, and their daughter, Virginia, was born several months later. As a single mother, Josefine believed that her only employment option was to find a housekeeping position where she could live with her daughter. It speaks well of the Hollingworths that they did not object to hiring a woman with a young child. Leta and Holly now had an unusually overqualified woman to cook and clean for them, and they also found that they had a person with whom they could share common interests. Leta, too, was an avid opera lover, and undoubtedly the two had many enjoyable conversations.

Josefine's daughter, Virginia, had keen memories of growing up in the Hollingworth household, and she remembers her good fortune in being "raised by three parents." Leta was a second mother to her, and Holly was a surrogate father. She remembered Leta as a kind woman, but that Leta often reminded her to be very quiet so that she could work without interruption. Leta was also the disciplinarian, setting strict rules of behavior for the young girl. On the other hand, Virginia described Holly as a sweet and generous man who never appeared angry and who never scolded her. Josefine and Virginia played an increasingly central role in Harry Hollingworth's life. It was perhaps not surprising that seven years after Leta's death, Holly re-married Josefine Weischer and became Virginia's official stepfather. Ben Florence, who later married Virginia and became Holly's son-in-law, also talked about Holly in the most glowing terms.[14]

Though she was not one to talk at length about herself, Leta did write occasionally about her interests outside of work. In a brief autobiography, she wrote, "For recreation I live in the country, talk to friends, go to the theater, and play bridge whenever and where I can; but I cannot yet afford enough time to become a good player."[15] Bridge was one of her great passions; she joined a bridge club and often entertained several tables of players at Hollywyck. Competitive in spirit and an excellent athlete, Leta was also an avid tennis player and horsewoman.

The Hollys were very sociable people and enjoyed entertaining. Their guest book contained the names of many prominent psychologists who visited and dined with them at Hollywyck. These included Lewis Terman, James McKeen Cattell, Henry E. Garrett, Anne Anastasi, Arthur Gates, Joseph Jastrow, Arthur Jersild, Carney Landis, Irving Lorge, Gardner Murphy, Henry Nissen, A.T. Poffenberger, and Edward Reisner. Leta's fellow Heterodites were also frequent visitors and included persons such as Katherine Anthony, Elizabeth

Irwin, Helen Hull and her partner, Mary Louise Robinson, a well known writer, and Alice Rohe. Leta's Ph.D. advisees Meta Rust and Winifred Scott visited, as did one student from her IQ above 180 group, Donald MacMurray—the Child E who had touched her soul so deeply once and had prompted her to turn her attention to gifted students. Even some Nebraskans were on the list; Leta and Holly's former undergraduate professors Louise Pound and Thaddeus Bolton came to visit, as did surrogate mother Nellie Pickup and Leta's old Valentine friend Ruth Quigley.

It is particularly noteworthy that Leta Hollingworth and Lewis Terman socialized. They are so often portrayed as geographic book-marks in the history of the gifted movement—she on the East Coast at Teachers College and he on the West Coast at Stanford. The fact that they actually knew each other and even shared a meal or two humanizes these luminaries in the field and certainly suggests a defi-nite respect for one another.

Despite their active social life at Hollywyck—and before—Leta and Holly made it a point not to attend Columbia University social events as a couple. They even marched separately at commencement exercises. Holly worried that if faculty and administrators knew that they were married, unkind questions would be raised such as, "Why was she hired, when he has such a fine position?" "She is taking money from someone else (a male) who has mouths to feed. They do not need two incomes." Holly was certain that the Dean of his college would not recognize Leta had he met her by accident. Although Holly suffered considerable angst from this subterfuge, Leta "...was less affected; she was more inclined to take things in her stride and make the best of them."[16] Holly revealed that several colleagues even referred to Leta as his daughter, so circumspect were they about their true relationship. And yet Teachers College and Columbia University professors lived in the Montrose Colony, and many others were invited to their home. Their marriage could not have been the great secret that the Hollys thought it was.

In a letter to her cousin in 1926, Leta reported, "We are both well, and busy as usual. Every week we go out to the country and chop wood for exercise. There isn't any real chance for exercise in the city."[17] In 1928, Holly and Leta were both awarded sabbaticals from their respective institutions. "It will not be a very long trip." Leta wrote her father, "but long enough for us, for we both like home better than any other place. However, we realize that we must go, for it has been seventeen years since we were in Europe, and things have changed greatly since the war. You remember that we were both in Europe in 1911, and stayed all summer."[18] They sailed on the "Deutschland" in the middle of February 1928 and spent several months touring Europe, visiting Hamburg, Berlin, Leipzig, Dresden, Stuttgart, Cologne, Belgium, England, Scotland, and Ireland.

Much of Europe was successfully recovering from the effects of World War I, but Germany was in dire straits. When the Hollingworths visited Germany in 1928, Adolph Hitler had already published *Mein Kampf* and had organized the Nazi Party and its youth movement, the Hitlerjugend; Goebbels was a rising star in Berlin, and many Jews were being persecuted. The Hollys spent a good deal of time in Germany. Perhaps this was partly because she spoke German, but also it was because she felt that Germany had given "more official administrative recognition to special education on the basis of innate mental endowment than any other country."[19] In Germany, Leta visited "all kinds of special schools and hob-nobbed with educational experts."[20] Her visit resulted in her gaining an even greater understanding of special education, particularly for the gifted.

In Berlin, for example, special schools for gifted children, (Begabtenschulen) had been established in 1917. Children were selected based upon mental tests and teacher recommendations. They completed the elementary school program in only three years. The cities of Hamburg, Breslau, Mannheim, Leipzig, Frankfort, Charlottenburg, and Göttingen also experimented with programs for gifted children. Leta was critical of the German programs in one area— gender discrimination. She noted:

> Both boys and girls participate in these special advantages, but in some cities only half as many girls as boys are permitted to be chosen.... . [P]sychologists...have pointed

out that in the tests used for selection, the girls equal the boys in performance, and that this raises questions of policy concerning the education of girls, which are, perhaps, especially distressing in view of German traditions of education.[21]

As she observed the work of European educators and psychologists first-hand, Leta gained new knowledge about how to educate gifted children. She must also have felt vindicated in her belief that differentiation and enrichment of curriculum was accepted pedagogical practice.[22]

At approximately this point in their marriage, most likely in the late 1920s or early 1930s, Holly felt that he and Leta were unable to sustain the intense close relations of their early married years. "The tender relation we established in those days was difficult to maintain in full depth when our separate professional careers came to pull us often in different directions or to different places, or to entangle us separately with different groups of people."[23] Gradually, they were developing contrasting social and political views, interests, and friends. Leta spent an increasing amount of time in the pied-à-terre they maintained in New York City, while Holly preferred the rustic life in Westchester County.

Leta attended theater, horse shows, concerts, and enjoyed her circle of friends. Holly remained overnight in the city only when it was unavoidable. There was one discernible cause of Leta's increasing remoteness from her husband. In 1929 or early 1930, Leta was diagnosed with an abdominal tumor; she told her family it was not malignant. It appears she was advised to do nothing about the tumor except "watch it." During the ten-year period between the diagnosis and her death, she refused to have any subsequent medical examinations, believing that they would result in a major operation. Years later, it was the opinion of her physicians that she had known for years that she had incurable cancer.

If there was a rift in their marriage, few people knew about it. According to Leta's cousin Helen and her niece Margaret, the Hollys had a happy marriage.[24] However, on the other hand, it is almost inconceivable that either Holly or Leta would confide such personal information as marital discord to anyone, family or not. They both had long experience with keeping secrets. Some may speculate that Holly and Josefine grew closer while Holly and Leta pulled apart. Perhaps that was the case; perhaps not. We simply do not know.

FAMILY

Leta remained a committed family member despite the long distances between New York City and Nebraska. "Through the years, she kept in touch with many relatives and friends who needed help, and shared her worldly goods, energies and devotion with them," wrote niece Margaret.[25] Her correspondence is filled with references to her sisters, brothers-in law, nieces, and nephews. The Hollingworths repeatedly sent money to relatives, even when they were young students and new faculty members living on a very limited budget. Despite their early financial problems, when family members needed to move in with them, there was no debate. Leta's sister Ruth did so from 1909 until 1911. During the winter of 1917, Holly's sister Gertrude stayed with them so she could study music.

Johnny Stetter remained a presence in Leta's life though they were rarely in each other's physical company. Despite the lifelong tension between them, Leta never stopped corresponding with her father or to others regarding his care. When the emotional bond between parent and child is "disrupted by abandonment, hostility, or severe physical and emotion abuse...usually the child feel that he or she has done something to bring this on, feels guilty, and makes repeated attempts to win the favor of the toxic parent."[26]

Leta's father continued to exert emotional influence upon her until her death. For example, she wrote to him about her upcoming sabbatical and gave him their address in London. She then added, "I will give it to you again before we sail, in case you might have lost this letter." Aware of his irresponsibility, she must have feared he would not be able to reach her if she was suddenly needed. Leta's father was very much on her mind Christmas Day, 1934. She wrote two letters that day—one to Papa, and one to her cousin "Kutz" (Anna Stetter Fischer). She informed Papa:

> We are busy this week, getting the house in shape for winter, storm doors on and the porch enclosed.... We are so <u>glad</u> we moved out of the city. Life in the country is so much more home-like [Leta's underline].[27]

Leta promised to visit Papa for his eightieth birthday. However, she did not find the time, or perhaps the will power, to do so. She wrote Anna of her concern for her father.

> I want to speak about "Uncle Johnny." I heard from him yesterday,—Hotel Arcade, Omaha. He spoke of having been sick, but was feeling all right again, according to his statement. He is very old now,—getting on for eighty,—and without any settled abode; so I'm beginning to sort of worry about him. I wish there were someplace where he would want to "stay put," amid familiar surroundings, where he would be looked after. I would gladly <u>pay</u> toward such an arrangement, and of course, as far as that goes he has resources of his own. But I could never undertake to manage him, myself, and neither could Maggie; for he <u>resents</u> all our advice or management, and would never do anything we might suggest. Furthermore, he wouldn't be congenial with either one of his sons-in-law. No use to make everybody miserable. I would never <u>undertake</u> anything that would make my husband wretched in his <u>own</u> home. But I would gladly pay toward some <u>suitable</u> arrangement. However, he will not "stay put" as long as he has legs to go on. He always did have those restless habits. He <u>never</u> used to stay home, even when he had a home.... Of course, I have written frequently to him to let me know if he needs <u>money</u>, but he always seems to have resources, even when corn fails. Maybe he's so old now, he doesn't <u>realize</u> when he <u>does</u> need money. Please keep an eye out, and

inform me. It only makes him angry for <u>us</u> to try to look into his affairs, but he does not resent <u>you</u>,—thinks you are wonderful [Leta's underlines].[28]

"I will feel easy about you," Leta wrote Papa on February 17, 1935, "if you are carrying my address on your person. There's no sense worrying about anyone—does no good, and takes the pleasure out of life. It seems to me that you must be in need of money by this time,—no corn crop, and the depression still on. Be sure to let me know if you need money. I will surely send it. I am among the lucky ones." She signed this letter, as she signed all the others to her father, "Your loving daughter, Leta." John Stetter never learned how to be a loving father. He continued to be a source of dismay and anxiety for Leta. She worried about him but could do nothing to ameliorate her concern. He had been an absentee father in Chadron and in Valentine, and he remained so for the rest of Leta's adult life. Emotionally she tried to be detached, but he continued to have the power to hurt and frustrate her.

RUTH

The family member who touched Leta the most deeply was her sister Ruth, also a teacher. In 1909, Ruth was diagnosed with pulmonary tuberculosis and moved to New York City to live with Leta and Holly. When her condition worsened a few years later, she was admitted to Loomis Sanitarium in the Catskill Mountains. During summers, Leta and Ruth shared a cottage at a nearby resort. Despite their poor financial state in this period, Leta and Holly paid all of Ruth's medical expenses. Leta hated to be alone, and her sister was a much-needed companion, particularly when Holly went "galloping over Europe" earning extra money as a companion to a mentally disturbed young man.[29]

Leta even involved Ruth in some of her research. In her writing on *Functional Periodicity*, Leta gave thanks to "my sister, Miss Ruth Stetter, [who] gave me much help in the matter of taking records in the Extensive Experiments, and in various other matters."[30] Writing to her cousin Anna on April 28, 1911, Leta notes, "We spent

Easter with Ruth. She is looking just as well as she always does, and is back at work. You know she had [the] grippe about two months ago, and had to give up work for a while."[31]

While working on her doctoral dissertation in 1915, Leta was devastated by a personal tragedy. "Holly and I went up to Loomis to spend Christmas day with Ruth. She is just about the same; no better and no worse. I was glad that we could be together at least."[32] Just as they returned home, they received a telephone call from the sanitarium informing them that Ruth had suddenly died. Leta and Holly decided Ruth ought to be buried in Nebraska, even though paying for her coffin and other funeral expenses would completely eradicate their savings. They had to endure a further upset, when striking truck drivers initially refused to transfer Ruth's coffin from one train to another. Their trip was made even more unpleasant because, during the three-day journey to Nebraska, they could not afford to buy any food. Leta Hollingworth's text, *Special Talents and Defects* (1923), is dedicated "To the Memory of Ruth Elinor Stetter—A Good Teacher."

Leta's surviving sister Margaret and her cousin Helen Stetter spent the summer following Ruth's death in Montrose with Leta. Helen remembered:

> You see, Leta was so broken up after Ruth died that she wanted us to come that first summer. She was alone and used to have Ruth come out to the house and stay with them for a while. It was just heartbreaking. I think in some ways Leta felt like her mother because she felt responsible for the two daughters, really her sisters, because the father just left them after the mother died.[33]

The intensity and sensitivity of emotional overexcitabilities last a lifetime; Leta was no exception.

MARGARET CHASE OVERTON

Another important family figure and a frequent visitor to the Hollingworths' was Leta's niece Margaret Chase Overton, who was Maggie's daughter. She lived with Holly and Leta for several summers in the early to mid 1930s. It was she who provided the most detailed description of Leta's physical appearance in the 1930s.

> She paid no attention to style in her choice of clothes, partly because she was rather heavy, and partly because she simply didn't want to take the time to shop for "fashionable" clothes, even when she could well afford to do so. She had a seamstress make most of her dresses, which were of a peasant style, with smocking or embroidery around the neckline and on the top of the dresses. They fit loosely with a sash around the waist. Her shoes were low-heeled and comfortable, so she could get places faster, and could be on her feet for long periods. Somehow, this manner of dressing suited her, and she always looked feminine and beautiful. The colors of the fabrics in her dresses were lovely colors—mostly pinks, roses, blues, and pale yellows and beiges—and they accentuated her clear skin, and lovely brown hair, which she wore combed back and in a bun at the nape of her neck. She had never cut her hair, and when she brushed it each night, it was so long, she could sit on it. She would always put it in a braid before going to bed. Her brown eyes were her most noticeable feature. They were full of expression—love, interest, compassion, humor—whatever emotion she was feeling at the moment. They were like Spaniel's eyes, soft and loving. Her hands were short and her fingers stubby, a physical characteristic, which, like her sturdy body, was inherited from her father, John G. Stetter. She was always writing something—letters, speeches, books in the making, ideas which she wanted to pursue. Her correspondence to her friends, colleagues, and family was voluminous through the years, and the amount of correspondence she received was just as astounding.[34]

Margaret worked at the Teachers College Library, and also at Barnard College helping her Uncle Holly record grades for his summer school students. She stayed in their New York apartment during the week while they commuted to their summer school duties from Montrose. When Margaret attended the University of Nebraska, it was her Aunt Leta who paid her tuition, book expenses, and provided a monthly living allowance. On her periodic New York visits, Leta took her niece shopping for her entire school wardrobe and also showed her the best things about living in New York City.

> She loved so many things, and since Uncle Holly was not interested in coming into the city to see entertainment, the two of us saw many things together and how she did enjoy it all—and so did I, of course. We would eat dinner at a different foreign restaurant each time we had dinner in the city, and would also try as many different restaurants for lunch on the days we went shopping. We saw musical comedies, plays, operas, operettas, tennis matches, and even the Carnero-Sharkey fight in Madison Square Garden... .We toured the museums, and all the foreign sections of the city. She was delightful to be with, full of humor, considerate, patient, eager to learn about something new, and we seemed to enjoy the same things, so that we thoroughly enjoyed each other's company.[35]

As much as Leta enjoyed New York City, Margaret believed:

> I think she loved her home—Hollywyck, at Montrose—the best of all. There, she could enjoy nature, tranquility, and find relaxation from a very busy schedule. When she and Uncle Holly were younger, they went swimming every day in the lake, and played tennis... . Sometimes you would hear the two of them singing, one in one part of the house, and the other joining in from another room... . They both enjoyed company and would quite often have a Sunday buffet and invite people in. Nearly every weekend, they would have guests at Hollywyck... . The guests were told to do as they pleased and relax, but everyone was to be at the table on time for the evening meal.[36]

She writes of her Aunt Leta: "She believed that <u>life</u> was very precious, <u>talent</u> was a blessing to be nurtured and shared for the good of others, and that <u>people</u> were to be cherished and helped" (Margaret's underlines). But while Margaret admired her aunt, she also found some of Leta's convictions to be frustrating. "She could be very determined. [Margaret here crossed out the words "strong willed" and penciled in "determined."]" For example, each fall, Margaret had to reinforce the stitching on the snaps and buttons of all of her new clothes because Leta insisted that "the store did not always do a good job."[37]

TEACHERS COLLEGE

In Leta's work environment, her persistence was sometimes regarded as obstinacy and dogmatism. Her professional obligations at Teachers College were typical of professors in institutions of higher education throughout the United States. She taught, advised students, attended departmental meetings, chaired master and doctoral committees, researched, and published. In addition, she was a speaker at many public events and gave a number of national radio addresses. Teaching and scholarship were her primary responsibilities, and she excelled at both. She rose quickly within the faculty ranks from instructor (1916-1919) to assistant professor (1919-1922) to associate professor (1922-1928) and finally to full professor (1928-1939). Only five years after receiving her doctorate, she was listed in *American Men of Science*—an honor which was accorded to only the top scientists in the country.

Colleagues and students often teased Dr. Hollingworth about the size of her tiny office in Room 334, Macy Hall, at Teachers College. Her office had a desk, one chair, filing cabinets, and a small set of bookshelves. Two people could not work in the office, and when she had graduate student assistants working on projects, they had to rotate office times. Often, conferences with students, teachers, and visitors would occur in the hallway. One afternoon, a psychologist who studied with Leta for his doctorate waited patiently in that hallway to see his mentor. He recalled:

> I came here today…to test against the most logical mind
> I know a plan for the quantitative testing of what I think
> is an important hypothesis… . Mostly, however, I come
> with little excuse except to renew the inspiration of even
> a brief contact with a rare person. Always I find more
> than I expect in this little three-cornered office. It may be
> the smallest office in Teachers College, but no room any-
> where is more significantly populated.[38]

THE PROFESSIONALIZATION OF PSYCHOLOGY

Leta Stetter Hollingworth was committed to professionalizing
the field of school psychology. During her early years on the Teachers
College faculty, she spent at least one day a week working in the Psychopathic Service at Bellevue Hospital. In 1917, she was a member of
a committee that founded the American Association of Clinical Psychologists. Appointed as the first psychologist for the newly organized
Classification Clinic under the auspices of the Neurological Institute
of New York City in 1921, her contributions to the fields of clinical
psychology and school psychology remained a constant in her professional life. She published several studies relating to the history of
psychological clinics, school psychology, and clinical practice, and
she lectured widely on these subjects.

Leta was an early proponent for the recognition of psychology as a
profession of merit, and one that could function independently from
physician oversight, particularly in the schools. She was opposed to the
common practice of assigning psychiatrists to direct school behavioral clinics. She addressed the Board of Education of the City of
New York on this matter on February 18, 1931:

> Any physician who decides to be a psychiatrist ipso facto is
> one. Yesterday he may have been an obstetrician, a sur-
> geon, or just a physician. Today he is a psychiatrist. That is
> all there is to the training required… . Do medical schools
> teach developmental psychology, child psychology, the
> psychology of habit formation and motivation, history of
> education, school organization, and all other bodies of

organized knowledge that are officially recognized as enabling a person to enter into the work of our schools? They do not...a survey of approved practice in leading cities and in the states will show that school clinics for pupil guidance and adjustment are typically under the direction of educators trained and experienced in education, not medicine. Let it remain so until there is reason for believing that it is better to be trained for child guidance in a medical school than in a school of education.[39]

She was central to the development of a school psychology program at Teachers College. However, as more school psychologists were certified by schools, she grew alarmed by the practice of group intelligence testing. Hollingworth was dismissive of what were, in her estimation, superficial practices employed by many school psychologists. In an address to the Child Study Club of Springfield, Massachusetts, she condemned the "widespread application of hastily constructed group tests by persons untrained in psychological techniques to large groups of children who cannot be seen individually while they are being tested." Always the advocate of the whole child, she believed that "no observation of individuals can be made in group testing."[40] She continued to do private, individual psychological testing, counseling, and consultations until her death.

A PASSION FOR QUALITY

Like so many gifted individuals, Leta Hollingworth was impatient with mediocrity. She had no tolerance for colleagues espousing theories without a scientific basis. Leta was not one to adapt her educational and psychological philosophy to the trends of her day. She had great disdain for "new" educational theories and "isms" that she did not think were based upon sound, scientific research. In an address to members of Kappa Delta Pi in 1932, she synthesized what she thought about the quality of contemporary research.

To do first-class research requires the best brains and the best training. Unfortunately, today too many people are doing so-called research who lack one or the other, or both of these requirements. This has led to some unfortunate conditions.... The first of these appears to be due to the demand to get knowledge quickly.... It has become a fashion in educational research to rush forth hastily with a huge load of pencil-and-paper tests; to spend an hour or two on a hundred children; to rush hastily home to the adding machine, there to tabulate the performance of children, not one of whom has even been perceived as an individual child by the investigator.... The fact is that much of this mass (or shall we call it "mess") research is not only not good, but is positively bad, in that it may lead to results which are precisely opposite from the truth.

She expressed concern about researchers sending teaching assistants into the field while they remained fixed in their offices, isolated from their subjects. Even worse were the researchers who investigated children by testing laboratory animals (such as rats) and then generalizing findings to include humans. "By this method we shall soon learn that children cannot sing, have beady pink eyes, and scamper about on all fours." Hollingworth then lambasted cooperative research, describing it as "a fashion for discovery by committee and by conference.... [A]s a student of the learning process, one cannot but doubt very deeply the value of attempts to carry on discovery and invention by cooperation. Research is by its very nature a highly individual and private matter—as is true of all creative effort."[41]

WILLIAM HEARD KILPATRICK AND LETA HOLLINGWORTH

The colleagues that Leta did respect were as meticulous in their research as she. But it was also true that she could be maddeningly uncompromising. Although Professor Leta Hollingworth had a collegial relationship with most faculty members, there was at least one notable and very telling exception. In 1934, a new "Foundations of Education" course, "Education 200," was introduced into the curriculum. It was taught jointly by professors from each division within Teachers College. A member of the Teachers College faculty recalled, "the college-wide representation didn't last, but it was a gallant and brave idea."[42] During the 1934-1935 academic year, four sections were offered. Seven professors were assigned to teach this course, with two professors teaching each section. Leta Hollingworth and the most popular professor at Teachers College, William Heard Kilpatrick (who had once been Leta's professor), were two of the seven professors assigned to collaborate and team-teach one section.

A *New York Times* reporter once described the Teachers College faculty as "one big unhappy family, in the best sense of the word." This unhappy family was one in which members were always adamantly arguing about philosophy, and this made the college one "of the most stimulating intellectual centers in New York City.... [It] may be said that when a Teachers College professor is in the morning papers, he is fighting the professor two doors down the hall."[43]

No doubt Leta Hollingworth and William Kilpatrick were among those at war. He was an avid Socialist turned Democrat, while she was an avid Populist turned Republican. She was a social conservative, and he was a social liberal. While they were both advocates of John Dewey's educational philosophy, they were on opposite ends of the progressive education continuum. Leta incorporated the learn-by-doing and child-centered pedagogy, but with educational content prescribed by the curriculum, which could then be enriched. Kilpatrick's "Project Method Approach" was more child-directed. In effect, the student determined a "purposeful" curriculum while the teacher simply played a facilitative role.[44] Expecting the two professors to teach together harmoniously was shortsighted.

In referring to Leta Hollingworth in his diaries, Kilpatrick consistently misspelled her last name "Hollingsworth." A day after Franklin Roosevelt's election in early November 1934, Kilpatrick wrote:

> We discussed Mrs. Hollingsworth's interest of individual differences and find we could not in the available

time agree on a course of action. There may be people who can…get things more thoroughly wrong than Mrs. Hollingsworth, but I hardly know any such. She can get more thoroughly wrong more consistently than any capable person known to me can.[45]

Several weeks later (November 20), Kilpatrick complained that the Syllabus Committee for ED 200 (the seven professors) could not agree upon the syllabus content. "I seem to lose out more often than I should. I do not understand." The following day, the disagreement among the collaborating professors continued, but this time they reached "an impasse regarding Mrs. Hollingsworth's paper on Race Differences. I count it greatly unscientific."[46]

On November 28, 1934, ED 200 met, and Kilpatrick observed: "Mrs. Hollingsworth is in great danger of making herself and her position ridiculous. The students really all laughed at her today when she took the position that the working classes did not revolt because they were lacking in native ability." He continued to denigrate Leta in his recollection of the class meeting the following week. "As usual Mrs. Hollingsworth made unscientific assertions and provoked the students. I was amazed."[47]

The spring semester did not find Kilpatrick in a less negative frame of mind concerning the course in general and some faculty members in particular.

January 9, 1935

Meet staff for Ed 200 F section I. Mrs. Hollingsworth got off on one of her pessimistic and fatalistic attacks on people generally. I tried to pin her down… .[48]

March 9, 1935

At 9:30 meet Ed 200 F. sectional staff… . I have less and less patience with our psychologists Stracey and Hollingsworth as all others who in the science follow the older Thorndike tradition.[49]

On the last day of the summer session in August 1935, Kilpatrick assessed his ED 200 colleagues. Few are treated kindly, but he reserves the most vitriol for Leta.

> Mrs. Hollingsworth…was true to form. She has a few obsessions, which she mistakenly calls psychology or science on "the facts." With these she brings forward with automatic sureness whenever certain cues are given. A more unscientific mind I have seldom observed. She rejects philosophy and so uses her own uncriticized philosophy unblushingly.[50]

He added, on August 17:

> Mrs. Hollingsworth gives [to me] a very annoying [undecipherable], stressing and elaborating the obvious, implying but not asserting positions many would like to combat; and with all using up much good time. I am much troubled.[51]

Leta's handwritten notes of a lecture, "The Nature of Human Nature" presented to the ED 200 staff on October 3, 1935, and later presented to the students, revealed why Kilpatrick and she were at such odds. She began her lecture to her colleagues by quoting two college presidents whose views were compatible with her own. First she cited Columbia University (and Teachers College) President Butler, who said:

> Not only is it a fact that individuals are not and can not be equal in respect to physical force or technical skill or intellectual power or moral excellence, but that all progress would come to an end if they were…. Almost all the radical movements and undertakings of the moment aim at the suppression of <u>individual excellence</u> and are therefore in flat contradiction with Liberalism in any of its forms. They are not only reactionary but gravely damaging to the highest and largest interests of society as a whole [Leta's underline].

She then cited the president of Colgate College as remarking:

> Nothing could threaten the race as seriously as social leg-
> islation. It is begging the unfit to be more unfit.

In her subsequent lecture, she presented what she believed were scientifically verifiable facts that she said may run

> ...counter to the American social philosophy, and to the
> hopes of reformers of mankind, including them. For it is
> to be <u>remembered firmly</u> that educational psychologists
> are the very ones who have the deepest professional
> interest in uplifting mankind. Their interest differs from
> that of the idealistic social philosophers only in being
> more profound and urgent. It has been so urgent as to
> lead to the strenuous work of actual experiment with
> real human beings, under controlled conditions; to the
> hard and thankless task of holding human beings under
> cumulative observation over long period of years, keeping
> track of their addresses, sustaining the burden of personal
> contact, and meeting them at intervals experimentally
> stated, in spite of wind and rain...[Leta's underline].

Not one to mince her words, Leta asserted to her colleagues that: (1) human beings, from birth and throughout their lives, differ in all measurable physical and mental traits; (2) differences in mental traits are of a greater range than differences in physical abilities; (3) human variations can be plotted on a bell-curve distribution, and that each individual has a place on that curve that will probably be maintained; and (4) the principles of individual differences apply to the general intelligence trait. She then added:

> Now these are <u>not opinions</u>. They are <u>facts</u>, which can be
> verified by anyone who will take the pains to become
> technically qualified, and will then go forth and measure
> human beings. No one doubts these facts who has ever

done this. They are doubted only by those who have not had opportunity to verify them [Leta's underline].

While educators agreed that children differ in the ways that they learn, Hollingworth noted:

> ...the idea is quite wide-spread that "environment," "will-power," "the ability of the teacher," "physical ailments" are the most potent determiners of the differences. That a given child simply cannot learn fractions, or reading, or algebra, or grammar because his native intelligence is insufficient and always will be, is hardly ever admitted in the formulation of scholastic policies. Yet this can be proved by anybody who will sincerely undertake to teach a six-year-old of IQ 50 to read, or a 14-year-old of IQ 185 to master algebra or Latin construction.

She suggested that the unresolved conflict in America between liberty and equality had resulted in major problems within education and in society generally. Because of this unresolved conflict, she said, there existed:

> ...malice toward excellence. Excellence is hated in America today.... Any one whose professional interest has led him much into contact with the education of very gifted children will readily agree with this. The most unpopular request one can make of foundations for the promotion of human welfare is for funds to study or promote the welfare of gifted children.

She faulted the American school system, elementary through high schools, for coercing students of low IQ to "suffer instruction in reading and [when in high school to]...enter classes in algebra, at public expense, there to suffer the ignominy of failure, or else to deceive the general public later with a high school diploma." She then asked,

…[if] the public schools simply send all alike, from imbecile to genius, thro' twelve years of schooling, with the same diploma for all at the end, what next? Shall the college and the medical school receive imbecile and genius alike? And graduate them? And shall we then be treated in our hour of illness by imbecile and genius, indiscriminately? Or must the line be drawn somewhere?[52]

William Heard Kilpatrick was one of the professors designated to lead the discussion that followed Leta's lecture. His diary the next day makes no mention of what, for him, must have been an odious task. His strong beliefs in the importance of environmental factors and the malleability of intelligence were diametrically opposed to those of Leta.

Whether at home or at work, Leta's life was characterized by an intensity and passion. She cared deeply about her family and friends. She, like Harry, thoughtfully sought truth in her endeavors, and she recognized that she had an obligation to courageously and forthrightly set forth her views when she believed them to be well reasoned. As a result, sometimes she was an irritant to others, and she did not "suffer fools gladly."

❧ CHAPTER 9 ❧

Homecoming

The East is too alien for purposes of eternal sleep.[1]
—Leta Stetter Hollingworth, 1936

The last nineteen months of Leta Stetter Hollingworth's life can be described in two words—triumphant and tragic. In 1938, Leta and Harry Hollingworth were notified by their undergraduate alma mater, the University of Nebraska, that they were both to receive honorary doctor of laws degrees. Harry believed that the granting of this honor to Leta and him was the very pinnacle of their lives.

> I shall never be granted any deeper satisfaction than came from this act of our Old University. The early struggles to survive and to study, on that very campus, would not be washed from memory. Almost on the very spot where we had pledged our "forty years" together, a grand new stadium and auditorium had been built since our days. On the platform of this auditorium, before many of our former teachers, and many of our local friends, and the people of Nebraska, L.S.H. and H.L.H. would stand side by side. The Chancellor would speak words of commendation about our work and would hand out our identical and gorgeously colored hoods, in quaint but significant symbolism of the approval of our joint endeavor.[2]

They requested leaves of absence from their respective institutions and headed west. Leta brought her movie camera to film favorite Nebraska people and places and to make a record of their childhood homes. Before Commencement Day, they drove to Dewitt and filmed Holly's aunts and his homestead. On the return trip to Lincoln, Leta asked Holly to make one more stop. He was surprised that she took them to Wyuka Cemetery. They then selected a burial plot. It was

> ...on the eastern slope of a grassy mound. L.S.H., in a mood that was strangely foreign to her up to that time, had become seriously concerned over the provision for our final resting-place, and she expressed a desire to make such an arrangement now. The prescient nature of this act was then, by me at least, wholly unsuspected, and I little dreamed that in another eighteen months I would be bring her there to rest forever in the spot she had chosen.[3]

Harry was unaware of Leta's illness and its seriousness, but Leta was not. Two years earlier, she had written a letter to the *Nebraska State Journal*, affirming:

> Sometime I shall come back to Nebraska for good. I was born there, I was reared there, and I was educated there. I shall take the last long sleep there. The East is too alien for purposes of eternal sleep.[4]

The program for the Sixty-Seventh Annual Commencement, "The Oration and the Conferring of Degrees," was dated "Monday June sixth, nineteen hundred and thirty-eight at ten-fifteen o-clock." Leta was escorted by her sponsor, Professor Louise Pound, the English instructor and close friend who had inspired and motivated her to write. Holly's escort was his sponsor Professor J.P. Guilford, the eminent statistician who was chair of the University of Nebraska Department of Psychology. They received their degrees with great pride and gratitude. Next to each of their names on the program were the identical words, taken from the Minutes of the Board of Regents:

> Psychologist, writer of important contributions to science, educator, distinguished alumnus of the University of Nebraska.[5]

Each honorary degree recipient had prepared notes for speeches that they anticipated presenting at various functions following the awards ceremonies. As it developed, only one speech was presented, and Leta was selected to give it. Using some of Holly's notes in addition to her own, she quickly pieced together the speech for the Alumni Dinner. It was titled "The Participation of Nebraska in the Intellectual and Artistic Leadership of the Nation." The address was so well received that it was subsequently reprinted by the University of Nebraska.

> The Nebraskans…participating in the mental life of the nation were born on the average above 45 years earlier than the decade of their notability. They were born between 1875 and 1885, or earlier… . They came into being under pioneering conditions. Do rigors of pioneering teach habits of hard work? Or was there something in the breed of the people who first settled the plains of Nebraska that was exceptional? Was the result perhaps a joint outcome of both of these conditions? Is Nebraska today producing the American notable for the future in the same ratio…? No one knows. Have pioneering conditions disappeared? Has the human stock of the state changed in kind or quality?

Leta's conclusion was that of a fiercely proud Nebraskan:

> In its early days, Nebraska produced many more intellectual persons per million of the population that the state could itself use. So it exported the surplus for the use of the nation as a whole. Just as it exported its corn, so

it exported its youths. When the state thinks of its crops, let it think of its gifted children, one of its main products. The sower that tops the Capitol sows not only the corn for the United States, but he sows also ideas into the intellectual life of America, everywhere, through Nebraskans scattered all over the nation.[6]

The new honorary doctors of law set out for Valentine and Chadron as soon as the ceremonies and festivities ended. It was Leta's first homecoming since she buried her sister Ruth in 1915. In Valentine, they attended a family reunion, which Helen Stetter remembered well, but not with pleasure.

> [Holly] thought we didn't know anything, and so he didn't accept us. And he came out here to visit, and he just didn't have any use for us.[7]

After the family reunion, Leta and Harry toured and filmed the city of Chadron and then attempted to discover the sites of the dugout and log-house of Leta's childhood. The homestead was gone. Holly and Leta returned to Hollywyck and to their careers at Barnard College and Teachers College, but they would return to Nebraska much sooner than anyone—except Leta—ever anticipated.

Throughout 1938 and most of 1939, Leta grew more fatigued, thinner, and increasingly remote from colleagues, families, and friends. She told no one about her failing health, but it was becoming obvious to those around her that something was wrong. Holly believed she was suffering from a lingering depression, but he was unable to identify a specific event that might have triggered Leta's emotional decline. She tried to continue working are her usual hectic pace as long as it was physically possible; she wrote, published, presented papers and lectures, and advised students. Finally, too exhausted to continue functioning at Teachers College, Leta requested and received another leave of absence. She planned to go away for a long rest with a friend who was also a trained nurse. As it turned out, she was too ill to leave her home.

During this period, Holly often found Leta sitting alone quietly reading books of poetry. Throughout her adulthood, she continued to read and compose poetry. Among her possessions at the time of her death were several undated poems, and while it is not possible to attach a particular life event to any of them, themes of love, loss, death, and religiosity are discernible. She was a woman of deep Christian faith. While she listed her religion as "Protestant" in a biographical dictionary of notable women, it is not known whether she was a church member or if she attended church, but her letters to Holly and many of her poems reflect a deeply held belief in the divinity of Jesus Christ, and they show familiarity with both the Old and New Testaments. Some of her poems clearly reflect the depth of her spiritual beliefs.

I Have Heard Song

In the hot night when everything is still,
And on the sleepless eyeballs looms the square
The dull gray window makes, and everywhere
Life flickers, speaks a whisper stern and chill,
That seems the listening silences to fill—

"Thou too must find the grave" I think on these:
I have heard song,—I even heard a lark
Sing on a barren grave,—and seen the trees
Bear fruit; and after deep black dark
Seen dawn; and felt the swift sea breeze
Salty as life blood; loved white butterflies;
Watched Autumn flush the silent, solemn land;
And have felt my hand within thy hand
And know thee wonderful, and found thee wise.

Thy Letters

I read in many an old and famous book
How many warrior heroes perished, crying
That love had taught them not to shrink from dying,
And felt this to be great. Lately I took
Thy letters, love, thy tedious absence giving

Me no peace, and read them thro' and thro',
And as I read, a great love I knew,—
Thy love, which taught me not to shrink from living.

The Bride and the Ring

Oh, we must be dear friends, little ring,
Through all days and winds and weather,
For some day you and I, little ring,
Must lodge in a grave that the years will bring,
Together.
Must lodge in a grave? You and I?
Nay, Christ, nay! That cannot be!
But a strange, dim woman, faded and old,
And a strange, thin, worn little band of gold,—
Not we!

Her poem, "Prairie Love" is her most romantic. How she loved Holly, and how she missed her home state of Nebraska!

Prairie Love

I love you as I love the strength of wings
That bear the hawk up even with the sun,
And hold it floating at a height that none
Unwinged may reach. So, sure and strong it flings
Itself into the ether. Thin, bright things
That form from vapor hover on that flight.
The first of heaven burn more redly there,
When sunset kindles. In that far blue air
Soars rapture. So your love with light
Strong pinions holds me to the height.[8]

When she could no longer conceal the extent of a long illness, an alarmed and frightened Harry Hollingworth persuaded Leta to permit a physician to examine her. The doctor ordered immediate hospitalization. With sirens wailing, an ambulance rushed her some forty miles to Columbia Presbyterian Medical Center. An exploratory operation revealed what Leta already knew. She had incurable cancer. There was no hope. Stunned by this terrible news, her family could not believe that their Leta was dying. Diagnosed with a progressive, incurable disease ten years earlier, she had chosen to tell no one—not her husband of thirty-two years, not her family, not her friends and colleagues. Although she was in agony, Leta refused pain-killing injections because she wanted to remain alert. Within days, she slipped into a coma and died on November 27, 1939 at the age of fifty-three.[9]

Not a particularly vain woman, Leta had maintained two conceits throughout her adult life. First, she refused to wear publicly her much-needed eyeglasses. Because she considered driving the car to be a public outing, she had, on more than one occasion, sat—agitated and sweating—behind the steering wheel of their Hupmobile. Her second conceit was her waist-long hair, which was invariably worn in a bun, gathered at the nape of her neck, which Leta plaited before going to bed. Shortly before she was hospitalized, she sheared off her beloved braid because it made her uncomfortable when she lay on the pillow. Surely, if nothing else, this was a statement of her despair. Yet everyone dear to Leta was shocked that she died. "We just didn't know how very sick she was," her cousin Helen Stetter recalled.[10]

Fifteen years elapsed before Harry Hollingworth was emotionally able to record in detail the final moments of her life. He chose the fifteenth anniversary of his devastating loss to do so.

> To be precise, on November 17, 1939, at 6:05 P.M. in Harkness Pavilion I saw and heard L.S.H. draw her last breath. I stood with folded arms in apprehensive gloom against the wall of the room near the foot of her bed while Drs. Richards and Van Etten and Nurse Kupfer busied themselves over her person and issued orders for the oxygen tent, which was never used because the end came in a few minutes. Her last activity was a tossing movement of the right arm on the bed, toward the place where I had usually leaned when visiting her in the last few helpless days.[11]

Leta Hollingworth returned one last time to the state she loved so much; she was buried in the Wyuka cemetery plot she had selected only eighteen months previously. John Stetter's behavior the day of Leta's funeral was described by his granddaughter Margaret:

> He still commanded attention in the restaurant where we ate, and afterwards jigged on the street. His mind had begun to fail, though, and as he had done so many times in his life, he unwittingly put his worst foot forward, thereby incurring further scorn. It was when we were riding to the cemetery, and naturally everyone riding was bowed with grief. All of a sudden he forgot where he was an and hollered, "My God, this new-fangled car rides easy—don't hardly bother your belly at all." A couple of minutes later he realized where he was and he said, "My God, I'm at Leta's funeral, ain't I? Guess I'm talkin' too much again."

Margaret Overton understood the family dynamics well as she concluded writing about the incident: "Some understood that he was just old, and his mind got mixed up at times, and others felt as they had always felt—that this was just one final proof that he had never been capable of any real affection and never would be."[12]

On November 28, 1939, a memorandum note was sent to the faculty and staff of Teachers College.

> It is with deep regret that I announce the death of Professor Leta S. Hollingworth on Monday, November 27. The funeral service will be held in Lincoln, Nebraska. There will be no service here. Flowers are being sent on behalf of the Faculty and Staff of Teachers College.[13]

The news of Leta Hollingworth's death shocked her colleagues. Even her collegial adversary, William H. Kilpatrick, wrote in his diary:

I am much surprised to see that Mrs. Leta Hollingsworth has died. I did not know she was ill. She was a strange person to me. She accepted the Thorndike of 1915 as the last word in fundamental psychology and coupled with it an equally strong social economic conservatism. The result was that while she and I remained good friends—she seemed to feel cordial to me—I differed from her on nearly every distinctive position she took. Where she was a member of my section of ED 200, it got to the place that the students smiled whenever she spoke. They knew in advance what she would say and had already rejected it. She was vigorous—and in that sense [an] attractive personality.[14]

It was an honest description of their relationship.

Obituaries in *The New York Times* and *The Herald Tribune* in the days following her death recounted her Nebraska childhood, education, and her work with gifted children at the Speyer School. *The Tribune's* obituary headlined:

Dr. Leta Hollingworth, 53, Dies: Experimental Education Leader
Columbia Professor and Writer Founded Speyer School Where Special
Curriculums Are Provided for Unusually Bright Children

The New York Times noted:

Mrs. Hollingworth of Columbia Staff Teachers College
Professor Had Been Head of Speyer School

Mrs. Leta S. Hollingworth, Professor of Education at Teachers College, Columbia, died yesterday afternoon in the Columbia Presbyterian Medical Center after an illness of two months. She was 53 years old. Her husband is Harry L. Hollingworth, Professor of Psychology at Columbia. The Hollingworth home is at Montrose, N.Y.

Born at Chadron, Neb., a daughter of John G. Stetter, Mrs. Hollingworth received her Bachelor of Arts degree from the University of Nebraska in 1906, in the same class with her husband. Both were awarded the honorary degree of Doctor of Laws by their alma mater last June.

For the last three and a half years, Mrs. Hollingworth has been executive head of the Speyer School, an experimental institution specializing in the training of exceptionally gifted children.

In 1940, the journals *Science* and *American Journal of Psychology* contained news of her death and detailed accounts of her scientific contributions and accomplishments. *Teachers College Record* published a memorial issue in her honor. The famous psychologist Arthur I. Gates, wrote in *Science*:

> Professor Hollingworth's work with exceptional children gave expression to the fundamental traits of their character and personality. Her decisions and opinions were based on cold facts; she was a staunch and courageous opponent of all forms of educational wishful thinking. Although her judgment was always impervious to the appeal of sheer sentimentality, which she despised, she was capable of the deepest affection for human beings and intense devotion to human welfare. The subjects of her studies were never human guinea pigs to her; they were the individual objects of her deepest concern... . This intense interest and devotion to the living individual, undistorted by sentimentality, and coupled with the clear-eyed vision of the scientist, of whose tools she was a master, account for the unique scientific validity and practical value of Professor Hollingworth's work.[15]

Her death was viewed as a "scientific tragedy" by Teachers College colleague and dear friend A.T. Poffenberger, who had co-authored with Harry the first applied psychology textbook. He believed that

...her work in it [the field] had really just begun...to be sure, some of the material in manuscript can and will be prepared for publication, and some of the research under way will be completed, but the more ambitious part of the program will scarcely survive the loss of her intelligent, enthusiastic and courageous direction.[16]

In December 1940, Teachers College convened a conference on gifted education in honor of Leta Hollingworth. The conference goals were to contribute to the solutions of the problems that most concerned her. The focus of this conference was on:

- Promoting a wider understanding of the importance of improving ways of discovering leadership.

- Appraising present accomplishments in the discovery and education of the gifted.

- Identifying the issues involved in education of gifted students.

- Furthering next steps in research, instruction, guidance, and other procedures that would lead to better methods of finding and making use of the abilities of the gifted.

The conference planners hoped that suggestions and materials would be brought forth that would enable the work of Leta Hollingworth to continue. "This task is worthy of our best efforts; for as Professor Hollingworth has said, 'Gifted minds have a positive value beyond all price.'"[17]

Earlier, Holly had notified Dean Russell that he would like to attend; however, he preferred not to sit at the head table but rather to sit with the seminar leaders.

I want to keep in touch so far as possible with the people in the P.S. 165 group, because there is unfinished work from the project which I hope to be able to bring to some degree of completion... .I am deeply touched by the appreciation shown in holding this Conference in my wife's memory and much hope that the program will do genuine good for the work of the College....[18]

The "unfinished work" to which he alluded was a major thrust of the conference—and afterward as well. When the project was completed, it was titled, *Children above 180 IQ: Stanford-Binet Origin and Development*. This important book—still read today—was a lasting legacy of Leta's vision and efforts.

Leta had begun writing this text in the mid 1920s, reviewing the literature on gifted children and documenting the five cases of children with IQ's above 180 that she had personally encountered to this point (and written about in Chapter 9 of *Gifted Children: Their Nature and Nurture*). In the Foreword to *Children Above 180 IQ*, Harry Hollingworth explained: "As the years went by she held back the manuscript from publication and one by one found seven more cases to be included in her list. At the time of her death in 1939, she had begun to revise the manuscript, bringing the survey up to date and adding new cases." The Preface and first three chapters of *Children Above 180 IQ* were written by Leta. The seven 'new' case studies of high IQ children were pieced together from her notes and presented "as she might herself have written, patterned after her reports of earlier cases." The last five chapters consist of reproductions or selections from her published writings "on what she considered to be the implications of her observations of children with rare intelligence."[19]

Dean Russell received another message. It was from Professor Lewis Terman. Unable to attend the Teachers College Conference because of ill health, Terman wrote:

> It is hard indeed to refuse an invitation I so much wanted to accept. Among all the psychologists I have known, none stands higher in my professional or personal esteem than the gifted and intrepid one in whose memory this conference has been called.[20]

Lewis Terman was right on both counts.

Epilogue

Leta Hollingworth's writings about gifted and highly gifted children remain current not only because of her keen insights, but also because she was a researcher who worked directly in the classroom with children and teachers. She knew gifted children well, and she understood their social and emotional constitutions as well as their academic needs. Much of her knowledge was intuitive, derived from her own experiences as a profoundly gifted person that she simply confirmed through her research. A model of a "scientist-practitioner," Leta's research was impeccable and considered multiple sources—observations in the field, standardized achievement and mental testing, detailed family histories, and teacher observations.[1]

On January 29, 1939, Leta wrote a memorandum to Dr. Paul Mort, Director of the Advanced School of Education (Teachers College), in which she reiterated her passion about the education of the highly gifted. She noted:

> I beg to submit the following memorandum on a must—
> an imperative duty—that rests at present upon Teachers
> College, as a result of advances in knowledge during the
> past twenty-five years. This...relates to the improve-
> ment of the education and guidance of the most highly
> educable children in our public schools.[2]

A precise writer, Leta understood that the phrase "imperative duty" was redundant. She was highlighting a point. Under the not very subtle heading, "The Necessity of Educating Highly Intelligent Children Instead of Merely Sending Them to School," she wrote:

> One of the most imperative musts of American education and of society at large today is this: <u>Very gifted children must be educated in accordance with what we have learned about their relative abilities, and in accordance with their availability for serving society at large in posts where intelligence of a high order is a sine qua non</u> [Leta's underline].[3]

She advocated that Teachers College formally establish a school for the "scientific study and education of children who test in the top percentile of the juvenile population." That school should be, in her opinion, separately endowed or financially supported by Teachers College, covering "all the costs of experimentation, research in psychology, and maintaining public relations." Leta reminded Dr. Mort that Speyer School

> …has been running for three years without any financial resources except such as are routinely provided for teaching pupils in any public school. Neither Teachers College nor the Board of Education has provided any research funds, or fund for handling public relations. Such work of these kinds as has been accomplished has been done on spare time [Leta Hollingworth's spare time].… . An ideal school would call for a different building, adequate assistance, and facilities for recording the work in print, in graphs, in moving pictures, in still pictures, and possibly in other works.[4]

The second "imperative must" outlined by Leta was the "Need for a revolving fund to aid and develop tested individuals."

> Whether the percentage of the needy gifted is at thirty or forty or ten, the fact is that many of these children are in economic situations which preclude any family provision

for appropriate education, while mediocre children of well-to-do parents go forward to occupy the facilities for higher learning, and hence into the learned professions and business management, and into public affairs.

What is needed is an <u>impersonal fund</u> from which the gifted young, scientifically selected, could obtain…the means for self development… . The establishment of a revolving fund for tested children would be a great experiment in social science… . It is an urgent must for school and society [Leta's underline].[5]

Leta feared that her work would not continue after her death.

We need now to make wider studies, and especially to establish long-time researches as institutional responsibilities. Up to the present, each research in this field has been the responsibility of a single, precarious human life. If the individual investigator dies, the group being observed is lost, and the research must start all over again, in a different connection. This should not be the case.[6]

GIFTED EDUCATION TODAY

In 1939, Leta Hollingworth estimated that about forty percent of gifted children had "no adequate or sure means of self development."[7] If Leta investigated the state of gifted education in the United States today, what would she find? In 1988, the Federal Government established The Jacob K. Javits Gifted and Talented Students Education Act. Colangelo and Davis noted that by the mid 1990s,

…every state has passed legislation on behalf of gifted children. Schools and districts across the U.S. and Canada and in dozens of foreign countries have created programs and services. Enthusiasm for creating a suitable education for the gifted—tomorrow's leaders and professionals—remains high among most educators and, particularly, among parents of gifted children.[8]

State, national and international organizations are devoted to the gifted child, such as The National Association for Gifted Children and the World Council for Gifted Children. These and other groups actively support parents and educators of this special population.

Highly and profoundly gifted children are being given some attention as well. Patricia Bremmer, the parent of a profoundly gifted child, established the National Gifted Children's Fund for the "sole purpose of assisting profoundly gifted children with their education," and in 1999, Bob and Jan Davidson established The Davidson Institute for Talent Development. Leta Hollingworth was the inspiration, and Leta's dream of a revolving fund for gifted children is now a reality, thanks to foundations such as these. An annual Hollingworth Conference has been held for almost fifteen years, and the National Association for Gifted Children has a designated Hollingworth Award to encourage research. Psychologists, such as Linda Kreger Silverman, devote their entire practices to working with highly and profoundly gifted children and their parents, and there are listservs on the Internet specifically for parents of these children.

Unfortunately, the basic issues identified by Leta Hollingworth still exist despite the progress that has been made. There are still persistent problems of under-identification, un-modified curriculum, and under-funding for gifted students. Most gifted programs today remove the child from the classroom for a modest "enrichment" program that lasts only for an hour or so during the school week. Gifted education specialists are overworked and overextended and frequently must use their own finances to enhance skimpily funded programs. Minority children and female gifted students remain particularly under-identified, despite recent research findings relating to multi-cultural differences in gifted expression.

So much of what Leta Hollingworth said and did in the early 1900s has made a significant mark on how we educate gifted children today. Even so, Leta's work continues to be under-funded and under-appreciated, and—most regrettably—Leta Hollingworth's voice is too often forgotten.

Endnotes

Introduction Endnotes

1 Leta S. Hollingworth, *Prairie Years, Verse by Leta Stetter Hollingworth* (New York: Columbia University Press, 1940), 34.

2 Julian Stanley, "A Toast, October 19, 1989," *Roeper Review* 12 (1990): 236.

3 Joel Shurkin, *Terman's Kids* (Boston: Little Brown & Company, 1992), 37.

4 Brian Thorne, *Carl Rogers* (London: Sage Publications, 1992), 7.

5 Howard Kirschenbaum, *On Becoming Carl Rogers* (New York: Delacorte Press, 1979), 48.

6 Ibid., 55.

7 Carolyn G. Heilbrun, *Writing a Woman's Life* (New York: Ballantine Books, 1988), 31.

8 Barbara A. Kerr, *Smart Girls* (Dayton, OH: Ohio Psychology Press, 1985); Barbara A. Kerr, *Smart Girls: a New Psychology of Girls, Women, and Giftedness* (Scottsdale, AZ: Great Potential Press, 1994); Rosalind Rosenberg, *Divided Lives* (New York: Hill and Wang, 1992); Rose Rudnitski, "Patty Smith Hill, Gifted Early Childhood Educator of the Progressive Era," *Roeper Review* 18 (1995): 19-24.

9 Wilma Vialle, "'Termanal' Science? The Work of Lewis Terman Revisited," *Roeper Review* 17 (1993): 32.

Chapter 1 Endnotes

1 Leta S. Hollingworth, *Children above 180 IQ Stanford-Binet: Origin and Development* (Yonkers-on-Hudson, New York: World Book Company, 1942), xi-xii.

2 Ibid.

3 Ibid., xiii.

4 Leta S. Hollingworth, "Bright Students Take Care of Themselves," *North American Review* 243 (June 1937): 272.

5   Martha A. Morelock, "On the Nature of Giftedness and Talent: Imposing Order on Chaos," *Roeper Review* 19 (1996): 8.

6   L. Hollingworth, *Children above 180 IQ*, 282.

Chapter 2 Endnotes

1   Harry L. Hollingworth, *Leta Stetter Hollingworth: A Biography* (1943; reprint, Boston: Anker Publishing, 1990), 32.

2   Lori C. Bland, Claudia J. Sowa, and Carolyn M. Callahan, "An Overview of Resilience in Gifted Children," *Roeper Review* 17 (December 1994): 77-80.

3   Paula Olszewski-Kubilius, "The Transition for Childhood Giftedness to Adult Creative Productiveness: Psychological Characteristics and Social Supports," *Roeper Review 23* (December 2000): 71.

4   H. Hollingworth, *Leta Stetter Hollingworth: A Biography*, 32.

5   George Condra, *Geography of Nebraska* (Lincoln, NE: University Publishing Co., 1921), 127-28.

6   Dorothy Weyer Creigh, *Nebraska, A Bicentennial History* (New York: W. W. Norton, 1977), 62.

7   Ibid., 71.

8   Johanna L. Stratton, *Pioneer Women, Voices from the Kansas Frontier* (New York: Simon & Schuster, 1981), 48.

9   James C. Olson, *History of Nebraska*, 2nd ed. (Lincoln, NE: University of Nebraska Press, 1966), 158.

10   Sod House Society, *Sod House Memories* (Hastings, NE: Sod House Society, 1974), 6.

11   Ibid., 164.

12   Ibid., 163.

13   Ibid., 39

14   Anonymous source.

15   First Congregational Church, "Chadron, Seventy Five Years, 1885-1960," (Chadron, NE, 1960), 1.

16   Chadron Centennial Souvenir Program, "Celebrating Chadron's 100th Year," (Chadron, NE, July 10-12, 1985), 43.

17   *Democratic Blade*, 1 January 1886.

18   W. C. Lee, *Wild Towns of Nebraska* (Caldwell, IA: Caxton Printing, 1988), 119.

19   Ibid., 114.

20   Helen Stetter, interview with author, Valentine, NE, August 1996.

21   *Compendium of History, Reminiscence, and Biography of Western Nebraska, Containing a History of the State of Nebraska* (Chicago: Alden Press, 1909), 647.

22   Margaret Chase Tatroe, "Grandpa Stetter's Life," (unpublished memoirs, c. 1960), 3.

23   Grant L. Shumway, ed., *History of Western Nebraska and its People* (Lincoln, NE: Western Publishing and Engraving Co., 1921), 2:556.

24   Helen Stetter, interview.

25   Tatroe, "Grandpa Stetter's Life," 1.

26   William A. Danley, "Autobiography of the Danley Family as Remembered by W. A. Danley," (unpublished memoir, 18 November 1917) 2.

27   Tatroe, "Grandpa Stetter's Life," 1.

28   *Compendium*, 647.

29   Tatroe, "Grandpa Stetter's Life," 3.

30   Gertrude Lutz, *Sketches of Some Pioneers* (Chadron, NE: Chadron Printing Co., 1953), 14-15. Fannie O'Linn was one of the first women lawyers in Nebraska, admitted to the Nebraska Bar in 1887. In 1893, William Jennings Bryan (one of Nebraska's senators) presented her to the United States Supreme Court. She was also a journalist for the *Omaha Bee*, a notary public, and the founder of the town of O'Linn, near Chadron.

31   H. Hollingworth, *Leta Stetter Hollingworth*, 20.

32   Ibid., 15-20.

33   Leta S. Hollingworth, "Facts about Bright Children," *Babyhood* 45 (December 1929): 365.

34   Infant Margaret was premature; she was so small, she could fit in a cigar box. A neighbor, Mrs. Carley, kept the infant in a warm oven for six weeks, and in her honor, Margaret's middle name was Carley.

35   Hope Edelman, *Motherless Daughters: The Legacy of Loss* (Reading, MA: Addison-Wesley Publishing Co., 1994), xxv.

36   Annemarie Roeper, "Reflections from Annemarie Roeper, A Personal Statement of Philosophy of George and Annemarie Roeper," *Roeper Review* 19 (1996), 18-19.

37   Leta S. Hollingworth, letter to John Stetter, 11 November 1934.

38   Leta S. Hollingworth, *Prairie Years: Verse by Leta Stetter Hollingworth* (New York: Columbia University Press, 1940), 25.

39   Ibid., 20.

40 Durward Howes, ed., *American Women: The Standard Biographical Dictionary of Notable Women, 1939-1940* (Los Angeles: American Publications, Inc., 1939), 3: 420.

41 Margaret Lillian Chase Tatroe, "Mother's Early Life," (unpublished memoirs, c. 1960), 3.

42 H. Hollingworth, *Leta Stetter Hollingworth*, 25-26.

43 L. Hollingworth, *Prairie Years*, 31-32.

44 *The Dawes County Journal*, 11 September 1896.

45 Ibid.

46 Ibid., 4 September 1896.

47 Ibid., 11 September 1896.

48 H. Hollingworth, *Leta Stetter Hollingworth*, 26.

49 Ibid., 31, 33-34.

50 Leta S. Hollingworth, "Bright Students Take Care of Themselves," *North American Review* 243 (1937), 268.

51 Mihaly Csikszentmihalyi, *Creativity: Flow and the Psychology of Discovery and Invention* (New York: Harper Collins, 1996), 332.

52 H. Hollingworth, *Leta Stetter Hollingworth*, 32.

53 L. Hollingworth, *Prairie Years*, 26-27.

54 Tatroe, "Mother's Early Life," 2.

55 Patricia Johnson, interview with author, Waterville, OH, 1999.

56 Abraham J. Tannenbaum, "The Meaning and Making of Giftedness," in eds. Nicholas Colangelo and Gary Davis, *Handbook of Gifted Education*, 2nd ed. (Boston: Allyn & Bacon), 37.

Chapter 3 Endnotes

1 Leta S. Hollingworth, *Prairie Years, Verse by Leta Stetter Hollingworth* (New York: Columbia University Press, 1940), 12.

2 Maxine Seller, "G. Stanley Hall and Edward Thorndike on the Education of Women Theory and Policy in the Progressive Era," *Educational Studies* 11 (1981): 373.

3 Ibid., 369.

4 Rosalind Rosenberg, *Beyond Separate Spheres, Intellectual Roots of Modern Feminism* (New Haven, CT: Yale University Press, 1982), 11.

5 Ibid., 8.

6   Barbara Miller Solomon, *In the Company of Educated Women: A History of Women in Higher Education in America* (New Haven, CT: Yale University Press, 1985), xviii.

7   Rosalind Rosenberg, *Divided Lives* (New York: Hill and Wang, 1992), 26.

8   Agnes O. O'Connell and Nancy Felipe Russo, *Models of Achievement, Reflections of Eminent Women in Psychology* (Mahwah, NJ: Lawrence Erlbaum, 1988), 11.

9   Harry L. Hollingworth, *Leta Stetter Hollingworth: A Biography* (1943; reprint, Boston: Anker Publishing, 1990), 39-40.

10 *The Sombrero: The Undergraduate Book of the University of Nebraska* (Lincoln, NE: University of Nebraska Press, 1905), 16.

11 Robert E. Knoll, *Prairie University: A History of the University of Nebraska* (Lincoln, NE: University of Nebraska Press, 1995), 48.

12 H. Hollingworth, *Leta Stetter Hollingworth*, 32.

13 Robert N. Manley, *Frontier University (1869-1919)*, vol. 1, *Centennial History of the University of Nebraska* (Lincoln, NE: University of Nebraska Press, 1969), 148.

14 *The Sombrero*, 108.

15 L. Hollingworth, *Prairie Years,* 21, 3, 10-11, 21, 9, 16, 17, 22, 24.

16 *The Sombrero*, 71.

17 *The Senior Book of the Class of '06 of the University of Nebraska* (Lincoln, NE: University of Nebraska Press, 1906), 10.

18 Ibid.

19 *The Sombrero*, 190.

20 Leta Stetter, "An Incident at Devlin's," *Senior Book of the Class of '06 of the University of Nebraska* (Lincoln, NE: University of Nebraska Press, 1906), 63-64.

21 Leta Stetter, "The Skull," *Senior Book of the Class of '06 of The University of Nebraska* (Lincoln, NE: University of Nebraska Press, 1906), 65-69.

22 *Daily Nebraskan,* 24 May 1906.

23 Ibid.

24 Harry L. Hollingworth, *Born in Nebraska* (original unpublished manuscript, 1940), 279-80. Private collection of Virginia Florence.

25 Harry L. Hollingworth, *Born in Nebraska* (unpublished manuscript, essay revision, n.d.), 45. Private collection of Virginia Florence.

26 Ibid., 4.

27 H. Hollingworth, *Born in Nebraska* (original), 80, 80a.

28   Harry L. Hollingworth, *Prairie Schoolmaster* (unpublished manuscript, c. 1940), 92. Private collection of Virginia Florence.

29   H. Hollingworth, *Born in Nebraska* (essay revision), 44.

30   H. Hollingworth, *Born in Nebraska* (original), 182-83.

31   H. Hollingworth, *Born in Nebraska* (essay revision), 49-150.

32   H. Hollingworth, *Prairie Schoolmaster*, 42.

33   Ibid., 45.

34   Ibid., 53.

35   Ibid., 126.

36   Harry Hollingworth was able to afford the private (Methodist-run) preparatory school because he was given a fifty percent reduction in tuition. Several years earlier, Holly had contemplated becoming a minister. His tuition reduction was based upon his professed religious calling. By 1900, he lost interest in theological studies, but he deliberately withheld this fact in order to attend the school.

37   H. Hollingworth, *Born in Nebraska* (essay revision), 211.

38   Ibid., 219.

39   Ibid., 253.

40   L. Hollingworth, *Prairie Years*, 12.

41   H. Hollingworth, *Born in Nebraska* (essay revision), 230.

42   H. Hollingworth, *Born in Nebraska* (original), 281.

43   Ibid.

44   Leta S. Hollingworth, *The Psychology of the Adolescent* (New York: Appleton & Co., 1928), 212-13.

45   Ibid., 213.

46   H. Hollingworth, *Born in Nebraska* (original), 303.

47   H. Hollingworth, *Leta Stetter Hollingworth*.

48   H. Hollingworth, *Prairie Schoolmaster*, 183.

49   H. Hollingworth, *Leta Stetter Hollingworth*, 57.

50   H. Hollingworth, *Prairie Schoolmaster*, 162.

51   H. Hollingworth, *Leta Stetter Hollingworth*, 34.

52   Ibid., 63.

Chapter 4 Endnotes

1   Leta S. Hollingworth to Emma Zanuch Fischer, 5 March 1917.

2   Harry L. Hollingworth, *Leta Stetter Hollingworth: A Biography* (1943; reprint, Boston: Anker Publishing, 1990), 91.

3   Dorothy Schneider and Carl J. Schneider, *American Women in the Progressive Era*: 1900-1920 (New York: Facts-on-File, 1993).

4   Harry L. Hollingworth, *Born in Nebraska* (unpublished manuscript, essay revision, n.d.), 260. Private collection of Virginia Florence.

5   Harry L. Hollingworth, *Years at Columbia* (unpublished manuscript, c. 1940), 113, 195, 231. Private collection of Virginia Florence.

6   Leta S. Hollingworth to Emma Zanuch Fischer, 5 March 1917.

7   H. Hollingworth, *Years at Columbia*, 57-58.

8   Ibid. 58.

9   H. Hollingworth, *Years at Columbia*, 34.

10 Helen Stetter, interview with author, Valentine, NE, August 1996.

11 James McKeen Cattell, "The School and the Family," *Popular Science Monthly* 74 (1909): 92-93.

12 Helen Stetter, interview.

13 Leta S. Hollingworth to Emma Zanuch Fischer, 30 January 1909.

14 H. Hollingworth, *Years at Columbia*, 77.

15 Rosalind Rosenberg, *Beyond Separate Spheres: Intellectual Roots of Modern Feminism* (New Haven, CT: Yale University Press, 1982), 87.

16 Rheta Childe Dorr, "Is Woman Biologically Barred from Success?" *New York Times Magazine* (19 September 1915): 15-16.

17 Ibid., 73.

18 H. Hollingworth, *Years at Columbia*, 77.

19 Ibid., 90.

20 Harry L. Hollingworth, "The Influence of Caffein [*sic*] Alkaloid on the Quality and Amount of Sleep, *American Journal of Psychology*, 23 (January 1912): 89-100.

21 Ludy T. Benjamin, Jr., Anne M. Rogers, and Angela Rosenbaum, "Coca-Cola, Caffeine, and Mental Deficiency: Harry Hollingworth and the Chattanooga Trial of 1911," *Journal of the History of Behavioral Sciences* 27 (January 1991): 42-55.

22 Ibid., 47.

23   Harry L. Hollingworth, "The Influence of Caffeine on Mental and Motor Efficiency," presented to The College of Physicians of Philadelphia, 23 October 1911.

24   Harry L. Hollingworth, "Preliminary Reports of an Experiment Designed to determine the Influence of Caffeine on Mental Processes" (working paper, 5 March 1911).

25   Benjamin, et al., "Coca-Cola."

26   H. Hollingworth, *Years at Columbia*, 97.

27   Leta S. Hollingworth to Frank and Anna Fischer, 28 April 1911.

28   Founded in 1754 as King's College, Columbia University is the fifth oldest higher education institution in the United States. In 1784, it was renamed Columbia College in the spirit of the newly won American Revolution. In 1897, the campus moved to where it now stands, in Morningside Heights at 116th Street and Broadway. In the late nineteenth century, Columbia broadened its mission to that of a university and placed the then loosely affiliated Teachers College and Barnard College for Women under its administration. Women were barred from admission to Columbia University as undergraduates. When this policy was challenged, a compromise permitted women to take Columbia University examinations, but they were forbidden to attend the lectures. This arrangement proved unsatisfactory. The President of Columbia, Frederick Barnard, then proposed that the institution become co-educational. The faculty and alumni objected to this plan as well. In 1889, the decision was approved to create an all-female annex to Columbia. Barnard College became the "sister" school to Columbia University.

29   H. Hollingworth, *Years at Columbia*, 39.

30   Michael M. Sokel, "The Unpublished Biography of James McKeen Cattell," *American Psychologist* 26 (1971): 633.

31   Lawrence Cremin, David A. Shannon, and Mary Evelyn Townsend, *A History of Teachers College Columbia University* (New York: Columbia University Press, 1954), 43.

32   Ibid., 295.

33   Robert L. Thorndike, "Edward L. Thorndike: A Professional and Personal Appreciation," in *Portraits of Pioneers in Psychology*, eds. Gregory A. Kimble, Michael Wertheimer, and Charlotte L. White (Washington, DC: American Psychological Association, 1991).

34   G. Stanley Hall (1844-1924) studied with William James and received the first Ph.D. in Psychology in America. He has been called the founder of organized psychology, the father of the child-study movement, and a national leader in educational reform.

35   Dorothy Ross and G. Stanley Hall, *The Psychologist as a Prophet* (Chicago: University of Chicago Press, 1972), 348.

36 Ibid.,140.

37 Edna Heidbreder, *Seven Psychologies* (New York: Appleton-Century-Crofts, 1933), 297-98.

38 Cremin, et al., *A History of Teachers College*, 44.

39 Ibid., 46.

40 John A. Beineke, *And There Were Giants in the Land: The Life of William Heard Kilpatrick* (New York: Peter Lang, 1998).

41 After a decade of teaching at the University of Chicago, John Dewey arrived in New York City in 1904 to become a faculty member in the Columbia University Philosophy Department. He also taught courses at Teachers College. When the Department of Educational Research was created at Teachers College, Dewey one of seven professors appointed.

42 Rosenberg, *Beyond Separate Spheres*, 88.

43 In a letter to Dean James Russell, Thorndike explained: "No doubt that Miss Norsworthy will be a better psychologist, as good a teacher, and a far more energetic and devoted worker with the students personally than any one else we can hope to get... . From the point of view of economy, she is certainly better than a man. If a woman is to be appointed, I should have no hesitation recommending her and in holding myself responsible for the conduct of the work... . From the point of view of economy, she is certainly better than a man."

44 Geraldine Jonchich, *The Sane Positivist: A Biography of Edward Lee Thorndike* (Middleton, CT: Wesleyan University Press, 1968), 222.

45 James Russell to James McKeen Cattell, 30 November 1909, James Russell Papers, Special Collections, Milbank Memorial Library, Teachers College, Columbia University.

46 James Russell to Nicholas Murray Butler, 17 December 1908, James Russell Papers.

47 Elizabeth Scarborough and Laurel Furumoto, *Untold Lives: The First Generation of American Women Psychologists* (New York: Columbia University Press, 1987), 193.

48 H. Hollingworth, *Years at Columbia*, 10.

49 Beineke, *And There Were Giants in the Land*, 100.

50 Ibid., 30.

51 Leta S. Hollingworth, *The Psychology of Subnormal Children* (New York: Macmillan, 1922), 64.

52 Nicholas Colangelo and Gary A. Davis, eds., *Handbook of Gifted Education*, 2nd ed. (Boston: Allyn & Bacon, 1997), 4.

53 May Seagoe, *Terman and the Gifted* (Los Altos, CA: Kaufmann, 1975), 47.

54   Max G. Schlapp and Leta S. Hollingworth, "An Economic and Social Study of Feeble-Minded Women," *Medical Record* 85 (1914): 1025-28.

55   Leta S. Hollingworth, *Prairie Years, Verse by Leta Stetter Hollingworth* (New York: Columbia University Press, 1940), 33.

56   H. Hollingworth, *Years at Columbia*, 95-96.

57   Leta S. Hollingworth, "The Vocational Aptitudes of Women," chap. 10 in *Vocational Psychology* (Harry L. Hollingworth, New York: D. Appleton, 1916), 224-25.

58   J. P. Mobius, "The Psychological Mental Weakness of Woman," *Alienist and Neurologist* 22 (1901): 626-32.

59   Stephanie A. Shields, "Functionalism, Darwinism, and the Psychology of Women," *American Psychologist* 30 (1975): 739.

60   Ibid., 739-40.

61   Leta S. Hollingworth, "Variability as Related to Sex Differences: A Critique," *American Journal of Sociology* 19 (1914): 511.

62   Leta S. Hollingworth, "The Frequency of Amentia as Related to Sex," *Medical Record* 84 (25 October 1913): 753-56.

63   Schlapp and L. Hollingworth, "Study of Feeble-Minded Women," 1028.

64   L. Hollingworth, "Variability as Related to Sex Differences," 523-24.

65   Ibid., 525-27.

66   Helen Montague and Leta S. Hollingworth, "The Comparative Variability of the Sexes at Birth," *American Journal of Sociology* 20 (1914): 342.

67   Ibid., 369.

68   Rosalind Rosenberg, "Leta Hollingworth: Toward a Sexless Intelligence," chap. 4 in *The Shadow of the Past: Psychology Portrays the Sexes* (New York: Columbia University Press, 1984), 88-89.

69   Rheta Childe Dorr, *A Woman of Fifty* (New York: Arno Press, 1980), 252.

70   Victoria S. Roemele, "Leta Stetter Hollingworth," in *Notable American Women 1607-1950*, vol. 2 (Cambridge, MA: Belknap Press, 1971), 207.

71   Leta S. Hollingworth, *Functional Periodicity: An Experimental Study of the Mental and Motor Abilities of Women during Menstruation* (New York: Teachers College, Columbia University, 1914), v.

72   Ibid., vi.

73   Ibid., vii.

74   Ibid., 97, 99.

Chapter 5 Endnotes

1 "Heterodoxy to Marie," private photograph album, 1920, the Arthur and Elizabeth Schlesinger Library, Radcliffe Institute, Cambridge, MA.

2 Ibid., 91-92.

3 Lynn Sherr, *Failure Is Impossible: Susan B. Anthony in her Own Words* (New York: Random House, 1995), xviii.

4 Valuable sources about Heterodoxy and the Heterodites include Inez Haynes Irwin's unpublished autobiography, *Adventures of Yesterday*, in the Inez Haynes Irwin Papers at the Arthur and Elizabeth Schlesinger Library, Radcliffe Institute; the "Heterodoxy to Marie," private photograph album, 1920, Schlesinger Library; the papers of Mary Ware Dennett, Schlesinger Library; Judith Schwarz, *Radical Feminists of Heterodoxy: Greenwich Village 1912-1940* (Norwich, VT: New Victoria Publishers, 1986); June Sochen, *The New Woman: Feminism in Greenwich Village, 1910-1920* (New York: Quadrangle Books, 1972).

5 June Sochen, *The New Woman: Feminism in Greenwich Village, 1910-1920* (New York: Quadrangle Books, 1972), 8.

6 Judith Schwarz, *Radical Feminists of Heterodoxy: Greenwich Village 1912-1940* (Norwich, VT: New Victoria Publishers, 1986).

7 Leta S. Hollingworth, *Children above 180 IQ* (Yonkers-on-Hudson, NY: World Book Company, 1942), 263.

8 Inez Haynes Irwin, *Adventures of Yesterday* (unpublished manuscript, n.d.), 416, the Arthur and Elizabeth Schlesinger Library, Radcliffe Institute, Cambridge, MA.

9 Mabel Dodge Luhan, *Mover and Shakers* (New York: Harcourt, Brace and Company; 1971), 143.

10 Inez Haynes Irwin, *Adventures of Yesterday*, 414.

11 Ibid., 422.

12 Rheta Childe Dorr, *A Woman of Fifty* (New York: Arno Press, 1980), 279.

13 Schwarz, *Radical Feminists,* 40.

14 "Heterodoxy to Marie."

15 Harry L. Hollingworth, *Years at Columbia* (unpublished manuscript, c. 1940), 112-13. Private collection of Virginia Florence.

16 H. Hollingworth, *Years at Columbia*, 113, 195, 231.

17 *The New York Times*, 5 April 1914, sec.4.

18 Ibid.

19 *The New York Times,* 13 April 1914.

20 *The New York Times*, 22 April 1914.

21 Rheta Childe Dorr, "Is Woman Biologically Barred from Success?" *New York Times Magazine* (19 September 1915).

22 Sochen, *The New Women,* 52-56.

23 Henrietta Rodman had written a letter to the editor of the *New York Tribune* urging a sports columnist to visit a game played at the New York City Board of Education—a game she called "mother baiting." She went on to compare the Board's actions with wife-beating, i.e., it was for the "good" of the woman that she was treated in this manner. This was cause for suspension.

24 Winona Evan Reeves, ed., *The Blue Book of Nebraska Women* (Mexico, MO: Missouri Printing and Publishing Company, 1914), 81.

25 Robert Lowie (1993-1957) and Leta Hollingworth were members of the Feminist Alliance and co-chaired the sub-committee "The Biological Status of Women." He also was a Columbia University alumni, studying anthropology under Franz Boas.

26 Robert H. Lowie and Leta S. Hollingworth, "Science and Feminism," *Scientific Monthly* 3 (1916): 277-84.

27 Ibid., 277.

28 Ibid., 282.

29 Ibid., 279, 281-84.

30 Leta S. Hollingworth, "Phi Beta Kappa and Women Students," *School and Society* 4 (1916): 932-33.

31 Janet Farrell Brodie, *Contraception and Abortion in Nineteenth Century America* (Ithaca, NY: Cornell University Press, 1994), 256, 281.

32 *The Woman Rebel*, vol. 1 (March 1914), the Arthur and Elizabeth Schlesinger Library, Radcliffe Institute, Cambridge, MA.

33 Leta S. Hollingworth, *The Psychology of the Adolescent* (New York: D. Appleton and Company, 1931), 78.

34 Leta. S. Hollingworth, "Social Devices Impelling Women to Bear and Rear Children," *American Journal of Sociology* 22 (1916): 19-29.

35 Ibid., 26.

36 Ibid., 25.

37 Ibid., 29.

38 Leta S. Hollingworth, "For and Against Birth Control," *New Republic* 11 (October 1922): 178.

39 Ibid.

40 Francis Galton (1822-1911) coined the term "eugenics" from the Greek meaning good in birth or "noble in heredity."

41 The practice of involuntary sterilization continued in the United States until at least 1979.

42 Leta S. Hollingworth, *The Psychology of Subnormal Children* (New York: Macmillan, 1920), 236-38.

43 Interestingly, her views about child-bearing by gifted women are not greatly dissimilar to statements spoken today by many advocates of amniocentesis, gene-splicing, or cloning.

44 Leta S. Hollingworth, *Gifted Children: Their Nature and Nurture* (New York: Macmillan, 1927), 198-200.

45 Helen Stetter, interview with author, Valentine, NE, August 1996.

46 H. Hollingworth, *Years at Columbia*, 48, 49, 89.

47 Ibid.

48 Schwarz, *Radical Feminists*, 37-38.

49 Helen Stetter, interview.

50 Leta S. Hollingworth, "The New Woman in the Making," *Current History* 27 (October 1927-March 1928): 15, 18, 20.

Chapter 6 Endnotes

1 Leta S. Hollingworth, "How Should Gifted Children Be Educated," *Baltimore Bulletin of Education* 50 (May 1931): 196.

2 Leta S. Hollingworth, "Bright Students Take Care of Themselves," *North American Review* 243 (June 1937): 272.

3 Miriam C. Pritchard, "The Psychology and Education of Subnormal Children," *Teachers College Record* 42 (1940): 228-29.

4 Leta S. Hollingworth, "The Psychological Examination of Poor Spellers." *Teachers College Record* 20 (1919): 131.

5 Leta S. Hollingworth. Printed address delivered before the Section for the Study of Retarded Children of the New York State Teachers Association, Albany, NY, 24 November 1919, Archives of the History of American Psychology, Akron, OH.

6 Ibid., 234.

7 Ibid., 273.

8 Leta S. Hollingworth, "Differential Action upon the Sexes of Forces which Tend to Segregate the Feebleminded," *Journal of Abnormal and Social Psychology* 17 (1922): 57.

9 L. Hollingworth, "How Should Gifted Children Be Educated," 196.

10   Nicholas Colangelo and Gary Davis, eds., *Handbook of Gifted Education,* 2nd ed. (Boston: Allyn & Bacon, 1997); Leta S. Hollingworth, "Experiments in Gifted Education," typed manuscript, Archives of the History of Psychology, Akron, OH.

11   Leta S. Hollingworth, *Gifted Children: Their Nature and Nurture* (New York: Macmillan, 1927).

12   Louise Specht, "Terman Class in Public School No. 64 Manhattan," *School and Society* 9 (29 March 1919): 393.

13   Ibid. The discomfort experienced by the P.S. 64 staff relating to using the words "superior" and "gifted" persists. Leta Hollingworth, a meticulous writer who selected her words with care, tended to use the word "gifted" in much of her academic writing, e.g., *Gifted Children: Their Nature and Nurture* (1926). In popular magazines, she often referred to this population as "very bright." The classes of gifted children in her experiments were described in several ways: "Special Opportunity," "Terman Classes," or "Rapid Learner."

14   Specht, "Terman Class in Public School No. 64," 393, 395, 396.

15   Margaret V. Cobb, Leta S. Hollingworth, Jane E. Monahan, Grace A. Taylor, and Jacob Theobald, *Summary Report on Pupils of Two Special Opportunity Classes of Very Bright Children: Instructed for Three Years in Public School 165 Manhattan and High School Careers Followed Up for Four Additional Years.* (New York: Board of Education of the City of New York, 31 October 1929), 7.

16   Ibid.

17   Eighteen of the children in each class of twenty-four were Jewish.

18   Leta S. Hollingworth and Margaret V. Cobb, "Children Clustering at 165 IQ and Children Clustering at 146 IQ Compared for Three Years in Achievement," in *The Twenty-Seventh Yearbook of the National Society for the Study of Education, Nature and Nurture: Part II, Their Influence on Achievement* (Bloomington, IL: Public School Publishing Company, 1928), 10-11.

19   Leta S. Hollingworth, "An Introduction to Biography for Young Children who Test above 150 IQ," *Teachers College Record* 2 (1924): 281.

20   Cobb, et al., *Summary Report,* 8.

21   Hollingworth managed to secure a small grant from the Carnegie Corporation enabling her to hire additional help testing students and serving as teacher assistants. The students were tested regularly over the three years. Each student was administered the Stanford-Binet IQ test yearly, as well as the Stanford Achievement Test. Some of the equipment for the Special Opportunity Classes was purchased with monies from the grant. This was a rare instance when she had "outside" funding.

22   Howard Gray and Leta S. Hollingworth, "The Achievement of Gifted Children Enrolled and Not Enrolled in Special Opportunity Classes," *Journal of Educational Research* 24 (November 1931): 261.

23   L. Hollingworth and Cobb, "Children Clustering at 165 IQ," 32.

24   Leta S. Hollingworth and Jane E. Monahan, "Tapping-Rate of Children who Test above 135 IQ (Stanford-Binet), *The Journal of Educational Psychology* 17 (November 1926): 517-18; Jane E. Monahan and Leta S. Hollingworth, "Neuro-Muscular Capacity of Children who Test above 135 IQ (Stanford-Binet)," *Journal of Educational Psychology* 18 (February 1927): 88-96; Leta S. Hollingworth, "Do Intellectually Gifted Children Grow toward Mediocrity in Stature?" *Journal of Genetic Psychology* 37 (1930): 356; Leta S. Hollingworth and Howard A. Gray, "Juvenile Achievement as Related to Size," *Teachers College Record* 32 (1930): 236-44.

25   L. Hollingworth and Monahan, "Tapping-Rate of Children," 517-18.

26   Cobb, et al., *Summary Report*, 15-16.

27   Leta S. Hollingworth, "Musical Sensitivity of Children who Test above 135 IQ (Stanford-Binet)," *Journal of Educational Psychology* 17 (1926): 108-09.

28   Ibid., 209.

29   Leta S. Hollingworth, *Special Talents and Defects* (New York: Macmillan, 1931), 162.

30   L. Hollingworth, *Gifted Children: Their Nature and Nurture*, 216.

31   Ibid., 218.

32   L. Hollingworth, *Special Talents and Defects*, 210.

33   Lewis Terman, typed manuscript, 3-4, Vineland Papers, Archives of the History of American Psychology, Akron, OH.

34   L. Hollingworth, *Gifted Children: Their Nature and Nurture*, 130.

35   Ibid., 75.

36   Leta S. Hollingworth, "The Child of Very Superior Intelligence, as a Special Problem in Social Adjustment," paper presented at the First International Congress on Mental Hygiene, Washington, DC, 8 May 1939. [Reprinted from *Mental Hygiene*, 15 (January 1931), 3.]

37   Ibid., 4-5.

38   Ibid., 5-6.

39   Ibid., 8-9.

40   L. Hollingworth, *Gifted Children: Their Nature and Nurture*, 346-47.

41   Ibid., 349.

42   L. Hollingworth, "The Child of Very Superior Intelligence," 9-10.

43   Ibid., 11.

44 Leta S. Hollingworth to Colleagues, 28 May 1934, Special Collections, Milbank Memorial Library, Teachers College, Columbia University.

45 Leta Hollingworth to Paul Mort, 14 August 1934, Special Collections, Milbank Memorial Library, Teachers College, Columbia University.

Chapter 7 Endnotes

1 Speyer School, owned by Teachers College, Columbia University, was designated "Public School 500" by the New York City Board of Education for the duration of the experiment in gifted education, which entailed a collaboration between Teachers College and the New York City public schools. It was an experiment in public education.

2 Leta. S. Hollingworth, "Mental Tests in Schools—Their Use as a Basis for Vocational Guidance," *Home and School* 9 (1925), 4.

3 Leta S. Hollingworth to Colleagues, 28 May 1934, Special Collection, Milbank Memorial Library, Teachers College, Columbia University.

4 A donation to be applied for the purchase of land and construction of a school was given to Teachers College in 1901 by Mr. and Mrs. James Speyer. It was anticipated that Speyer School "should speedily become one of the most important experimental stations in the field of education." In 1915, the school was reorganized as a junior high school for boys; in 1925, the building housed the Institute for Child Welfare Research (later the Institute of Child Development).

5 Leta S. Hollingworth, *Public Addresses* (Lancaster, PA: The Science Press, 1940), 124-26.

6 Leta S. Hollingworth to Paul Mort, 14 August 1934, Special Collections, Milbank Memorial Library, Teachers College, Columbia University.

7 Leta S. Hollingworth, "Outline of Plans for the Development of the Speyer School as a Joint Enterprise," memorandum to Professor P. R. Mort, 13 August 1934, 1.

8 Leta S. Hollingworth to Dr. Mort, 17 September 1934; Leta S. Hollingworth to Dr. Mort, 5 October 1934.

9 Leta S. Hollingworth to Dr. Del Manzo, 3 May 1935; Arthur Gates to Milton C. Del Manzo, 4 May 1935.

10 Memorandum by Leta S. Hollingworth to the Board of Superintendents of the Public School of New York City and to the Director of the Advanced School of Education, Teachers College, Columbia University, 1 January 1937, 2.

11 Harry L. Hollingworth, *Leta Stetter Hollingworth: A Biography* (1943; reprint, Boston: Anker Publishing, 1990), 129.

12   Leta S. Hollingworth, "The Terman Classes at Public School 500," *Journal of Educational Sociology* 10 (1936): 86-90.

13   Miriam C. Pritchard, "The Contributions of Leta S. Hollingworth to the Study of Gifted Children," chap. 4 in *The Gifted Child* (Boston: D.C. Heath, 1951), 61.

14   It is important to recognize that the Binet classes followed a similar educational and social philosophy. Children learned at their own pace; field trips were an integral part of their program as well. The Speyer School pedagogy was based upon the individual learner. In its way, the experiments with the children with special needs was as radical as the rapid learners' projects.

15   Leta S. Hollingworth, "The Terman Classes at Public School 500," *The Journal of Educational Sociology* 10 (1936): 88

16   Leta S. Hollingworth, "What We Know about the Early Selection and Training of Leaders," *Teachers College Press* 40 (1939): 575-92.

17   Leta S. Hollingworth, "An Enrichment Curriculum for Rapid Learners at Public School 500, Speyer School," *Teachers College Record* 39 (January 1938): 297-99.

18   Board of Education of the City of New York, Division of Elementary Schools, "Final Report of the Public School 500 (Speyer School), 1935-1940," publication no. 12., chap. 3 in *Education of the Rapid Learner in Public School 500* (1941), 91.

19   This would later be termed "cooperative learning" in the 1990s.

20   Pritchard, "Contributions of Leta Hollingworth," 63.

21   Board of Education, "Final Report," 97.

22   H. Hollingworth, *Leta Stetter Hollingworth*, 123.

23   L. Hollingworth, "An Enrichment Curriculum for Rapid Learners," 300.

24   Ibid.

25   Leta Hollingworth to Thad Hungate, 11 March 1938.

26   H. Hollingworth, *Leta Stetter Hollingworth*, 130.

27   Leta Hollingworth to Thad Hungate, 11 March 1938.

28   Correspondence from Amsterdamsche Montessori-School to Leta Hollingworth, 2 July 1938, Special Collection, Milbank Memorial Library.

29   Modern evidence indicates that Leta's strict hereditarian belief is not well founded. There are some extremely gifted children who have been born to parents of average or below-average intelligence.

30   "The Positive Aspect of the Preservation of Hereditary Strength," memorandum by Leta S. Hollingworth to Committee on Social-Economic Goals, National Education Association, Sub-Committee on Hereditary Strength, 1939.

31 Gretta Palmer, "Junior Brain-Trusters" *Literary Digest* (19 February 1938): 9-11; "Clever Children also Good Looking," *New York Times* (31 October 1937); Leta S. Hollingworth, "The Positive Aspect in the Preservation of Hereditary Strength," in *Public Addresses*, 98-103; L. Hollingworth, "What We Know about the Early Selection and Training of Leaders," 572-92.

32 Robert J. Sternberg and Elean Grigorenko, eds., *Intelligence, Heredity, and Environment* (New York: Cambridge University Press, 1997), preface, xi.

33 Willard L. White and Joseph S. Renzulli, "A Forty Year Follow-Up Study of Students who Attended Leta Hollingworth's School for Gifted Students," *Roeper Review* 10 (1987): 90, 94.

34 L. Hollingworth, *Public Addresses*, 48.

35 Leta S. Hollingworth to Dr. Benjamin Greenberg, 1 May 1939, Special Collections, Milbank Memorial Library, Teachers College, Columbia University.

36 Leta S. Hollingworth, *Prairie Years, Verse by Leta Stetter Hollingworth* (New York: Columbia University Press, 1940), 26-27.

37 *New York Times*, 1941, 2.

Chapter 8 Endnotes

1 Leta S. Hollingworth, *Prairie Years, Verse by Leta Stetter Hollingworth* (New York: Columbia University Press, 1940), 35.

2 "Gorton Codfish Cake Cans and History," www.columbia.edu/barnard/psych/museum/b_cod.html, 1.

3 Leta S. Hollingworth to John Stetter, 17 January 1928.

4 "History of the Barnard College Psychology Department," , 3-5.

5 Harry L. Hollingworth, *Years at Columbia* (unpublished manuscript, c. 1940), 114. Private collection of Virginia Florence.

6 Ibid., 114, 201-02.

7 Ibid., 153.

8 Ibid., 177.

9 Ibid., 183.

10 Leta S. Hollingworth to Anna Fischer, 1 January 1922.

11 Leta S. Hollingworth to Anna Fischer, 20 December 1924.

12 Virginia Weischer Florence, interview with author, 2 February 1998.

13 H. Hollingworth, *Years at Columbia*, 216.

14 Benjamin Florence, phone interview with author, 2000.

15 L. Hollingworth, *Prairie Years,* 35.

16 Ibid., 191.

17 Leta S. Hollingworth to Anna Fischer, 16 July 1926.

18 Leta S. Hollingworth to John Stetter, 17 January 1928.

19 Leta S. Hollingworth, "Provisions for Intellectually Superior Children," chap. 14 in *The Child: His Nature and His Needs,* M. V. O'Shea, ed. (New York: The Children's Foundation, 1924), 295.

20 H. Hollingworth, *Years at Columbia*, 217.

21 L. Hollingworth, "Provisions for Intellectually Superior Children," 277-99.

22 If Leta was aware of the educational discrimination against the Jews, it likely would have posed a dilemma for her, since so many of the children she had selected for her school programs in the United States were Jewish, as were some of her fellow Heterodites.

23 H. Hollingworth, *Years at Columbia*, 114.

24 Helen Stetter, interview with author, Valentine, NE, August 1996; Margaret Chase Overton, memoirs, 1975.

25 Margaret Chase Overton, memoirs, 1975, 4.

26 Michael Piechowski, "Emotional Giftedness: An Expanded View: Connecting the Gifted Community World-Wide," Selected Proceedings from the 12th World Conference of the World Council for Gifted and Talent Children, Seattle, WA, July 29-August 2, 1997, 253.

27 Leta S. Hollingworth to John Stetter, 25 December 1934.

28 Leta S. Hollingworth to Anna Fischer, 25 December 1934.

29 H. Hollingworth, *Years at Columbia*, 48. Hollingworth was hired to be a companion by a wealthy businessman because "his only son...did not seem then to be making effective adjustment to the difficult conditions of his motherless life." Holly first went to Europe with the young man and his family in the summer of 1908 and made enough money to enable Leta to join him that December in New York. He again accompanied the family to Europe in 1909; in 1911, Leta joined her husband and the family for the third summer abroad.

30 Leta S. Hollingworth, *Functional Periodicity* (New York: Teachers College, Columbia University, 1914), vii.

31 Leta S. Hollingworth to Kutzie and Frank, 28 April 1911.

32 Leta S. Hollingworth to Anna, 29 December 1915.

33 Helen Stetter, interview with author, Valentine, NE, August 1996.

34 Margaret Chase Overton, memoirs, 1975.

35 Ibid.

36 Ibid.

37   Ibid.

38   Douglas Spencer, "Clinical Psychology and Mental Adjustments," *Teachers College Record* 42 (1940): 196.

39   Leta S. Hollingworth, "Who Should Direct the Behavior Clinic?" delivered before the Board of Education, 18 February 1931; printed in *The Principal* (April 1931), 10-12.

40   Leta S. Hollingworth "Psychological Service for Public Schools," *Teachers College Record* 34 (1933): 376.

41   Leta S. Hollingworth, *Public Addresses* (Lancaster, PA: Science Press, 1940), 50.

42   R. F. Butts, *In the First Person Singular: The Foundations of Education* (San Francisco: Caddo Gap Press, 1993).

43   Lawrence A. Cremin, David A. Shannon, and Mary Evelyn Townsend, *A History of Teachers College Columbia University* (New York: Columbia University Press, 1954), 247.

44   A recent biography of William Heard Kilpatrick by John A. Beineke (*And There Were Giants in the Land: The Life of William Heard Kilpatrick*, 1998) is illuminating in several ways beyond the detailed descriptions of Kilpatrick's important contributions to teaching and learning. Leta Hollingworth is a non-entity. Her name never appears in the 500-page text. Naomi Norsworthy is referred to once, and Patty Smith Hill is accorded two citations. Kilpatrick's was a male-centered world. It is not surprising that no females were invited to join the Kilpatrick Discussion Group that met at the Teachers College Faculty Club. That philosophically diverse group included William Bagley, Harrison Elliot, Jesse Newlon, George Counts, Percival Symonds, Goodwin Watson, Bruce Raup, Harold Rugg, Isaac Kendel, and John Dewey.

45   William Heard Kilpatrick, diary, vol. 30, 261, Special Collections, Milbank Memorial Library, Teachers College, Columbia University.

46   Kilpatrick Diary, 271.

47   Kilpatrick Diary, 276, 279.

48   Kilpatrick Diary, vol. 31, 15.

49   Ibid., 58.

50   Ibid., 179.

51   Ibid., 213.

52   Leta S. Hollingworth, "The Nature of Human Nature," handwritten lecture, Hollingworth Papers, Archives of the History of American Psychology, Akron, OH.

Chapter 9 Endnotes

1   Harry L. Hollingworth, *Leta Stetter Hollingworth: A Biography* (1943; reprint, Boston: Anker Publishing, 1990), 3.

2   Harry L. Hollingworth, *Years at Columbia* (unpublished manuscript, c. 1940), 246. Private collection of Virginia Florence.

3   Ibid., 258.

4   H. Hollingworth, *Leta Stetter Hollingworth*, 3.

5   Minutes of the Board of Regents of the University of Nebraska, 26 April 1938, vol. 14, part 1, Archives of the University of Nebraska, Lincoln, NE.

6   Leta S. Hollingworth, "The Participation of Nebraska in the Intellectual and Artistic Leadership of the Nation," address presented to the University of Nebraska Alumni Association, 6 June 1938, Archives of the University of Nebraska, Lincoln, NE.

7   Helen Stetter, interview with author, Valentine, NE, August 1996.

8   Leta S. Hollingworth, *Prairie Years, Verse by Leta Stetter Hollingworth* (New York: Columbia University Press, 1940), 13, 14, 8, 18.

9   H. Hollingworth, *Years at Columbia*, postscript, 1945.

10   Helen Stetter, interview.

11   H. Hollingworth, *Years at Columbia*, postscript, 1945.

12   Margaret Chase Tatroe, "Grandpa Stetter's Life," (unpublished memoirs, c. 1960), 4-5.

13   "To the Faculty and Staff of Teachers College," memorandum, 28 November 1939, Special Collections, Milbank Memorial Library, Teachers College, Columbia University.

14   William Heard Kilpatrick, diary, 18 November 1939, vol. 35, 267.

15   Arthur I. Gates, "Obituary, Leta Stetter Hollingworth," *Science* 91 (1941): 9-11.

16   A. T. Poffenberger, "Leta Stetter Hollingworth: 1886-1939," *American Journal of Psychology* 53 (1940): 299-301.

17   "Conference on the Education for the Gifted in Honor of Professor Leta S. Hollingworth," program for the Conference on Education for the Gifted, December 13-14, 1940, Teachers College, Columbia University, Special Collections, Milbank Memorial Library, Teachers College, Columbia University.

18   Harry Hollingworth to William F. Russell, 10 December 1940.

19   Leta S. Hollingworth, *Children Above 180 IQ: Origin and Development* (Yonkers-on-Hudson, New York: World Book Company, 1942), iii-v.

20   Lewis Terman to William Russell, 29 August 1940.

Epilogue Endnotes

1   Barbara Kerr, "Leta Stetter Hollingworth's Legacy to Counseling and Guidance," *Roeper Review* 12 (1990): 178.

2   Leta S. Hollingworth to Paul Mort, 29 January 1939.

3   Ibid.

4   Ibid.

5   Ibid.

6   Leta S. Hollingworth, "The Importance of Studying Mental Deviates," *Journal of Consulting Psychology* 1 (1937): 75.

7   Leta S. Hollingworth to Paul Mort, 19 January 1939.

8   Nicholas Colangelo and Gary A. Davis, eds., *Handbook of Gifted Education*, 2nd ed. (Boston: Allyn & Bacon), 7.

Notes on Sources

Within months of Leta's death in 1939, Harry L. Hollingworth wrote a two-volume autobiography, *Born in Nebraska*, and *Years at Columbia*. The work was revised several times—abridged, re-organized, and re-paginated. Both volumes are invaluable sources. The first, *Born in Nebraska*, consists of at least two versions.

1. Original version, 1940, typed and unbound, 338 pages. Handwritten page numbers occasionally crossed out and new ones, not necessarily chronologically arranged, are substituted.

2. "Essay Revision," (no date), typed and bound, 257 pages. Handwritten page numbers are occasionally crossed out and new ones, not necessarily chronologically arranged, are substituted.

The second volume of Hollingworth's autobiography, *Years at Columbia*, is a typed and unbound 279-page manuscript. Handwritten page numbers are occasionally crossed out and new ones, not necessarily chronologically arranged, are substituted. Other versions may exist.

Yet a third autobiographical summary, *Prairie Schoolmaster*, is a typed and bound 237-page manuscript; it is a condensation of *Born in Nebraska* and contains new information about Harry Hollingworth's early teaching experiences. It, too, was never published.

Harry periodically updated his autobiography through postscripts (1944, 1949, 1952, 1953, 1954). It was in these postscripts that he revealed details of Leta's death and that he had destroyed her personal correspondence. The remainder of her uncompleted studies and laboratory notes were given to colleagues. They have never surfaced.

These works were loaned to the author by Virginia Florence, Harry Hollingworth's stepdaughter. Additional copies of *Born in Nebraska* and *Years at Columbia* are in the Nebraska Historical Society, Lincoln, Nebraska and in the Archives of the American Psychological Association in Akron, Ohio.

Prairie Years, Verse by Leta Stetter Hollingworth (1940), compiled by Harry Hollingworth, contains many of her poems, as well as the only known autobiography of Leta Hollingworth. Only five pages long, this first-person account provides a tantalizing example of Leta's voice. Harry then extrapolated material from his autobiographical notes for *Leta Stetter Hollingworth, A Biography* (1942), which remained the only published biography of Leta until this work.

Archival Collections

Arthur and Elizabeth Schlesinger Library, Radcliffe Institute, Cambridge, Massachusetts
> Mary Ware Dennett Papers
> Inez Haynes Irwin Papers
> "Heterodoxy to Marie" Album and Photographs
> "The Woman Rebel"

Special Collections, Milbank Memorial Library, Teachers College, Columbia University
> Leta S. Hollingworth Papers
> Speyer School Papers
> William Russell Papers
> William Heard Kilpatrick Diary
> Naomi Norsworthy Papers

Archives of the History of Psychology, Akron, Ohio
> Hollingworth Papers (Leta S. and Harry L.)
> Vineland Papers
> Florence Goodenough Papers

Archives of the University of Nebraska, Lincoln, Nebraska
> Senior Book of the Class of 1906
> Sombrero (Class of 1906)
> University of Nebraska Sixty-Sixth Annual Commencement Program, June 6, 1938
> *Daily Nebraskan*
> Minutes of the Board of Regents, University of Nebraska, April 26, 1938 (vol. 14, part 1)

Pamphlet, "The Participation of Nebraska in the Intellectual and Artistic Leadership of the Nation, by Leta Stetter Hollingworth, '06, '38, Delivered in part on June 6, 1938, as an address before the Alumni of the University of Nebraska, at Lincoln, Nebraska."

The Nebraska Historical Association, Lincoln, Nebraska
Miscellaneous historical material

Uncollected Papers

Leta Hollingworth's letters to the Stetter/Fischer families were obtained from Kathleen Rutledge. The following materials were given to me by Patricia Johnson:

"Grandpa Stetter's Life" by Margaret Chase Tatroe
"Mother's Early Life" by Margaret Lillian Chase Tatroe
"Lineage and Paternal Ancestry of Margaret Lillian Chase Tatroe, Daughter (and only child) of Roy Chase and Margaret Stetter Chase," by Margaret Chase Tatroe (1943-1945, 1960)
Untitled reminiscences about "Aunt Leta" by Margaret Chase Tatroe
"Autobiography of the Danley Family as Remembered by W.A. Danley, Chadron, Nebraska, November 18, 1917

Permissions

Quotations from Harry L. Hollingworth, *Leta Stetter Hollingworth, A Biography*, (1943; reprint, Boston: Anker Publishing, 1990) by permission of Anker Publishing Company.

Quotations from Judith Schwarz, *Radical Femisists of Heterodoxy: Greenwich Village 1912-1940*, (Norwich, CT: New Victoria Publishers, 1986) by permission of New Victoria Publishers.

Quotations from Sod House Society, *Sod House Memories* (Hastings, NE: 1972), and *Sod House Memories* (Henderson, NE: 1991) by permission of the National Sod House Society.

Personal Interviews

Richard Boyer, Valentine, 1996
Benjamin Florence (by phone), 2000
Virginia Florence, Weston, Connecticut, 1997, and also by phone, 1997-2002
Patricia Johnson, Waterville, Ohio, 1999
Kathleen Rutledge, Lincoln, Nebraska, 1996, 1997
Helen Stetter, Valentine, Nebraska, 1996

Picture Credits

Arthur and Elizabeth Schlesinger Library, Radcliffe Institute, Cambridge,
   Massachusetts
Virginia Florence
Richard Fischer

Selected Bibliography of Works by Leta Stetter Hollingworth

Books

Functional Periodicity. Contributions to Education, No. 69. New York:
   Bureau of Publications, Teachers College, Columbia University,
   1914.

The Psychology of Special Disability in Spelling. Contributions to Education,
   No. 88. New York: Bureau of Publications, Teachers College,
   Columbia University, 1918.

The Psychology of Subnormal Children. New York: The Macmillan Company, 1920.

Special Talents and Defects: Their Significance for Education. New York:
   The Macmillan Company, 1923.

Gifted Children: Their Nature and Nurture. New York: The Macmillan
   Company, 1926.

The Psychology of the Adolescent. New York: D. Appleton, 1928.

Public Addresses. Lancaster, PA: The Science Press, 1940.

Children above 180 IQ. Yonkers, NY: World Book Company, 1942.

Chapters and Articles in Books

"The Vocational Aptitudes of Women." Chap. 10 in *Vocational Psychology*,
   by Harry L. Hollingworth. New York: D. Appleton, 1916.

"Experiments in Education of the Gifted." In *Contributions to Education,
   New York Society for Experimental Education,* Vol.1, 139-48. Yonkers, NY: World Book Company, 1924.

"Provisions for Intellectually Superior Children." Chap. 14 in *The Child,
   His Nature and His Needs.* New York: Children's Foundation, 1924.

"The Size and Strength of Children who Test above 135 IQ." In *Twenty-
   Third Yearbook of the National Society of Education, Part I. The
   Education of Gifted Children,* edited by Guy Montrose Whipple.
   Bloomington, IL: The Public School Publishing Company, 1924.
   (With Grace A. Taylor.)

"Getting Away from the Family: The Adolescent and His Life Plans." In *Concerning Parents: A Symposium on Modern Parenthood*. New York: New Republic, Inc., 1926.

"Children Clustering at 165 IQ and Children Clustering at 146 IQ Compared for Three Years in Achievement." In *Twenty-Seventh Yearbook of the National Society for the Study of Education, Part II. Nature and Nurture: Their Influence Upon Achievement*, edited by Guy Montrose Whipple, 3-33. Bloomington, IL: The Public School Publishing Company, 1928. (With Margaret V. Cobb)

"Psychology of the Family." In *Encyclopedia Britannica*, 205-6. 14th ed. 1929.

"Special Gifts and Special Deficiencies." Chap. 20 in *Handbook of Child Psychology*. Worcester, MA: Clark University Press, 1931.

"The Adolescent Child." Chap. 23 in *Handbook of Child Psychology*. Worcester, MA: Clark University Press, 1931.

"Education." Chap. 20 in *The Problem of Mental Disorder*. New York: McGraw-Hill Book Company, 1934.

"Problem Children." In *Childcraft: Teacher's Problems* (Reprinted in *Childcraft*, Vol. 8: *Guidance of the Child*). Chicago: The Quarrie Corporation, 1939.

"The Significance of Deviates." *The Thirty-Ninth Yearbook of the National Society for the Study of Education: Intelligence, Its Nature and Nurture, Part I: Comparative and Critical Exposition*, edited by Guy Montrose Whipple, 43-66. Bloomington, IL: The Public School Publishing Company, 1940.

"The Problem of Comparing Races." *The Thirty-Ninth Yearbook of the National Society for the Study of Education: Intelligence, Its Nature and Nurture, Part I: Comparative and Critical Exposition*, edited by Guy Montrose Whipple, 257-61. Bloomington, IL: The Public School Publishing Company, 1940.

"Intelligence as an Element in Personality." *The Thirty-Ninth Yearbook of the National Society for the Study of Education: Intelligence, Its Nature and Nurture, Part I: Comparative and Critical Exposition*, edited by Guy Montrose Whipple, 271-75. Bloomington, IL: The Public School Publishing Company, 1940.

"Personal Reactions to the Thirty-Ninth Yearbook." *The Thirty-Ninth Yearbook of the National Society for the Study of Education: Intelligence, Its Nature and Nurture, Part I: Comparative and Critical Exposition*, edited by Guy Montrose Whipple, 451-54. Bloomington, IL: The Public School Publishing Company, 1940.

"The Course of Mental Development in Slow Learners Under an Experience Curriculum." *The Thirty-Ninth Yearbook of the National Society for the Study of Education: Intelligence, Its Nature and Nurture, Part II: Original Studies and Experiments*, edited by Guy Montrose Whipple, 245-54. Bloomington, IL: The Public School Publishing Company, 1940. (With Pritchard and Horan)

Articles in Journals

"The Frequency of Amentia as Related to Sex." *Medical Record* 84 (October 25, 1913): 753-56.

"Variability as Related to Sex Differences in Achievement, A Critique." *American Journal of Sociology* 19 (January 1914): 510-30.

"An Economic and Social Study of Feeble-Minded Women." *Medical Record* 85 (June 6, 1914): 1025-28. (With Max G. Schlapp)

"The Comparative Variability of the Sexes at Birth." *The American Journal of Sociology* 20 (November 1914): 335-70. (With Helen Montague)

"The Mentally Defective as Cases in the Courts of New York City." *Medical Record* 87 (February 27, 1915): 337-41. (With Max G. Schlapp)

"Social Devices for Impelling Women to Bear and Rear Children." *American Journal of Sociology* 22 (July 1916): 19-29.

"Science and Feminism." *The Scientific Monthly* (September 1916): 277-84. (With Robert H. Lowie)

"Phi Beta Kappa and Women Students." *School and Society* 4 (December 1916): 932-33.

"Echolia in Idiots: Its Meaning for Modern Theories of Imitation." *Journal of Educational Psychology* 8 (April 1917): 212-19.

"The Psychology of the Prodigious Child." *Journal of Applied Psychology* 1 (June 1917): 101-10. (With Charlotte G. Garrison and Agnes Burke)

"The Psychological Examination of Poor Spellers." *Teacher College Record* 20 (March 1919): 126-32.

"Special Disabilities that Contribute to the Retardation in School Status." *Ungraded* 5 (December 1919): 49-54. (Also presented as an address delivered before the Section for Study of Retarded Children of the New York State Teachers Association, Albany, NY, November 24, 1919.)

"Psychological Clinics in the United States." *Teachers College Record* 22 (May 1921): 221-25.

"Differential Action upon the Sexes of Forces which Tend to Segregate the Feebleminded." *Journal of Abnormal and Social Psychology* 17 (April-June 1922): 35-57.

"Subsequent History of E: Five Years after the Initial Report." *Journal of Applied Psychology* 6 (June 1922): 205-10. (With Charlotte G. Garrison and Agnes Burke)

"For and Against Birth Control." *The New Republic* 11 (October 1922): 178.

"The Special Opportunity Class for Gifted Children Public School 165 Manhattan." *Ungraded* 8 (March 1923) 121-28.

"An Introduction to Biography for Young Children above 150 IQ." *Teachers College Record* 26 (December 1924): 277-87.

"The Regression of Siblings of Children who Test at or above 150 IQ (Stanford-Binet)." *Journal of Educational Psychology* 16 (January 1925): 1-7. (With Margaret V. Cobb)

"Intellectually Superior Children." *Mclure's Magazine* 1 (May 1925): 51-61.

"Development of Intelligence in the First Six Years." *Ungraded* 10 (June 1925): 204-7.

"Mental Tests in Schools." *School and Home* 9 (November 1925): 1-4.

"Vocabulary as a Symptom of Intellect." *American Speech* 1 (December 1925): 154-58.

"The Adolescent in the Family." *Child Study* 27 (January 1926): 5, 6, 13.

"The Musical Sensitivity of Children who Test above 135 IQ (Stanford-Binet)." *Journal of Educational Psychology*, 17 (February 1926): 95-109.

"Tapping-Rate of Children who Test above 135 IQ (Stanford-Binet)." *The Journal of Educational Psychology* 18 (November 1926): 505-18. (With Jane E. Monahan)

"Neuro-Muscular Capacity of Children who Test above 135 IQ (Stanford-Binet)." *Journal of Educational Psychology* 18 (February 1927): 88-96.

"Subsequent History of E—Ten Years after the Initial Report." *Journal of Applied Psychology* 11 (October 1927): 385-90.

"Who Are Gifted Children?" *Child Study* 5 (October 1927): 3-5.

"The New Woman in the Making." *Current History* 27 (October 1927-March 1928): 15-20.

"The Discipline of Highly Intelligent Children." *Mclure's Magazine* 1 (June 1928): 19, 41-42.

"After High School—What?" *Parents Magazine* 4 (June 1929): 21, 60.

"The Production of Gifted Children from the Parental Point of View." *Eugenics* 2 (October 1929): 3-7.

"Facts about Bright Children." *Babyhood* (December 1929): 359, 365, 371, 375-76.

"The Systematic Error of Herring-Binet Rating Gifted Children." *Journal of Educational Psychology* 21 (January 1930): 1-11.

"Do Intellectually Gifted Children Grow toward Mediocrity in Stature?" *Journal of Genetic Psychology* 37 (September 1930): 345-60.

"Juvenile Achievement as Related to Size." *Teachers College Record* 32 (December 1930): 236-44. (With Howard A. Gray)

"Playmates for the Gifted Child." *Child Study* 8 (December 1930): 103-4.

"The Child of Very Superior Intelligence as a Special Problem in Social Adjustment." *Mental Hygiene* 11 (January 1931): 3-16.

"Personality Development of Special Class Children." *Eighteenth Annual Schoolmen's Weekly Proceedings* 31 (June 20, 1931): 442-46.

"Who Should Direct the Behavior Clinic?" *The Principal* (April 1931): 10-12.

"How Should Gifted Children Be Educated?" *Baltimore Bulletin of Education* 50 (May 1931): 195-98.

"Developmental Problems of Middle Adolescence." *Westminster Leader* 5 (October 1931): 23-24, 29.

"The Achievements of Gifted Children Enrolled and Not Enrolled in Special Opportunity Classes." *Journal of Educational Research* 24 (November 1931): 1-7. (With Howard A. Gray)

"Late Adolescence." *Westminster Leader* (November 1931): 24-25.

"Who Is the Gifted Pupil?" *Nineteenth Annual Schoolmen's Week Proceedings* (University of Pennsylvania Bulletin) 32 (1932): 239-46.

"How One Race Judges the Other for Physical Attractiveness." *Journal of Social Psychology* 3 (November 1932): 463-69. (With R. Madden)

"Recognizing Gifted Children." *The League Script* (Minneapolis Teachers League), 13 (December 1932): 7-9.

"Psychological Service for Public Schools." *Teachers College Record* 34 (February 1933): 368-79.

"The Centile Status of Gifted Children at Maturity." *Journal of Genetic Psychology* 45 (September 1934): 106-20. (With R. M. Kaunitz)

"The Comparative Beauty of the Faces of Highly Intelligent Adolescents." *Journal of Genetic Psychology* 47 (December 1935): 268-81.

"Psychological Weaning." *The Red-Book* 70 (December 1935): 268-81.

"Binet's Contribution to Social Science." *The Consulting Psychologist* 2 (March 1936): 9-12.

"The Development of Personality in Highly Intelligent Children." *National Elementary Principal* 15 (July 1936): 272-81.

"Adult Status of Highly Intelligent Children." *Journal of Genetic Psychology* 49 (September 1936): 215-26. (With Irving Lorge)

"The Terman Classes at Public School 500." *Journal of Educational Sociology* 10 (October 1936): 86-90.

"The Founding of Public School 500: Speyer School." *Teachers College Record* 38 (November 1936): 119-28.

"A New Deal for Ability." (Editorially changed to "Some Suggestions on Scholarships.") *The Independent Journal of Columbia University* (December 4, 1936).

"Bright Students Take Care of Themselves." *North American Review* 243 (June 1937): 261-73.

"The Importance of Studying Mental Deviates." *Journal of Consulting Psychology* 1 (September-October 1937): 73-75.

"Application of the Bernreuter Inventory of Personality to Highly Intelligent Adolescents." *Journal of Psychology* 4 (October 1937): 287-93. (With Metta M. Rust)

"An Enrichment Curriculum for Rapid Learners at Public School 500: Speyer School." *Teachers College Record* 39 (January 1938): 296-306.

"What We Know about the Early Selection and Training of Leaders." *Teachers College Record* 40 (April 1939): 572-92.

"Problems of Relationship between Elementary and Secondary Schools in the Case of Highly Intelligent Pupils." *Journal of Educational Sociology* 13 (October 1939): 90-102.

Pamphlets and Memoranda

"Helping the Nervous Child." Pamphlet published by the Lincoln School of Teachers College, 1927.

"Summary Report on Pupils of Two Special Opportunity Classes of Very Bright Children." Pamphlet published by the Board of Education of the City of New York, October 31, 1929.

"The Positive Aspect of the Preservation of Hereditary Strength:" Memorandum to Committee on Social-Economic Goals, National Education Association, Sub-Committee on Hereditary Strength, 1939.

Selected Addresses

"Who Should Direct the Behavior Clinic?" Delivered before the Board of Education of the City of New York, February 19, 1931.

"The Creative Work of Intellectually Gifted Children." Delivered before The Massachusetts Civic League, Ford Hall, Boston, MA, October 21, 1931.

"Observations on Current Educational Research." Delivered before Kappa Delta Pi, New York City, July 14, 1932.

"The Participation of Nebraska in the Intellectual and Artistic Leadership of the Nation." *University of Nebraska Special Bulletin*. Delivered before the alumni of the University of Nebraska on receiving the L.L.D., June 6, 1938.

"What We Know about the Early Selection and Training of Leaders." *Teachers College Record 40* (April 1939): 572-92. Delivered before the Fifth Advanced School Conference on Educational Policies, November 11, 1938.

"Problems of Relationship between Elementary and Secondary Schools in the Case of Highly Intelligent Pupils." Delivered before the National Committee on Coordination in Secondary Education at a Symposium on "The Education of Pupils of High Intelligence," Cleveland, OH, February 27, 1939.

"To the Graduates of Speyer School, Spring of 1939." Delivered at the graduation exercises at the close of the school year, New York, 1939.

Radio Broadcasts

"Adolescence: The Difficult Age" Address over NBC National Network, sponsored by the National Advisory Council on Radio in Education, December 19, 1931 .The text of this address was published by University of Chicago Press, December 1931.

"Facts and Fancies about the Adolescence." Address over Station WEVD, New York, October 13, 1933.

Poetry

Prairie Years: Verse by Leta Stetter Hollingworth. New York: Columbia University Press, 1940.

Major Events In Leta Stetter Hollingworth's Life
1886-1939

May 25, 1886   Leta is born to Margaret Elinor Danley and John G. Stetter.

February 8, 1890   Margaret Stetter dies in childbirth.

1890-1899   Leta and her two sisters are sent to live with Danley grandparents by their father; he leaves the home and returns sporadically.

1899-1902   Leta and two sisters move to Valentine into the "fiery furnace" of their father and stepmother.

1901   Leta's poem, *The Lone Pine,* is published in local newspaper.

1902   Graduates from Valentine High School.

1902-1906   Undergraduate years, University of Nebraska, Lincoln, Nebraska.

1905   Engaged to Harry (Holly) Levi Hollingworth.

1906   Awarded B.A. degree (and teaching certification) and is elected to Phi Beta Kappa.

1906-1908   Teaches high school in DeWitt and McCook, Nebraska.

December 31, 1908   Marries Harry L. Hollingworth and moves to New York City.

1908-1911   Unable to find teaching job because she is a married women, she also fails to obtain financial aid for graduate study because of her sex.

1911   H.L. Hollingworth secures research grant from Coca-Cola to study the effects of caffeine on human health. He hires Leta Hollingworth to be a research assistant on the project, one of first studies in applied psychology. Leta enters graduate school at Columbia University and Teachers College, Columbia University.

1912   Charter member of the Heterodoxy Club.

1913   Receives Master of Arts from Columbia University and the Master's Diploma in Education from Teachers College. Hired as psychologist by Clearinghouse for

	Mental Defectives in New York City administering mental tests.
1914	Appointed the first psychologist in the Civil Service of New York City.
1915	Appointed clinical psychologist at Bellevue Hospital and consulting psychologist to the New York Police Department.
1916	Earns Ph.D. at Teachers College, Columbia University. Appointed Instructor in Educational Psychology and Principal of the School for Exceptional Children, Teachers College.
1919	Promoted to rank of Assistant Professor of Education. Certified as Examiner in Mental Defect by the New York State's Commission for Mental Defectives. Teaches first college-level course in gifted education and inaugurates the field.
1920	Publishes *The Psychology of Subnormal Children*.
1922	Appointed to the rank of Associate Professor of Education. P.S. 165 experiment with gifted and profoundly gifted children begins.
1923	Publishes *Special Talents and Defects: Their Significance for Education*.
1926	Publishes *Gifted Children: Their Nature and Nurture*.
1928	Publishes *The Psychology of the Adolescent*.
1929	Promoted to the rank of Professor.
1935	New York City Board of Education establishes the experimental Speyer School with Hollingworth as Director of Research.
1938	Leta Stetter Hollingworth and Harry L. Hollingworth receive honorary Doctor of Law degrees from the University of Nebraska.
November 27, 1939	Death at the age of 53 of cancer.
1942	Posthumous publication of *Children above 180 IQ Stanford-Binet* (compiled from her notes by Harry Hollingworth and others).

Index

About the Author

Dr. Ann Klein is professor Emerita from the University of Wisconsin-Eau Claire. She holds a bachelor's degree in secondary education from the University of Wisconsin-Madison, a master's degree in history from University of California, Los Angeles, and a doctorate in Curriculum and Instruction from the University of Massachusetts.

Dr. Klein taught history and English in middle and secondary schools in New Jersey, New York, and Massachusetts for twenty years before earning her doctoral degree. Subsequently, she taught in the Department of Curriculum and Instruction at the University of Wisconsin-Eau Claire, where, in 1997, she was recognized with the University's Excellence in Teaching Award. She has shared her findings about gifted education in such national arenas as the National Association for Gifted Children, the Henry B. and Jocelyn Wallace International Research Symposium on Talent Development, and the World Council for Gifted Children.

For many years, Dr. Klein was director of a summer institute for teachers titled "Celebrating Gifted Education." In 2000, the Wisconsin Association for Talented and Gifted presented her with the Outstanding Service Award in recognition of her work on behalf of the organization.

She first became intrigued with Leta Hollingworth after reading about Leta in *Roeper Review*, a gifted education journal, which dedicated the March 1990 issue to Hollingworth's life. In researching material for this book, she interviewed Leta's relatives, researched archives at Columbia University, the Nebraska Historical Society, the University of Nebraska, the American Psychological Association, the

Arthur and Elisabeth Schlesinger Library at Radcliffe Institute, and even corresponded with an individual who at one time owned the Hollingworth home in Montrose, New York.

Raised in Newark, New Jersey, Dr. Klein currently resides in Eau Claire, Wisconsin and Elk Rapids, Michigan and is the parent of two (now-adult) gifted children.